1992

BALANCING
JOB SATISFACTION
& PERFORMANCE

BALANCING JOB SATISFACTION & PERFORMANCE

A Guide for Human Resource Professionals

WILLA M. BRUCE
and
J. WALTON BLACKBURN

Q

QUORUM BOOKS
Westport, Connecticut • London

Library of Congress Cataloging-in-Publication Data

Bruce, Willa M.
    Balancing job satisfaction and performance : a guide for human
resource professionals / Willa M. Bruce and J. Walton Blackburn.
        p.   cm.
    Includes bibliographical references and index.
    ISBN 0–89930–658–6 (alk. paper)
    1. Job satisfaction.   2. Quality of work life.   3. Performance.
HF5549.5.J63B74   1992
658.3'14—dc20   92–15989

British Library Cataloguing in Publication Data is available.

Library of Congress Catalog Card Number: 92–15989
ISBN: 0–89930–658–6

First published in 1992

Quorum Books, 88 Post Road West, Westport, CT 06881
An imprint of Greenwood Publishing Group, Inc.

Printed in the United States of America

The paper used in this book complies with the
Permanent Paper Standard issued by the National
Information Standards Organization (Z39.48–1984).

10   9   8   7   6   5   4   3   2   1

For Dr. Maryanne Stevens, R.S.M.
May her hope that all people have good work be fulfilled.

Contents

Tables

Acknowledgments

We acknowledge the special contributions to this book of the Reverend Michael G. Morrison, S.J., President of Creighton University, and of Patricia Callone, Assistant to the President. Their involvement in the design and management of a participative planning effort was critical to its success and provided the context and inspiration for our discussion of participation in Chapter 6. The strategic planning program at Creighton University pulled together hundreds of recommendations from every part of the university community to shape the university's plans for the future. We also acknowledge the invaluable assistance of Roger Stuhmer, Director of Public Affairs of U.S. West Communications, who facilitated our planning conference and advised us on our planning implementation process.

We also thank graduate students in the Master of Public Administration program at the University of Nebraska at Omaha, particularly Elise Hubbard for her assistance with data input and analysis, and Janice Walker for her contributions to the workshop on diversity training described in the text. Others, too numerous to mention, assisted with bibliographic identification and preparation. We also appreciate the willingness of so many people to share their job experiences with us.

_____ **Chapter 1** _____

Satisfied Employees Make a Difference

We have to teach ourselves again to relate pleasure to work instead of connecting it with drudgery, dullness, and stupidity.

Dorothy Soelle[1]

Do you remember the 1957 film *The Bridge on the River Kwai*, prisoners of war toiled to build the fabled bridge for their enemy captors? Alec Guiness, portraying a dedicated military officer who led the prisoners, even urged them to take pride in their efforts. And Sessue Hayakawa, portraying the enemy leader, extolled the prisoners, "Be happy in your work," as though satisfaction in work alone would compensate for all their other hardships.

Indeed, the desire to have satisfied employees is widely pervasive among human resource managers. The belief that satisfied employees are also productive employees is naturally appealing. Managers and workers alike pursue job satisfaction in the often naive belief that it leads directly and surely to that other workplace ideal—high performance. The fact is, however, that sometimes satisfied employees perform better, and sometimes they do not.

This book addresses performance issues common to the public, private, and nonprofit sectors. It is a book to assist human resource managers to maximize employee increasingly diverse work force. Other books that address job satisfaction are more academic than practical, with the issues of job satisfaction and productivity buried in scholarly discussions of the psychology or sociology of work. Books that deal with performance focus more on how to measure it or why we need to improve it than on how to encourage it. Current books simply do not provide very practical advice to the human resource manager. This one does by showing how to balance job satisfaction and performance as one deals with the rapidly changing labor market, technology, and environmental conditions.

A study of two state-owned liquor stores illustrates the complexity of the satisfaction/performance relationship. The stores were similar in terms of purpose, number of employees, and geographic locations. Job descriptions and job characteristics were very much alike. One store (we'll call P for productive) was a profitable enterprise; breakage was low and the books balanced at each audit. The other store (call it O for opposite) cost more to run than the revenues it generated. Its high breakage rates, books that did not balance, and customer complaints were a serious concern of state auditors.

At first blush, those called in to study the situation thought that the difference in the performance at the two stores was one of job satisfaction. Employees at Store P, they assumed, were more highly satisfied with their jobs, and therefore were more dependable and more productive. To the researchers surprise, just the opposite was true.

Apparently, Store P–employees worked so hard and diligently that they felt overworked and unappreciated. Store O–employees, on the other hand, were truly "happy" in their work. Supervision was lax. They came and went to suit themselves and enjoyed socializing with one another—both on and off the job. In these two stores, performance and job satisfaction were not correlated at all.[2]

Job satisfaction often seems like an ultimate, perhaps unattainable, goal of both managers and employees. Research conclusions such as those of the study of the two state liquor stores suggest the difficulty of achieving job satisfaction while maintaining high performance.

The desire to find the secret formula can lead to bizarre efforts. In one experiment, researchers placed volunteers in front of a computer screen and fitted them with a face mask that delivered either a puff of peppermint or fresh air every five minutes. The subjects were tested in their performance of "vigilance tasks," which required them to pay strict attention during a forty-minute test. Those who sniffed fresh air detected only 65 percent of certain signal changes on the computer screen. Those who sniffed peppermint detected the altered signal about 85 percent of the time. Overall, peppermint inhalers did about 15 to 20 percent better.

Other desperate efforts to increase productivity are occurring overseas, as well as in the United States. "Fragrance scientists" report that pleasurable smells are already being tested on clerical workers in Japan, on straphangers in the London subway, and on patients having brain scans, which require them to lie motionless in claustrophobic tunnel-like contraptions. One expert found that air fresheners bought at the grocery store produced positive effects in the performance of clerical tasks and face-to-face negotiations.[3]

Because of the growing concern about the ability of American firms to succeed in an increasingly competitive world economy, and for public and nonprofit organizations to become more productive and efficient, the quest for means of enhancing worker productivity will continue to intensify. A counterforce that makes the quest more and more challenging is the increasing sophistication of much of the American labor force. Most of today's workers expect to derive much more satisfaction from their work than their grandparents ever dreamed was possible. In addition, today's work force is constantly growing more diverse—demographically, culturally, and racially. New technologies, such as the computer, enhance performance but also introduce new challenges to managers who wish to maintain job satisfaction and a safe and healthy work environment. Thus, though the challenge of enhancing performance becomes more urgent, the difficulties of increasing productivity while maintaining job satisfaction become more complex.

THE IMPORTANCE OF JOB SATISFACTION

Despite its tenuous, often contradictory relationship with performance, job satisfaction is a complex and important concept for human resource managers to understand. "Most employees do not believe their work is being properly rewarded. Nor do they believe that their companies are doing enough to attract high quality performers, train them, or manage them effectively."[4]

Companies that do satisfy employees' desires for good managerial relations, respect, fair and adequate compensation, and opportunities for growth and development through training, are reaping the benefits. Research conducted by the Hay Group, Inc., found "distinct relationships between (good) human resource management practices and improved performance."[5] A vice president for personnel of International Business Machines (IBM), speaking at a conference of university planners, repeatedly stressed the importance of respect for the individual.[6] A newspaper editor reported that educators are finding that the values needed in the "new workplace" include caring, commitment, loyalty, and teamwork.[7]

Despite the evidence that concern for employees is important, a report in the *Wall Street Journal* indicates that trust and loyalty run low at U.S. companies: a survey of 400 managers showed that fully one-third distrust their direct bosses, and 55 percent do not believe top management.[8] At a time when trust and loyalty are becoming increasingly important, they are generally declining. That is not only a sad commentary but also an impetus for this book.

In large organizations where pay levels are high, successful companies put an emphasis on pay for performance, training, and career development. In smaller successful companies, employee performance has been improved through providing challenging assignments, respectful treatment, and the willingness of managers to listen.[9] In both cases, employees who report satisfaction also produce more. As one company supervisor states, "When you let an employee know you are glad of the association, you automatically get more effort from that person. . . . Promoting happiness among workers is an important part of being a successful supervisor."[10]

The notion that satisfied employees make a difference was spurred by what has been called the "third industrial revolution,"[11] which began with the Hawthorne studies of the 1930s calling for a humanization of the workplace. Designing "enriched" jobs that created employee satisfaction, as opposed to providing only a day's pay for a day's work, became one part of the workplace humanization movement. This movement is based on the premise that "the work force assures long-term productivity if it is well cared for."[12] This movement presupposes the desirability of having satisfied employees.

Since Herzberg's 1959 work on "satisfiers" and "dissatisfiers" in the workplace,[13] job satisfaction has frequently been held up as a means of improving employee motivation. With that improvement come increasing individual productivity, job longevity, and organizational efficiency. The salience of the concept of job satisfaction has become so ingrained in thinking about jobs and employees that its importance is now taken for granted, as though it is a tenet of managerial faith. Today, human resource managers want to know *how* to have satisfied employees, not *why* employees should be satisfied.

In truth, employees and managers may have different reasons for wanting organizational conditions that foster job satisfaction. Today's employees "seem concerned with life values, fulfillment, a sense of wholeness, and fundamentally with love; in addition, they are concerned about purpose, contribution and meaning."[14] Just as the organization expects optimum performance from its workers, employees have come to expect job satisfaction as a right.[15]

Employees—and you yourself, after all—spend most waking hours at work, thinking about work, resting up from work, or preparing for work. Work is an intrinsic part of most lives, frequently our reason for being, a place from which we get our identity. Work provides "daily meaning as well as daily bread."[16] Yet work is not always a place where workers feel satisfied. In fact, a great many believe

work, is, by its very nature, about violence—to the spirit as well as to the body. It is about ulcers as well as accidents, about shouting matches as well as fistfights, about nervous breakdowns as well as kicking the dog around. It is above all (or beneath all), about daily humiliations. To survive the day is triumph enough for the walking wounded among the great many of us.[17]

The "walking wounded" are not just at the lower levels of the organization or among those who are not well educated. Some overly committed professionals produce at such high levels they do harm to themselves. One physician we talked with acknowledged, "It's a wonder that I and the nurses who work with me don't all have bladder infections. We see so many patients in such a short time, we don't stop long enough to go to the toilet." This doctor was describing work place "violence" to her body and to the bodies of those who work for her.

One of the authors of this book subjected herself to similar violence. In order to meet a deadline, she sat for such long periods of time at her word processor that her kneecap slipped off her knee. Six months and several hundred dollars worth of physical therapy later, she began to realize the value of balance—balance that can actually enhance performance because it acknowledges the humanity as well as the competence of the worker.

Have you ever worked so hard, performed so outstandingly, that your body suffered? Many have, and some do on a regular basis. As a part of the research for this book, we surveyed a group of employees who had been designated by a large multinational company as "outstanding achievers." (See Appendix A for a description of the research.) We thought that these employees, who had been identified as extremely productive could shed light on the performance/satisfaction relationship. Indeed, they did shed light on it. Their responses also pointed to the harm that can occur at work as a result of high productivity.

Ninety-one percent of the respondents stated they were unable to achieve balance in their lives. Of that group, 45 percent report that their health has been negatively affected because of their high productivity, and 44 percent say their job creates high stress. A large group of these superstars report that they think their health is at risk because of the high levels of performance expected of them. Those between the ages of thirty-one and fifty have lives more out of balance than do their younger and older cohorts.

Respondents to our survey, between the ages of thirty-one and fifty are working hard, experiencing stress, and worrying that opportunities will decline as they age. Some of their stress is caused by overwork. Some of it is caused by a lack of respect from supervisors. Some of it is because of poor relations and mistrust between supervisors and employees.

Human resource managers may be concerned about employee job satisfaction for different reasons than their workers. Altruistic managers want satisfied employees because they care about their employees. Re-

sult-oriented managers want satisfied employees because satisfied workers may perform better and have less absenteeism and greater longevity.
Satisfied workers also tend to produce higher-quality work than their
dissatisfied cohorts. In fact, over two thousand studies on humanizing
the workplace indicate that satisfied workers are more productive and
that organizations with satisfied workers are more efficient.[18]

Satisfied employees are more likely to experience high internal work
motivation, to give high-quality work performance, and to have low
absenteeism and turnover.[19] Simply put, organizations that have instituted programs to improve job satisfaction have found them to be "successful in terms of both human and economic standards."[20]

As might be expected with scholarly research, other findings have
contradicted these "satisfaction equals performance" conclusions. One
textbook asserts:

Job satisfaction and output are virtually independent of each other. There seem
to be at least two possible reasons for this. The first is that in many jobs, variations
in satisfaction cannot lead to variations in productivity. In machine-paced assembly work, for instance, the speed of the production line is constant whatever
the level of job satisfaction of people working on the line. Secondly, even when
correlations do appear . . . the association may be spurious since both may be
associated with another factor. In other words, job satisfaction and productivity
may well have largely separate causal paths; one set of factors (e.g., investment
in technology) determines productivity, another set (e.g., perceived equity of
rewards) produces job satisfaction.[21]

With the obvious confusion and disagreement about the relation of
job satisfaction to performance, you probably wonder what to believe
and where to focus your efforts. You know that when satisfied employees go too happily about their work, organizational efficiency and
effectiveness may falter. You also know that today's work force wants
a workplace that provides satisfying terms and conditions of employment. You recognize the violence that occurs in your own organization,
yet you know that performance equates to dollars and maximizes profits.

Herein lies the balancing act. Satisfaction and performance benefit
both the organization and the worker. When the scales tip in either
direction, and the life of the worker and the terms and conditions of
employment are not in balanced proportions, something suffers. Either
the worker experiences demoralizing, demotivating, and debilitating
pain, or the organization suffers a downturn in productivity.

This discussion is not about accidents and conditions that are covered
by Workman's Compensation legislation, nor about stipulations moni-
tored through the Occupational Safety and Hazards Administration. To
their purview fall the gross abuses and the accidental injuries and conditions. Our discussion refers to the everyday situations of employees

who perform work that gives them both "daily meaning and daily bread."

The 1987 Hudson Institute report sponsored by the U.S. Department of Labor, *Workforce 2000*, indicated that work-force growth would slow and employers "will have to compete for workers in a less skilled and more diversified labor market."[22] More and more employers will also be dealing with employees who are now more skeptical about their concern for them as human beings. This, we think, underscores the need for learning to balance satisfaction with performance expectations.

Whether or not satisfaction and performance are directly and strongly correlated is not the issue. The issue is that in order to attract and retain qualified employees in the upcoming tight labor market, employers will have to treat people as their most important asset. Employers will need to assess their organization and the jobs in it to see where violence might occur, and to see how it might be eliminated or prevented. This will require efforts by employers in several areas, as this text will explain. As employers, you will have to

1. Manage a newly emerging diverse work force in which white males will be a minority;

2. Learn how a rapidly changing environment will affect your organization;

3. Accommodate workers' family responsibilities so they do not detract from performance;

4. Provide consistent and constant skill and behavioral education and training;

5. Encourage participative management;

6. Provide satisfying employment that encourages people to become and to remain a viable part of the work force;

7. Achieve a balance between performance and satisfaction for both yourself and the workers in your organization; and

8. Identify and eliminate workplace violence that threatens the well-being of all employees.

CONFUSION ABOUT JOB SATISFACTION

The great variety of studies about, and approaches to, job satisfaction attest to its importance; however, those who try to understand what enhances employee job satisfaction and how it benefits the workplace frequently disagree on how to foster it. Job satisfaction is so complex and dependent upon so many different factors that managers and scholars alike seem confused about why job satisfaction occurs and whether or not it is a relevant workplace issue.

Certainly, in times of economic hardship when the supply of workers far exceeds the demand for their talents, people are frequently so glad to be employed that the issue of being satisfied with a job is immaterial to them. Their performance may relate more to a determination to insure financial security than to any personal satisfaction they may derive from a job.

In the 1990s and beyond, however, we suspect that the demand for qualified, competent workers may exceed the supply. Workers will be able to shop for jobs as opposed to employers being able to select among many applicants. *Workforce 2000* indicates that the number of available workers, and their literacy and skill levels, will continue to decrease while newly emerging jobs will require greater knowledge, skill, and ability than did those in previous decades.[23]

Some employers are already seeing this trend toward a decreasing supply of skilled labor. A hiring authority at a major medical facility reported her dilemma this way:

Last month I hired a new data entry operator. She's been late almost every day she's been employed. But, I don't want to fire her. She can do the job. Only two people applied for the position when we advertised it. The other applicant was a single parent of three who told me she was going through a divorce and wasn't sure if she could make it to work every day. She assured me she'd get in as often as she could. She also wanted $8.00 per hour for a position budgeted at $4.50.

What is an organization to do? What do you think? The competitive edge in hiring will depend on how well organizations attract good workers. The competitive edge in survival will depend on how long those good workers are retained. We have traditionally thought that to remain healthy, organizations need a turnover rate of about 25 percent a year. As the supply of qualified workers declines, however, retention will become a greater concern.

At first thought, you might conclude that the medical facility with only two job applicants needs to upgrade the data-entry position to a higher-paying one. You might worry that your organization does not have the slack resources for pay upgrades. But higher pay is not the complete solution either to attracting or retaining productive employees.

A recent survey of American workers found that "job security, high pay, and good benefits are not even on the top ten list" of what people want in a job.[24] Interestingly, since social scientists started studying those things, these items never have been the highest priorities. Herzberg, as early as 1966, found that conditions like pay, benefits, fair policies and procedures, and comfortable working conditions are neither satisfiers nor motivators for most workers. These elements of a job must be in place before a worker will take the job (unless the person is desperate and the job market tight). If these conditions do not prevail, the employee will shortly become dissatisfied, contribute as little as feasible, and leave as soon as possible.

Herzberg called conditions like pay, security, and good working conditions "hygiene factors." Workers want them as a right of employment. Workers, however, do not respond to them with either motivated performance nor increased satisfaction. Unions frequently haggle over issues of pay and benefits. Many companies deal with their employees as though "security, pay, and benefits were the only ways to motivate them."[25] Yet these job components are insufficient in themselves to enhance performance. If they are not in place, workers become dissatisfied. If they are in place, workers need additional conditions for their own satisfaction and motivation.

At upper levels of the organization, satisfaction and performance may occur differently than at lower levels. Professional employees relate to the workplace and their responsibilities in different ways than do the rank and file of labor. While one cannot assume that professionals take total responsibility for their performance and satisfaction, it is a generally accepted fact that "the career problem for professionals usually centers around his [sic] ability to increase his [sic] skills and to make that increase visible to his [sic] colleagues."[26] Professional employees will negotiate acceptable salary and benefits. Then as they perform, they will find satisfaction in competition or collaboration with peers both inside and outside of the organization.

Unskilled laborers, on the other hand, often feel powerless because they are not as marketable as professional workers. Their skills are more readily available. They frequently resort to collective bargaining as a means of attaining acceptable terms and conditions of employment. In viewing collective action as a way of acquiring job and life security, employees at lower levels of the organization may also have unwritten norms about how much work is expected and how much is acceptable.

What was called "soldiering" in 1912 by Fredrick Taylor and what is still alive and well among today's workers is the proclivity toward establishing and maintaining group norms of production that may be substantially lower than the capabilities of individual workers. In a recent study of American workers, for example, half of those surveyed said that they "worked just hard enough to avoid getting fired" and "seventy-five percent said that they could be significantly more effective on the job."[27]

You may already be experiencing that kind of suboptimum performance in your organization. In fact, that experience may be why you are reading this book. Certainly, everyone is concerned about maximizing performance within reasonable expectations of job commitment and accomplishment, and everyone wants people to give a day's work for a day's pay. At the same time, we are concerned about such work-related problems as stress and burnout, which can harm employees both physically and mentally.

Some organizations, ranging from a retail store in downtown Baltimore to a large government agency in Nebraska, have actually taken steps to insure that their employees spend no more than forty hours per week in work-related activities. In each organization, the concern is the same. Employees who produce too much, who put work above other aspects of their lives, are in danger of stress-related illnesses.

Some human resource managers envy others who have problems with workers courting burnout from excessive devotion to the job and the organization. One multinational information services company, concerned with just getting lower level employees to appear at work, has instituted a "key employee" program. After a designated number of days in which the employee reports for work on time, the worker is awarded a gold-finished-key lapel pin. The employee can accumulate the keys and use them to purchase gifts in a "company store."

A large nursing-home human resource manager decided to encourage employees to come to work by using the motivation theory of Maslow, who postulated an ascending hierarchy of five human needs: physiological, safety and security, belonging, esteem, and self-actualization. To motivate an employee, according to Maslow, determine which needs are currently being met and appeal to the next higher level. Wages address physiological needs; benefits such as insurance, sick leave and vacations, and worker's compensation, meet safety and security needs.

The human resource manager at the nursing home decided that wages and benefits were such that the employees' first two levels of needs were being met. How to appeal to the next level, she wondered. A T-shirt was the solution. The manager announced that any employee who came to work on time every day for sixty days would receive a T-shirt with the nursing home's name emblazoned on both front and back, believing that the T-shirt would appeal to belonging needs, possibly even esteem needs. This was the desperate attempt of a desperate manager, but today, a year later, the shirts are worn by only a few. They may become collectors' items. The authors certainly hope so. One of us was the recipient of a shirt that nobody earned.

Just getting employees to report for work seems to be an increasing problem for human resource managers. As the supply of workers decreases, the problem may worsen. Human resource managers with whom we've talked identify this problem as one of their greatest concerns. Consistent attendance is a precondition of job satisfaction and performance. An employee who is not satisfied with a job may not come to work regularly or promptly, and an employee who does not come to work cannot perform.

Some measures used to ensure high performance may be counter-productive. Some employers are using devices that allow them to listen in on phone calls, count keystrokes, and gauge the amount of time workers spend on transactions. Computer monitoring is used to evaluate ten million American workers, many times without their knowledge or permission. While such monitoring is used to train workers and to pro-mote those who perform well, such electronic snooping causes fear and stress, which lead to illnesses. While a certain degree of monitoring is acceptable to workers, managers rely too heavily on it to assess worker efficiency.[28]

"Downsizing" is another approach being tried to enhance organiza-tional efficiency. It is an approach with a negative effect on employee morale and often on productivity as well. When companies reduce staffs with massive layoffs, early retirements, and other "grenade" approaches to cutting costs, employees who remain become frightened that their jobs will be next. Managers must pay sufficient attention to the human element, or the "downsized" companies will be less efficient, not more. In a modern company, people are critical to success; they are individuals with talents to be developed, not replaceable pegs to be shoved around from slot to slot—or out. In corporations with badly managed reductions, the remaining employees can experience increased conflict. You can expect a decrease in real communication, more rumors, less participa-tion, more power plays, more politics, more autocratic leadership, more turnover, and less innovation because that involves extra risk and costs.[29]

Several schools of thought have attempted, over the years, to explain what "causes" job satisfaction. We will discuss these explanations briefly in this chapter to introduce the various ways job satisfaction has been conceptualized and understood. With over ten thousand studies of job satisfaction having been conducted, the confusion about what fosters it runs rampant. Yet, the effort devoted to attempting to understand job satisfaction speaks to the importance given it by practitioners and aca-demics alike.

The purpose of this book is not a one-more-time rehash of the studies of job satisfaction. Rather, the bulk of this book is devoted to assisting employers to consider factors relevant to job satisfaction and perfor-mance. Some of these factors are the emerging demographic and tech-nological trends affecting the American work force and workplace. These trends are prompting personal self-assessment among those who must learn to manage workers from cultures other than their own, or with life-styles different than their own. These trends are pushing us to ex-amine our own biases and our own strengths.

Most research on job satisfaction has focused on the effects of job enrichment and job design, or on the Quality of Work Life. As a human resource manager concerned about balancing satisfaction with performance, you need to know how to foster an organizational climate that contains these elements. You also need to recognize that these components are only the tip of the iceberg in human resource management and are necessary but insufficient to balancing satisfaction and performance in the workplace of the 1990s and beyond. Let's examine current scholarly thinking about job satisfaction.

Job Enrichment

An "enriched" job is one in which an employee has opportunities for achievement, recognition, advancement, responsibility, and growth. Enriched jobs are those in which employees can be involved in the production of goods or services from beginning to end. Enriched jobs are not a series of limited, specialized activities, repeated over and over. Rather, enriched jobs are those in which the workers have the opportunity to see processes or tasks through from start to finish.

Enriched jobs contain five core work dimensions: *task identity, task significance, skill variety, autonomy,* and *feedback.* The presence of these components within the job will then lead to critical psychological states of meaningfulness of work, responsibility for work outcomes, and knowledge of work outcomes. The presence of these psychological states leads, ultimately, to motivation, high-quality performance, low absenteeism and turnover, *and* high job satisfaction.[30]

An employee who can point to a product and brag, "I made that" or "my efforts produced that" is experiencing task identity. If employees also consider the fruit of their labors to be important, then task significance is part of their job. A task is significant when employees believe that what they have done makes a real difference to someone or to society. Autonomy is experienced by those who are encouraged to work without close supervision; skill variety means they do a lot of different things on a regular basis; and feedback presupposes regular and accurate information on how work is perceived by those for whom it is done.

An example of an enriched job is that of a small-city municipal clerk who has responsibility for the general operations of government. The municipal clerk's job requires the traditional duties of a manager: "Planning, Organizing, Staffing, Directing, Coordinating, Reporting, and Budgeting (POSDCORB)." Clerks serve as "boundary spanners" between local government bureaucracy and the citizen. In many cases they are the embodiment of government for the citizen. They must be responsive to elected officials while maintaining political neutrality. In terms of the scope of their duties, over 90 percent of them are responsible for the following functions: maintaining official records and documents; answering inquiries from other departments and citizens; maintaining the official council minutes book; maintaining the official ordinance and resolution books; recording the council minutes; arranging and preparing for meetings; administering oaths; and supervising clerical staff. More than 75 percent of the clerks administer elections; 66 percent issue business and nonbusiness licenses; 33 percent maintain vital statistics; and 31 percent manage municipal finances.[31]

Thus, municipal clerks have jobs with task identity, task significance, skill variety, and autonomy, and sometimes feedback. Municipal clerks report a high level of job satisfaction. Over 81.4 percent of the almost two thousand clerks surveyed agreed with the statement, "Considering everything, I am very satisfied with my job at the present time,"[32] as did 86 percent of the professionals we surveyed.

Job enrichment among managerial and professional employees is often inherent in the nature of their work. Those who perform support functions and operate the organization's technology are those for whom job enrichment is difficult, though not always impossible.

Hospital employees are examples of those for whom routinized, specialized job requirements are being changed. Today, in many medical facilities, a patient is assigned a "Nurse Coordinator" who is involved from the beginning to end of treatment and is thus able to derive satisfaction from seeing a patient improve as a result of his or her ministrations. Responsibility for a maternity patient used to move from labor room staff to delivery room to recovery room to maternity ward, with no one knowing what happened after she left their care. In a situation in which employee jobs are enriched, the pregnant woman comes to a birthing area where the same staff provide continuity of service and see the results of their labors. This atmosphere enriches both the lives of the employees and the situation of the woman.

Your own organization will probably have employees for whom enrichment is possible. Can one account executive provide comprehensive services to a client? Can one social worker deal with all family members and assorted family needs? Can one craftsperson follow a construction project from start to finish? Can one data entry person be responsible for a group of the same customers? Only you can assess your own organization to see if the positions in it are candidates for job enrichment. Some will be. Some will not.

Enriched jobs do increase satisfaction among jobholders. The trade-off, however, is the retreat from specialization. As more people become a "jack-of-all-trades and a master of none," the superior knowledge needed for difficult situations or for solving unusually complex problems is not available.

While important and demonstrably effective in enhancing job satisfaction and improving performance, job enrichment is simply not appropriate for all organizational positions. As a human resource manager, you must assess where, when, and if enrichment activities are suitable in your organization. Enriched jobs, like the other conditions that foster satisfaction and enhance performance, usually can be created easily for managers and professionals. For employees in the organization's technological core, however, creating an enriched job is not such an easy undertaking.

In the traditional hierarchical organizational structure, three levels have been identified by theorists: the executive level, the managerial level, and the technological core. The technological core is the great underbelly of the organization where goods and services are produced, where the blue-collar and pink-collar workers are often the only employees, and where technology is routinized. In the technological core, unions often form as workers band together to attempt to achieve the strength in numbers that they lack in power or position. In the core, the specialization demanded by assembly lines makes enriching jobs difficult, and the greatest violence is committed against these workers who are cogs in the production process. They are not autonomous individuals, but anonymous interchangeable parts.

Technological workers are often forgotten by those who study and implement programs of job enrichment. They are often the forgotten employees when discussions about job satisfaction and performance take place. They are, however, the heart and soul of the organization. A 1991 *Fortune* magazine article suggests that to serve customers better and to make a company more competitive, one must "bust through the bureaucracy."

Instead of looking to the boss for direction and oversight, tomorrow's employee will be trained to look closely at the work process and to devise ways to improve it, even if this means leaving his [sic] regular job to join an ad hoc team attacking a problem. . . . [You must] Forget structures invented by the guys at the top. You've got to let the task form the organization.[33]

The chief executive officer at Xerox points out, "We're never going to outdistance the Japanese on quality. To win, we need to find ways to capture the creative and innovative spirit of the American worker. That's the real organizational challenge."[34]

To capture this spirit is indeed the challenge for organizations of the future. Enriching jobs is one way to capture it. But to capture and then deplete that spirit will not address organizational concerns. Job enrichment is only a small part of the solution. Balance is the crucial ingredient. Assist employees to balance their performances with their bodies' demands and with the rest of the responsibilities of their lives, and satisfied employees will be able to perform. Maybe, they will even outdistance the Japanese, who, as we write this book, are increasingly experiencing ill effects because of overwork. Some Japanese even died from causes attributed to excessive workplace demands, demands that put workers' lives out of balance.

Quality of Work Life

Another way to increase satisfaction among employees is to provide a high Quality of Work Life (QWL) environment,[35] in which employees may be productive because their work situation is one in which they find satisfaction. A QWL environment may contain either routinized jobs or enriched jobs. The key to QWL is the institutionalization of the following components, all within the employer's purview:

1. Fair and adequate compensation;
2. Safe and healthy work environment;
3. Opportunities to develop human capacities by performing meaningful work and suggesting new ways of doing job tasks;
4. Growth and security, which includes opportunities to improve knowledge, skills, and abilities, and a sense of job security;
5. Social integration, which includes the opportunity to interact favorably with both coworkers and manager;
6. Constitutionalism, which includes personnel policies that are administered fairly, a work environment free of harassment, and equal opportunities for all employees to advance;
7. Total life space, which includes the ability to balance the demands of home and work; and
8. Social relevance, which includes pride in both the job and the employer.[36]

Some scholars have found that a QWL environment leads to job satisfaction, employee growth, meaningful jobs, and employee well-being.[37] Others believe that QWL is not relevant in today's bureaucratic workplace.[38] We have found that the presence of QWL factors are conducive to job satisfaction. A high quality of work life can result from a determined effort on the part of a human resource manager. It may also exist simply as a result of concerned executives and skilled managers who display "good management."

The presence of QWL factors in an organization sets the stage for job satisfaction to occur. The factors are a backdrop against which the activities of both workers and supervisors take place. Without them the work environment can be uncomfortable, even hostile. With QWL factors in place, the real business of balancing job satisfaction and performance can begin. We believe that QWL factors are equivalent to what have been called "dissatisfiers."[39] If quality working conditions are not present, people will become dissatisfied. They may look for other jobs. They may simply perform at a minimal level. In either event, the organization will lose.

Thus before even beginning to think about balancing the satisfaction and performance of employees, a self-examination is in order; call it an "internal audit" of working conditions. Be as thorough in your analysis of the working conditions in your organization as the accountants who audit company debits and credits. If your organization is unionized, certainly the terms and conditions of employment for those who work in the technological core have been closely scrutinized. What about the working situations of the supervisors, middle managers, and staff advisors? What about the working situations of the clerical, secretarial, and support staff?

What employees at all levels of the organization want is "good work." "Good work" is not only a job, a source of financial support; it is

- Work that allows people to use the skills that are unique and special to them;
- Work that allows people to be in relationships with one another at the workplace; and
- Work that allows people to produce something that is "good," something to which they can look with pride, something that has social relevance.[40]

Is this the kind of work that takes place in your organization? Can it be? How?

Think for a minute about the recent sexual harassment investigation that emerged from the U.S. Senate review of Clarence Thomas for his appointment as Supreme Court Justice. The allegations and counterallegations suggest an example of the often-hidden work environment that impairs "good work." If Anita Hill's perception of her working environment is correct, then we can say that she sacrificed the QWL factors of Constitutionalism and social integration, so that she could have access to opportunities for growth and advancement. These are sacrifices that no employee should have to make. These are sacrifices that violate the ideal of "good work."

Alert and conscientious human resource managers, reviewing the working environment in their organizations, can discover and prevent uncomfortable conditions. Human resource managers cannot sit in an ivory tower of sorts, assuming that if no complaints are made, all is well in the organization.

As early as 1957, Chris Argyris noted that the very nature of organization tends to treat the workers with disrespect. He offers the following propositions:

Proposition I. There is a lack of congruency between the Needs of Healthy Individuals and the Demands of the Formal Organization.

Proposition II. The results of this Disturbance are Frustration, Failure, and Short-Time Perspective and Conflict.[41]

Unfortunately, now, some thirty years later, Argyris's propositions still ring true. People come to organizations with the expectation that they will contribute their knowledge, skills, and abilities in exchange for fair and adequate compensation and opportunities for advancement and prestige. In today's competitive environment, they soon find that the organization demands more and more, and that their lives are out of balance. Their "total life space" is violated.

While those with limited knowledge, skills, and abilities may be at the mercy of the organization or dependent on union negotiations for a satisfying set of working conditions where balance is possible, professionals are not. A recent *U.S. News & World Report* article notes:

After a decade of worshiping work, many successful professionals say they feel disheartened and dissatisfied with their careers—exhausted by the constant conflict between getting ahead at the office and building a satisfying life outside it—and left wanting by rewards that are strictly monetary. . . . [They] are looking to trade in their fast-track lives for more-balanced careers with greater psychic rewards.[42]

Should you be committed to helping workers at all levels of your organization achieve this balance? We think so. Will such commitment be costly? We think it will be an investment. "As more companies are discovering, what is rewarding for the individual, is also, ultimately, what is rewarding for the organization."[43]

The Role of Managers

The evidence that "good management" plays a part in affecting employee job satisfaction[44] puts a responsibility on both the managers and the supervisors in your organization. Our own research on what an individual supervisor or manager can do to foster job satisfaction is the impetus for this book. The job satisfaction of your employees is very much in your hands, although, some employees' personal characteristics and personal life situations can affect it from time to time.

In the surveys we completed for this book,[45] we asked respondents to report on the behavior of those who manage them in terms of the following criteria: treatment as an important person, help with solving problems, awareness of job difficulties, communication, frankness, consistency, ability to foster good relations with the work force, encouragement to make suggestions, consistency, and encouragement to seek educational opportunities. We then completed a statistical analysis of the responses and found that every one of these managerial behaviors had a statistically significant relationship with job satisfaction.[46]

Table 1.1 shows the strength of relationships between managerial behaviors and job satisfaction, as indicated by chi-square. It shows the percentages of those who were satisfied with their jobs in relationship to various managerial behaviors.

Respondents to our survey were asked to report on working conditions by answering questions that corresponded to the components of Quality of Work Life elements listed previously. Factor analysis was then conducted to determine which of the elements of QWL were the most important. Table 1.2 shows these elements in order by importance. Table 1.3 shows the percentage of respondents who indicated the presence of each factor in their work environment.

Study the tables. Which elements of QWL are present in your workplace? Are these elements present for all employees or just some? Which elements can you influence? How does your organization compare to the ones in this study? You can find out, if you want, by utilizing the questionnaire provided in Appendix A, which also contains a description of the research methodology. Elements of QWL that you can influence directly are total life space, good managerial relations, fair and adequate compensation, and safe and healthy work environment.

Total Life Space. You will notice that the people we surveyed valued most having a sense that their job did not violate their "total life space." That is, in order to feel satisfied with their jobs, these employees wanted to be able to balance the demands of work and home. To do this, workers want their managers to expect a reasonable amount of work, but not so much that the job interferes with personal life.[47] In a recent journal article, a vice president for personnel for IBM acknowledged the emerging importance of these issues. He emphasized the need to provide alternative work arrangements for families with both single and dual incomes to help them manage daily stress issues such as the care of children and elderly parents. He also emphasized the need for professional development and training.[48]

The idea of "total life space" is a new concept for human resource managers, growing in importance as the numbers of employed women

Table 1.1
Relationship between Managerial Behavior and Employee Satisfaction

Managerial Behavior	%Satisfied	df	chi-square	Significance
Treats employee as important person	90.8%	4	99.57093	.00000
Communication	86.2%	4	74.40409	.00000
Frankness	89.8%	4	70.12120	.00000
Consistence	89.9%	4	43.09997	.00000
Helps solve job-related problems	87.7%	4	41.83678	.00000
Encouragement to seek educational opportunities	86.4%	4	41.30284	.00000
Aware of employee difficulties	86.7%	4	27.04781	.00001
Encouragement to make suggestions	85.7%	4	22.06042	.00021
Ability to foster good relations with work force	89.1%	4	11.87339	.01832

Table 1.2
Quality of Work Life Elements in Priority Order

Factor	chi-square	df	Significance
Total Life Space*	24.5644	4	.00006
Good Supervisory Relations*	41.83678	4	.00000
Treated as Important Person*	99.57093	4	.00000
Adequate and Fair Compensation*	36.04748	4	.00000
Safe and Healthy Environment*	58.08503	4	.00000
Social Relevance**	46.62744	4	.00000
Involved and Informed Employees**	11.87339	4	.01832
Opportunities to Grow and Develop**	41.30284	4	.00000
Good Coworker Relations**	26.59374	4	.00002
Stress-free Environment**	31.93995	4	.00000
Fair Treatment for All**	36.84031	4	.00000
Job Variety**	28.05017	4	.00121

*   These factors have eigenvalues of 1.0 and higher.
**   These factors have eigenvalues of less than 1.0.

Table 1.3
Presence of Quality of Work Life

Factor	Percent of Respondents with Element Present
Total Life Space	52.2 %
Good Supervisory Relations	56.4 %
Treated as Important Person	84.9 %
Adequate and Fair Compensation	32.4 %
Safe and Healthy Environment	91.7 %
Social Relevance	69.4 %
Involved and Informed Employees	16.4 %
Opportunities to Grow and Develop	62.6 %
Good Coworker Relations	96.7 %
Stress free Environment	53.0 %
Fair Treatment for All	81.8 %
Job Variety	98.1 %

grow. Chapter 2 discusses the changing demographic nature of the work force, and Chapter 5 explains the impact of family responsibilities on both job satisfaction and performance. These are new issues for management, yet in today's work world, balancing performance with job satisfaction requires an understanding and a set of skills that neither workers nor their managers have acquired. One purpose of this book is to equip you with the knowledge and skills to facilitate that balancing act for yourself, and for your employees.

Good Managerial Relations. The second most important factor in fostering job satisfaction is "good managerial relations."[49] Those who act to maintain good relations with their employees exhibit the following behaviors: help with job-related problems, awareness of employee difficulties, good communication, and regular feedback about performance so that employees always know where they stand.[50]

Regular feedback is a key to good communications. It must occur to identify and assist with any job-related problems an employee might have. Whether employees are meeting and exceeding expectations, or whether they are performing in an unacceptable manner, they want their behavior assessed by management. Line supervisors are in a better position to give consistent, timely, and ongoing feedback than you are. "Keep up the good work" and "Great job" are usually easy for them to say. Unfortunately, "What you're doing is unacceptable" does not come so easily. We are always surprised at the reluctance of managers to provide regular feedback to their employees. One group of twenty-one managers who were participating in a training exercise to learn to give feedback listed the reasons why they are reluctant to tell employees how they are doing. The reasons they listed included:

- I don't want to judge the employee.
- I don't want to offend the employee.
- I'm afraid I'll make matters worse.
- I might say the wrong thing.
- I try to avoid arguments.

We call managers who protest like this "gutless wonders." By not communicating regularly with those who work for them they hamper job satisfaction and impede performance. They also shirk their responsibility. Even worse, we believe, they do not give their employees the opportunity to maximize performance and satisfaction.

To illustrate—one of the men with whom we spoke in creating material for this book is from a less-developed country but is currently working and studying in the United States. Because he is highly skilled, he easily acquired a job when he arrived in this country. A precise awareness of time and a penchant for promptness, however, are not a part of his culture, as they are in American culture. So, even though his working schedule was from 8 AM to 5 PM, the man went to work whenever he was ready; sometimes he arrived at work at 8:30, sometimes after 9. No one said a word to him about tardiness until the day he was fired. The supervisor who had failed to confront him about tardiness lost a competent employee. The employee learned about American timekeeping, but at the price of his job. How much simpler it would have been to have just given him feedback about his behavior soon enough to prevent both his and the organization's loss.

Even highly professional workers, such as university faculty members conducting research, value feedback. One study found that a leadership style emphasizing accurate, complete, and frequent communication was positively associated with faculty satisfaction.[51] In the Hawthorne experiments of the 1930s, researchers studied employees of Western Electric in an effort to determine the effects of decreasing or increasing light upon productivity. They found, however, that light was not the contributing factor to performance, but what was critical was the attention and feedback of managers. Almost sixty years later, our studies had similar results.

Employees want to have input into decisions that affect them and to feel important.[52] They want to be informed and involved.[53] When a job brings recognition and respect, employees experience satisfaction with it.[54] This is an easy condition to create with feedback. You and the supervisors throughout your company can simply seek and use employee input into decision making, and let employees know they are appreciated. In Chapter 6 we will talk about the role of employee participation in enhancing both performance and satisfaction and tell you how to manage a participative process.

Fair and Adequate Compensation. Adequate compensation is another important influence on employee job satisfaction.[55] Employees do expect fair and adequate compensation—a day's pay for a day's work. The component of compensation that influences satisfaction appears to be "equity" rather than "dollar amount," however.[56]

Satisfaction with wages is more dependent on relative than on absolute pay, on comparison with others, and on perceptions of fairness. While within organizations there is a correlation between job satisfaction and pay, it is very small.[57] People are consistently more satisfied because of equity than they are because of high wages.

Relative pay is a better predictor of job satisfaction than the absolute amount paid; in one study (published in 1963) supervisors earning over $12,000 a year were more satisfied than company presidents earning under $49,000. People at work have a clear idea of what they ought to be paid in comparison with others, and in relation to their skill, experience, and so forth. They want their performance, seniority, age, and education to be recognized and rewarded.[58]

Pay equity was a major recommendation in an organizational strategic planning effort that one of the authors directed. One planning committee wanted to "ensure that job titles, job descriptions, and salary levels are commensurate with job responsibilities and are equivalent across all . . . departments, and divisions."[59] Another committee stated that "working conditions, including compensation, fringe benefits, physical environment, and opportunity for advancement should be as beneficial as possible. Inequalities will exist; care must be taken so that inequities do not."[60]

Compensation comes in many forms other than financial remuneration. For instance, a major midwestern retail chain has an Honors Club in which membership is earned by sales clerks who, over a one year period, exceed their quota. Recognition comes in two simple ways. Clerks who are "members" of the Honors Club can wear a badge that announces their membership and are guests at a banquet held in Des Moines, Iowa, where a "motivational speaker" challenges them to continue to excel. Only 10 percent of the sales personnel achieve Honors status, and they point with pride to that achievement. Persons with whom we talked report that one of the things they appreciate most is the inspiration to do even better in the upcoming year. Simply put, organizations that have instituted programs to improve job satisfaction have found them to be "successful in terms of both human and economic standards."[61]

Work Environment. Employee job satisfaction is also influenced by the quality of the working environment—both its physical attributes and the degree to which it provides meaningful work. While a comfortable physical environment is correlated with job satisfaction, the relationship is not nearly as strong as the relationship between satisfaction and managerial behavior.

A survey of eighty-eight studies on the relationship between perceived control at work and several outcome variables concluded that "employees who perceive comparatively high levels of control at work are more satisfied, committed, involved, and motivated."[62] In this same vein, attitudes about the work group are important influences on job satisfaction.

Employees want certain conditions in their work. They want to believe that what they do will ultimately make a difference to someone in some way. They want to participate in decision making. They want opportunities to grow and develop, and they want these same opportunities for their coworkers, regardless of race, sex, or age.

Employee Characteristics. Several characteristics of employees have an influence on their job satisfaction. The employees whom we have surveyed and interviewed are a good group from which to develop an understanding of the relationship between personal attributes and life-styles, and job satisfaction. Eighty-six percent of them are highly satisfied with their jobs. They report commitment and positive feelings toward their jobs. They are people who have learned to balance satisfaction with productivity. In this book we will share with you what we have learned from them.

We found that older workers (51 + years) tend to be more satisfied than younger colleagues, and that greater length of time on the job correlated with higher job satisfaction.[63] Other scholars report that maturity may influence job satisfaction as much as biological age,[64] or career stage, or length of job tenure.[65]

THE BALANCING ACT

As human resource manager, you are a key "satisfaction maker" in your organization. When new employees are hired, you (or your staff) give the first impressions of the organization to them. If you give false expectations about the work setting, promotion opportunities, or salary possibilities, disillusionment will create dissatisfaction. In recruiting and promoting, be certain to "tell it like it is." Give no false hopes. Make no promises you cannot keep.

Remember that most American workers have an "inner need to do the very best job" possible.[66] What they want to help them balance performance with job satisfaction is a proactive manager with human relations skills. They want respect, honesty about their performance, assistance when they need it, and encouragement to better themselves.

For example, one group of employees with whom we have worked requested that their organization "provide professional counseling to staff on the promotion and development of career goals and opportunities." They also wanted a systematic training program to enhance the occasional staff training courses that have been very popular. Respondents to our surveys reflect this same desire. Forty seven percent of them agreed with the statement, "I wish I had more training for my job."

Simply put, people we have surveyed and talked with want to be able to balance satisfaction and performance. They want both to be high level. They ask for organizations to develop policies and conditions that will help them perform well and advance. They also ask for help in balancing the many demands on their time and energies. They are willing to meet organizations halfway—to do their part in the balancing act. Sometimes, however, our respondents feel hindered by policies and by supervisory behavior. In fact, 89 percent of them said that relationships between workers and managers need improving. What about the people in your organization?

AN OVERVIEW OF THIS TEXT

You have just been introduced to the conventional wisdom and confusion about job satisfaction and performance as well as our research on these subjects. We believe this information is necessary but insufficient for the management of workers in the coming decades. Traditional knowledge has been developed from studies of a workplace far different than that we now inhabit. The workplace of tomorrow will be populated with a diverse group of multicultural workers who must balance family responsibilities with career obligations. This workplace will rely on increasingly sophisticated technology that might overwhelm and alienate workers who are not adequately trained or involved. Thus your job as a manager of human resources will be more complicated.

Balancing job satisfaction and performance will become more necessary, and more difficult. You will be challenged in ways and by circumstances that did not exist in the 1970s and 1980s. You will have to accomplish more with fewer resources and with less human capital. Workers will expect more than their predecessors. You can expect that labor will have a sellers' market in which you as the buyer have fewer choices. Thus the general purpose of this book is to prepare you to successfully manage the work force of the upcoming decades by assisting them to balance satisfaction and performance.

Chapter 2, "The Changing Work Force," addresses the workplace complexities created by the diverse cultures represented by a new work force. These complexities are largely hidden from conscious awareness but are surfacing as the work force becomes more diverse. This chapter explains why the traditional means to foster job satisfaction and performance are necessary but insufficient for managing a diverse work force. It documents the changing realities of work force composition and explains how to deal with the four trends identified by the U.S. Department of Labor as forces that will "revolutionize tomorrow's work force."

Chapter 3, "Environmental Trends Affecting the Workplace," advises the human resource manager how to meet the challenges to job satisfaction and performance presented by a changing environment. This chapter describes the impact of technology and the changing nature of work and of socioeconomic conditions upon job satisfaction and performance. Because of the decreasing numbers of skilled workers available, employers will be forced to establish conditions that enhance job satisfaction. Dissatisfied employees are absent more often. Dissatisfied employees leave. This chapter explains how to achieve a workplace in which employees are both satisfied and productive in spite of environmental trends.

Chapter 4, "The Impact of Family Responsibilities," explains why traditional human resource management has not taken into consideration the impact of an employee's family on job satisfaction and performance, nor the interface between work and family. Rather, mainstream management pretends that employees can leave family concerns at the organizational gate. Yet, as more and more women enter the workplace with plans to stay and advance, family demands on both men and women spill over onto the organization, affecting both job satisfaction and performance. This chapter utilizes original research by the authors to educate you as managers about the competing demands of home and work, and to offer the notion of workplace as surrogate family. This chapter can assist you to make decisions about the organizational role in managing the work/family interface, and the text discusses options for accommodating employee needs.

Chapter 5, "The Power of Training and Education," explains how education for employees and their families can foster job satisfaction and performance. This chapter can assist you as managers to view employees as unique individuals whose personal needs for self-actualization can be integrated with organizational performance needs. For employees to be satisfied performers, they need assistance, education, and encouragement. This chapter explains how and why different kinds of training opportunities should be provided for both employees and their families. Specific instructions are given for utilizing federal training programs and for setting up arrangements for training in-house, by consultant, and by contract.

Chapter 6, "The Benefits and Methods of Participation," is based on the maxim of employee motivation, which affirms that "people accept what they help to create." This chapter discusses the role of participative management in enhancing job satisfaction and performance. The chapter is grounded in the planning literature, and both the experience and original research of the authors. For certain kinds of employees, participation in decision making enhances their commitment to the organization and draws upon their intimate knowledge of their work to introduce improvements that enhance performance and job satisfaction. The chapter discusses the utility of participation at different organizational levels, and describes some different approaches to participative planning and decision making. Most discussions of participative planning tell what to do, but give little instruction on how to manage the process. This chapter provides you with practical guidance on how to make the process work.

Chapter 7, "Portraits of Satisfied and Dissatisfied Employees," describes important differences between satisfied and dissatisfied employees. It is based on interviews with people who work in public, private, and nonprofit organizations. Few people are totally satisfied or totally dissatisfied. Part of how they feel depends on their own personality and expectations. This chapter utilizes personal stories to illustrate how much of job satisfaction and performance can be influenced by human resource management practices, and how much comes from the unique characteristics of individual employees.

NOTES

1. Dorothy Soelle, *To Work and to Love* (Philadelphia: Fortress Press, 1989): 72.

2. William Turcotte, "Control Systems Performance, and Satisfaction in Two State Agencies," *Administrative Science Quarterly* 19 (March 1974): 60–73.

3. "Need to Concentrate? Snort a Peppermint," *Omaha World-Herald* (Nebraska), February 20, 1991, 9.

4. Ronald Grey and Peter Gelfond, "The People Side of Productivity," *National Productivity Review* 9, no. 3 (Summer 1990): 301–12.

5. Ibid.

6. Patricia K. Fullagar and Werner K. Sensbach, "Mile High Planning: SCUP–24 Conference Report," *Planning for Higher Education* 18, no. 2 (1989–90): 66.

7. Ruth Walker, "A Larger Sense of Family—and Learning," *Christian Science Monitor*, May 17, 1990.

8. "A Special News Report on People and Their Jobs in Offices, Fields and Factories," *Wall Street Journal*, January 16, 1990, 1.

9. Ibid.

10. Alan Farrant, "You Need Good Subordinates," *Supervision* (May 1990): 17–19.

11. G. Hofstede "Humanization of Work: The Role of Values in a Third Industrial Revolution," Working Paper 77–16, EIASM Brussels, 1977.

12. Martin Mork, *The Work/Life Dichotomy* (Westport, Conn. Quorum Books, 1989): 16.

13. Fredrick Herzberg, B. Mausner, and B. B. Snyderman, *The Motivation to Work* (New York: Wiley, 1959).

14. R. Ferris, "How Organizational Love Can Improve Leadership," *Organizational Dynamics* 16, no. 11: 41–51.

15. F. Herzberg, "One More Time: How Do You Motivate Employees?" *Harvard Business Review* (January-February 1968).

16. Studs Terkel, *Working* (New York: Pantheon Books, 1974): xi.

17. Ibid.

18. S. Clegg and D. Dunkerley, *Organization, Class and Control* (London: Routledge & Kegan Paul, 1980): 512.

19. J. Hackman and G. Oldham, "Development of the Job-Diagnostic Survey," *Journal of Applied Psychology* 60, no. 2 (April 1975): 161.

20. A. Braendgaard, "Cultural-Normative Change or Interest Politics in Disguise?" Paper presented at EIASM Seminar on Cultural and Normative Change in Organizations, Brussels (April 20–21, 1978).

21. Robin Fincham and Peter Rhodes, *The Individual, Work and Organization* (London: Weidenfeld and Nicolson, 1988): 97.

22. Douglas M. Morrill, "Human Resource Planning in the 1990s" *Best's Review* (July 1990): 104+.

23. William Johnston and Arnold Packer, *Workforce 2000* (Indianapolis, Ind.: Hudson Institute, 1987).

24. John Naisbitt and Patricia Aburdene, *Reinventing the Corporation* (New York: Warner Books, 1985): 86.

25. Ibid.

26. J. Thompson, *Organizations in Action* (New York: McGraw-Hill, 1967): 114.

27. Naisbitt and Aburdene, *Reinventing the Corporation*, 85.

28. "Worker Advocacy Group Alleges Employee Surveillance Increasing," *Omaha World-Herald* (Nebraska), February 25, 1990, 18G.

29. David R. Francis, "Efficiency Gains Rare After Business Layoffs," *Christian Science Monitor*, May 25, 1990, 8.

30. See, J. R. Hackman, "The Design of Work in the 1980's," *Organizational Dynamics* 6 (Summer 1978): 3–17; J. R. Hackman and E. E. Lawler III, "Employee Reactions to Job Characteristics," *Journal of Applied Psychology Monograph* 55 (1971): 259–86; J. R. Hackman and G. Oldham, *The Diagnostic Survey: An Instrument for the Diagnosis of Jobs and the Evaluation of Job Redesign Projects* (New Haven: Yale University, 1974); J. R. Hackman and G. Oldham, "Development of the Job Diagnostic Survey," *Journal of Applied Psychology* 60 (April 1975); and J. R. Hackman and J. L. Suttle, *Improving Life at Work* (Santa Monica, Cal.: Goodyear Publishing Co., 1977).

31. W. Bruce, "Job Satisfaction and Quality of Work Life," *News Digest of the International Institute of Municipal Clerks* (January 1988).

32. Ibid., 15.

33. Brian Dumaine, "The Bureaucracy Busters," *Fortune* (June 17, 1991): 36–50.

34. Ibid., 38.

35. See, for example, Bruce, "The Quality of Work Life of the Nation's Municipal Clerks," *News Digest of the International Institute of Municipal Clerks* (April 1989): 1–4; J. W. Blackburn and W. Bruce, "Rethinking Concepts of Job Satisfaction: The Case of Nebraska Municipal Clerks," *Review of Public Personnel Administration* 10, no. 1 (Fall 1989): 11–29; C. Kerr and J. Rosow, eds., *Work in America: The Decade Ahead* (New York: D. Van Nostrand, 1979); D. Nachmias, "The Quality of Work Life in the Federal Bureaucracy: Conceptualization and Measurement," *American Review of Public Administration* 18 (June 1988): 166–73; W. Ouchi, *Theory Z* (Reading, Mass.: Addison-Wesley, 1981); T. Peters and R. Waterman, *In Search of Excellence* (New York: Harper and Row, 1983); and T. Cummings and E. Huse, *Organization Development and Change*, 3d ed. (St. Paul, Minn.: West Publishing Company, 1989).

36. Cummings and Huse, *Organization Development and Change*, 199–200.

37. See, R. Walton, "Perspectives on Work Restructuring," in W. Passmore J. Sherwood, eds. *Sociotechnical systems: A Sourcebook.* San Diego, CA: University Associates, 1978; Kerr and Rosow, *Work in America*; Ouchi, *Theory Z*; Peters and Waterman, *In Search of Excellence.*

38. See, S. Mohrman and T. Cummings, "Implementing Quality of Work Life

Programs by Managers," in R. Ritvo and A. Sargent, eds., *The NTL Manager's Handbook* (Washington, D.C.: NTL Institute, 1983): 320–28; and G. Strauss, "Is There a Blue Collar Revolt Against Work?" in J. O'Toole, ed., *Work and Quality of Life* (Cambridge, Mass.: MIT Press, 1974): 47–61.

39. Herzberg, Mausner, and Snyderman, *The Motivation to Work.*

40. Adapted from E. Schumacher, cited in Dorothy Soelle, *To Work and to Love.*

41. Chris Argyris, "The Individual and the Organization," reprinted in W. Natemeyer and J. Gilberg, *Classics of Organization Behavior,* 2d ed. (Danville, Ill.: The Interstate Printers and Publishers, 1989): 21–34.

42. Amy Saltzman, "The New Meaning of Success," *U.S. News & World Report* (September 17, 1990): 56–58.

43. Ibid., 58.

44. See, Cummings and Huse, *Organization Development and Change;* Blackburn and Bruce, "Rethinking Concepts of Job Satisfaction"; and Bruce, "Job Satisfaction and Quality of Work Life."

45. See Appendix A: Research Methodology for a complete description of the research and a copy of the survey instrument.

46. Cross-tabs established that the correlation of the statement "Overall, I am very satisfied with my job" with each question about the identified managerial behaviors was significant at the .00 level, except "ability to foster good relations with the work force", which was significant at the .01 level.

47. Cross-tabulation of Factor 1 with Q41, "Considering everything, I am very satisfied with my job at the present time," indicates a strong relationship between job satisfaction and "total life space" ($X^2 = 24.5644$) at a significance level of .00006.

48. Fullagar and Sensbach, "Mile High Planning," 66.

49. With an eigenvalue of 2.222, this variable explains an additional 5.8 percent of variance in job satisfaction.

50. Cross-tabulation of Factor 2 with Q41, "Considering everything, I am very satisfied with my job at the present time," indicates a strong relationship between job satisfaction and "good managerial relations" ($X^2 = 41.8368$) at a significance level of .0000.

51. William F. Glueck, and Gary D. Thorp, "The Role of the Academic Administrator in Research Professors' Satisfaction and Productivity," *Educational Administration Quarterly* 10 (1974): 72–90, cited in Marvin W. Peterson, ed., *Key Resources on Higher Education Governance, Management, and Leadership* (San Francisco: Jossey-Bass, 1987): 403–4.

52. Cross-tabulation of Factor 3 with Q41, "Considering everything, I am very satisfied with my job at the present time," indicates the strongest relationship with job satisfaction of any of the factors ($X^2 = 99.5709$) at a significance level of .0000.

53. Although this sense of "involved and informed" appears as seventh on the list, the significance of its relationship with job satisfaction is also .0000.

54. B. Posner, and W. Schmidt, "Values and Expectations of City Managers in California," *Public Administration Review* 47, 5 (September/October 1986): 404–9.

55. With an eigenvalue of 1.0000, Factor 4 explains only 3 percent of the

variance, yet has a strong relationship with Q41 ($X^2 = 99.5709$) at a significance level of .0000.

56. This expectation of pay equity has appeared in the literature on motivation since the days of Herzberg and also of J. Adams, "Inequity in Social Exchange," in L. Berkowitz, ed., *Advances in Experimental Social Psychology*, vol. 2. (New York: Academic Press, 1965).

57. Michael Argyle, *The Social Psychology of Work*, 2d ed. (London: Penguin Books, 1989): 94, 99).

58. Ibid., 94, 99, 238.

59. "Strategic Planning Committee Report: Staff Infrastructure Committee," (Omaha, Nebraska: Creighton University, 1989–90): 10.

60. "Support Services Committee Report," (Omaha, Nebraska: Creighton University, 1989–90): 5.

61. Braendgaard, in Clegg and Dunkerley, *Organization, Class, and Control*, 513.

62. P. Spector, "Perceived Control by Employees: A Meta-analysis of Studies Concerning Autonomy and Participation at Work," *Human Relations* 39, no. 11 (1986): 1005–16.

63. R. Katzell and D. Yankelovich, "Improving Productivity and Job Satisfaction," *Organizational Dynamics* 4 (Summer 1975): 69–80; and Blackburn and Bruce, "Rethinking Concepts of Job Satisfaction."

64. S. R. Rhodes, "Age Related Differences in Work Attitudes and Behavior: A Review and Conceptual Analysis," *Psychological Bulletin* 93 (1985): 328–67 describes psychosocial aging as "systematic changes in personality, needs, expectations, and behavior as well as performance in a sequence of socially prescribed roles." Biological aging has to do with sensorimotor performance and balance.

65. See, S. Stumpf and S. Rabinowitz, "Career Stage as a Moderator of Performance Relationships with Facets of Job Satisfaction and Role Perceptions," *Journal of Vocational Behavior* 18 (1981): 202–18.

66. D. Yankelovich, in Naisbitt and Aburdene, *Reinventing the Corporation*, 85.

APPENDIX A: RESEARCH METHODOLOGY

Our research was based on the following hypotheses:

- Employee job satisfaction is significantly related to the behavior of the employee's supervisor.
- Employee job satisfaction is significantly related to working conditions that a supervisor can influence.
- Employee job satisfaction is significantly related to feelings about the job that can be influenced by a supervisor.

To test these hypotheses, respondents were asked to answer fifty-two questions on a multi-page questionnaire. The first part of the questionnaire contained 11 questions regarding individual characteristics of respondents: gender, age group, education, and description of current job and family responsibilities. The second part included 14 statements relating to personal feelings about the job, 10 statements relating to supervisory behavior, 14 statements relating to working conditions, as well as a summary statement, "Considering everything, I am very satisfied with my job at the present time," and a statement naming the state of employment. Respondents were asked to read each statement, then to circle a number to indicate whether they "agree," "don't know," or "disagree." Only one statement specifically asked about job satisfaction, which is consistent with a number of other studies that used a single-item measure for overall job satisfaction. In addition, in previous research on municipal clerks, this single statement had an average correlation of .83, with fifty-six questions that asked about the five specific job conditions identified by Hackman and Oldham in 1975.

The validity of the questionnaire was assured by using multiple measures of the same concept. For purposes of validity, seven questions were asked in negative form, then re-coded for data analysis. Thus respondents were asked to think through their responses, and not just automatically "agree" or "disagree". The size of the sample and high response rate assured reliability within ± 4 percent.[1]

Survey data were nominal. Because of the complex interrelationships of conditions that impact job satisfaction, they were analyzed in two ways. First, the 39 questionnaire items that did not relate to individual characteristics were subjected to factor analysis based on a varimax procedure and a criterion of an eigenvalue greater than 1.0. This determined where clusters of relations exist and produced a rotated factor matrix that reduced the 36 items to 12 factors, of which four factors had eigenvalues greater than 1.000.

Second, Crosstabs tables were then constructed to determine the relationship between job satisfaction and the first variable of each of the four significant factors; and between job satisfaction and each questionnaire item that represented supervisory behavior. Chi-square was used as the test of statistical significance, with a significance of .11000 to .00000 considered worth reporting. Chi-square was also used to determine strength of relationship.

A copy of the actual questionnaire is on the following pages.

NOTE TO APPENDIX

1. When a population size of 10,000 yields a sample size of between 566 and 964, results have a reliability of ± 4 percent. Welch Susan and John C. Comer *Quantitative Methods for Public Administration* (Chicago: The Dorsey Press, 1983).

We are writing a book called <u>Job Satisfaction and Performance: Achieving a Balance</u>. This survey is designed to help us learn more about job satisfaction, performance, and quality of worklife. Would you please take a few minutes of your time to answer the following questions. All responses will be kept confidential. Your assistance will be greatly appreciated. Thank you very much for your help.

--Dr. J. Walton Blackburn   --Dr. Willa Bruce

PLEASE ANSWER THE FOLLOWING QUESTIONS ABOUT YOURSELF BY PUTTING AN X BESIDE THE CHOICE THAT DESCRIBES YOU.

1. I am   _____male   _____female

2. My age is   _____ under 30   _____ 31 to 40   _____ 41 to 50   _____ 51 to 60   _____ 60+

3. I am   _____African-American   _____White   _____ Asian   _____Other

4. The highest education I have completed is
    _____ less than 12 years of high school   _____ high school diploma or GED   _____ some college
    _____ a 4 year degree   _____ some graduate school   _____ a graduate degree

5. The length of time that I have worked in my current position is
    _____ less than one year   _____ 1 to 5 years
    _____ 6 to 10 years   _____ more than 10 years

6. Which of the following titles best describes you?
    _____ Executive   _____Department Head   _____Supervisor
    _____ Salesperson   _____Service Provider   _____Professional Staff
    _____ Computer Programmer   _____Clerical   _____ Other (describe) _____

7. My position is   _____ part time   _____ full time

8. I am: _____ married (or living in a significant relationship)   _____ not married

9. If you are married or living in a significant relationship, is your spouse or significant employed?
    _____yes   _____no

10. I have family responsibilities   _____yes _____no

11. I am a single parent   _____yes _____no

PLEASE RESPOND TO THE FOLLOWING STATEMENTS ABOUT YOUR JOB BY PUTTING A CIRCLE AROUND THE NUMBER UNDER YOUR RESPONSE.

	AGREE	DON'T KNOW	DISAGREE
12. I have a lot of variety in my job.	_____	_____	_____
13. I would like to be more informed about the operation of the organization.	_____	_____	_____
14. If I do my job well, I can expect to be promoted to a job with more prestige and salary.	_____	_____	_____
15. I have pleasant work surroundings.	_____	_____	_____
16. I have good relations with my coworkers.	_____	_____	_____

	AGREE	DON'T KNOW	DISAGREE
17. In my job I am treated as a responsible important person.	___	___	___
18. I don't believe there is too much pressure in my job.	___	___	___
19. I believe that too much work is expected of me.	___	___	___
20. My job is important.	___	___	___
21. I frequently see the results of my work.	___	___	___
22. The training I have received for my job is adequate.	___	___	___
23. I would like to be more involved in decision making in my organization.	___	___	___
24. I would rate my supervisor highly in helping with job-related problems.	___	___	___
25. If I continue to perform my job as I am now doing, I can expect to keep my job as long as I want.	___	___	___
26. My coworkers cooperate to get the job done.	___	___	___
27. I believe that my boss is aware of the difficulties I experience in my job.	___	___	___
28. People in my organization are treated fairly without regard to age.	___	___	___
29. Communication between me and my boss is good.	___	___	___
30. People in my organization are treated fairly without regard to gender.	___	___	___
31. I am well informed about personnel policies.	___	___	___
32. I believe personnel policies are almost always administered consistently.	___	___	___
33. I have input into decisions that are made in my department.	___	___	___
34. I have adequate authority to carry out my job.	___	___	___
35. I have so much to do for my job sometimes I don't have enough time for my personal life.	___	___	___
36. People in the community respect me because of my job.	___	___	___

	AGREE	DON'T KNOW	DISAGREE
37. I always know where I stand with my supervisor.	___	___	___
38. I am satisfied with the amount of free time I have outside of work.	___	___	___
39. I am bothered by others smoking in my workplace.	___	___	___
40. I perform work that is meaningful for me.	___	___	___
41. The organization has a good reputation as an employer.	___	___	___
42. I believe that management can do more to improve relations between themselves and the work force.	___	___	___
43. I believe my salary is about the same as I would earn elsewhere.	___	___	___
44. My supervisor encourages me to suggest new ways of doing work.	___	___	___
45. My supervisor actively encourages me to seek new educational opportunities.	___	___	___
46. I am under a great deal of stress because of my job.	___	___	___
47. I receive adequate and fair compensation.	___	___	___
48. Overall, my working conditions are safe and healthy.	___	___	___
49. I have opportunities to use and develop my skills and knowledge.	___	___	___
50. I am able to balance comfortably my job and my life away from work.	___	___	___
51. Considering everything, I am very satisfied with my job at the present time.	___	___	___
52. The state I work in is _____	___	___	___

THANK YOU VERY MUCH FOR TAKING THE TIME TO COMPLETE THIS SURVEY.

Please return your completed survey in the enclosed postage-free envelope
to: Dr. Willa Bruce
         Department of Public Administration
         University of Nebraska at Omaha
         Omaha, NE 68182

_____ Chapter 2 _____

The Changing Work Force

The framework established by our language and culture becomes
the playground of our creativity . . . and the prison of our continuing
prejudice.

Martha Gadberry Beaman

This chapter addresses how culture influences workplace relationships,
which in turn affect job satisfaction and performance. We want to provoke thought about the complexities created by culture, complexities
that are largely hidden from conscious awareness but that surface as the
work force becomes more diverse. We will provide you with information
and techniques to assist employees to work together in ways that benefit
themselves and your organization, despite cultural messages that inter-
fere with productive relationships. In this chapter we will talk about
cultural issues that surround diversity management, making it difficult
and challenging. We explain both the real and hidden costs of harassment and provide legal guidelines for preventing it.

We will talk mostly about employees who are supervisors, managers,
professionals, and executives in both the government and corporate
sectors, because almost all research has dealt with these categories of
workers. But we will also mention blue- and pink-collar workers. At the
lower levels of the organization where goods and services are actually
produced and delivered, educational levels will be lower and unions are
more likely to exist. There people are more apt to be afraid of what
management will do, thinking in terms of "them against us." There,
also, is where literacy is more likely to be a concern. But whether employees are at the pinnacle of the organization or labor in its bowels,
they are human beings with similar concerns, fears, and, frequently,
prejudices—all feelings that make it difficult to manage diversity.

As you probably know, the composition of the American work force is changing rapidly. More than half of the U.S. work force now consists of minorities, immigrants, and women.[1] In 1991, only 22 percent of new entrants into the job market were white males.[2] Typical workers in the twenty-first century will be more mature, more highly educated, and more technologically sophisticated than their counterparts in the twentieth century. Increasing numbers of new work force entrants will be nonwhite and from cultures other than European-American.

Consider the following statistics:

1. Regarding women—

   - In 1990, 57 percent of the work force were female,[3] and more than 46 percent were in professional or managerial positions.[4] "Women have been the dominant factor in labor-force growth over the past 30 years."[5]
   - "More than half of all college and university students are women."[6]

2. Regarding a mature work force—

   - The median age of the population will reach 36 by the year 2000, six years older than at any time in the history of the nation.[7]
   - Between the years 1986 and 2000, the number of Americans aged 48 to 53 will leap by a staggering 67 percent, compared with overall population growth of only 15 percent.[8]

3. Regarding the nonwhite work force—

   - In 1970, 10.9 percent of the work force was nonwhite. By 1985, that percentage had increased to 13.6, and by 2000, it will increase further to 15.7 percent.[9]
   - Between 1980 and 1985, the population of Hispanics increased by 22.9 percent, of blacks by 8.3 percent, and of Asian and other nonwhites by 36.1 percent.[10]
   - Over the next twenty years, the U.S. population is expected to grow by 42 million. Hispanics will account for 47 percent of this growth. Blacks will account for 22 percent. Asians and other people of color will make up 18 percent of this increase, while whites will account for only 13 percent.[11]

Because of changing work-force demographics, managing diversity has become the theme of the 1990s. People talk about it. Trainers develop films, questionnaires, and activities to help supervisors understand it. Educators conduct programs on it. Scholars write books about it. Everyone, it seems, is saying "manage diversity" or "value diversity." Diversity has become the latest buzzword, the newest mantra of management gurus. As one corporate executive explained when we broached the subject, "We've done diversity to death. Everybody's sick of hearing about it."

Yet, managing a diverse work force is going to be *the* challenge of the twenty-first century. The composition of the work force is changing. Futurists are certain of it. Many human resource professionals are seeing it happen. A popular business magazine urges us to "concentrate on trying to get different races and sexes to work together, without adding to the stereotypes."[12] An article in the *Harvard Business Review* queries, "Diversity is what makes America different. Why don't we turn it to our advantage?"[13] High schools and universities have adjusted their curricula "in reaction to criticisms that students' sense of history is skewed by a Eurocentric focus in the classroom."[14] Literally, as the executive said, diversity is being "done to death."

We believe that the cultural and ethnic diversity of the American nation is a key source of our economic dynamism and inventive creativity. Major scientific advances have been produced by refugees from totalitarian regimes. Workers of diverse nationalities and racial backgrounds did the heavy labor of constructing the nation's physical infrastructure. Workers of varied racial and ethnic backgrounds bring diverse value perspectives to the workplace, which often enhances workplace creativity.

One of the authors was struck with the ethnic diversity of America one day on a university campus when he met a student who was obviously a mix of African American, Asian, and Caucasian heritage and whose name was something like Simone Kleinholtz (names of French and German origin respectively). The student's friendliness suggested an outgoing appreciation for other people, perhaps in part a result of her own cultural heritage. When the author commented that her name was "an interesting mix of nationalities," the student replied, "My mother loved French names."

We are seeing more ethnic and racial diversity in the people we encounter in every day life. The paradox is, however, that despite the obvious trends and all of the hype and rhetoric, dealing with diversity is not in the action plans of most corporations.[15] Most people still are not certain whether to value diversity, to accentuate diversity, or simply to ignore it. For example, a recent survey of 645 national companies found that while 75 percent of the respondents expressed a concern about changing work-force demographics, only 29 percent offered a program on managing diversity.[16] Another survey of 121 human resource executives from Fortune 500 companies produced similar results. Twenty-seven percent of the companies provide some diversity training, mostly to top executives, but only 15 percent have formal written policies on diversity.[17]

Most corporate and government entities are still not certain what "managing diversity" means, nor have they really thought about the implications to them of the changing work force. This chapter and Chapter 3 address the challenges created by demographic and environmental changes over which human resource managers have no control. Like it or not, we are faced with rethinking how to interact with employees. We must learn how to balance the performance and satisfaction of a group of people who are different from those for whom traditional management practices were developed, that is, who are often different from us.

What is needed is "multicultural vision,"[18] says one authority. We would add multicultural *awareness* and *commitment to action*. People fear what they do not understand. Your vision will never be implemented unless others become aware of the vision *and* are provided with the tools and motivation to help to realize that vision with you. Your commitment will not be another's until together you share your dreams and fears.

ISSUES OF DIVERSITY

Managing diversity is not about Affirmative Action. Affirmative Action is about actively hiring and promoting those people defined by law as members of a "protected class" who are underrepresented in the workplace. "There are very few places in the country where you could dip a recruitment net and come up with nothing but white males. Getting hired is not the problem. . . . It's later on that their [those who are "protected"] manager's inability to manage diversity hobbles them and the companies they work for."[19]

Our dictionary defines the word *diversity* with two others: "different" and "variety." The thesaurus adds two more worth noting: "assortment" and "medley." Each of these words carries its own unique connotation, which is relevant as we begin this discussion about the changing nature of the work force.

"Different" means "not like me." It invites comparison. If I am good, then "not like me" must be bad. If I am successful, then "not like me" must be a failure. If I am intelligent, then "not like me" must be dumb, and so on. Because women, minorities, and older workers are "different" from the men who made up the traditional work force, comparison induces disapproval. A negative comparison is frequently made, even by those who are members of the "different" group.

"Variety," "assortment," and "medley," provide possibilities for creativity. No one disparages Baskin and Robbins' twenty-three "varieties" of ice cream. Most of us were pleased when that variety increased to include "low-fat" products and yogurt. "Variety" implies choices, a selection large enough to provide exactly what is needed to satisfy. So does "assortment," a word frequently used by chocolate manufacturers. An assortment of Whitman's, Russell Stover's, or Fanny Farmer's candy is a "good" gift. Each box is sure to contain the very piece that is your favorite, or ours. An "assortment" or a "variety" of workers, or applicants, ought to fill us with excitement not dread.

"Medley." Now, there's a word! A "medley" of songs brings smiles, often fine old memories. A "medley" of fragrances captures our heart as potpourri. A "medley" implies an amalgamation, in which, once joined, all elements blend to make the final product greater than the sum of its individual components.

So, then, the first issue in managing the diversity of the changing work force is to think of those changes as leading to variety, creating assortments never before thought possible, and a medley of workers whose final products will excel. The mixture of backgrounds and perspectives enhances a decision or the creation of a product. If you can see the possibilities, you can begin to create an environment where "we" is everyone, where all workers are enabled to perform to their potential, where job satisfaction and performance are in balance.[20]

Approaches to Valuing and Benefiting from Diversity

As a first step toward balancing the satisfaction and performance of the changing work force, you can initiate diversity training at all levels of your organization. We provide an outline for one such training session in the chapter's appendix. A number of commercial diversity management–training programs are currently available. In order to maximize the potential benefits of these training packages, however, we think it is necessary for you to understand the cultural influences that have shaped thinking and behavior about women, minority, and mature workers.

Although the United States variously has been described as "vegetable soup," a "stew pot," and a "garden salad," the assumptions seem to have been that the very act of throwing all the ingredients together into one place in time created one "melting pot" in which all blended together as one. Any deviation from the blend has been treated like a lump in the gravy, something to be smashed down and blended in, or removed.

Why that happens is important to understand if you want to balance the satisfaction and performance of your work force. Part of the answer lies in the cultural heritage of the United States. The next section elaborates on how cultural influences shape all our behavior below the level of conscious awareness.

CULTURAL INFLUENCES ON DIVERSITY MANAGEMENT

The culture of the United States is rooted in Judeo-Christian, Western European traditions of whites. It has historically had little tolerance or appreciation of other heritages. Even though Native Americans inhabited these lands when white Europeans arrived and blacks were an integral part of colonial life, mainstream scholars have chosen to devalue their cultures. One scholar, for example, thinks that

black Americans have realized that whites have not only deprived them of material wealth but also of the invaluable facts of their own culture. In the past, white America has taken the most skillfully crafted and beautifully expressive artifacts of black American culture and labeled them "American:" thus jazz is viewed as "America's gift to the world." Well, that just is not so; jazz, like the rich folklore, the skilled literature, and the countless other facets of the body of intellectual and imaginative work reflecting black American culture is simply not America's to give. Black jazz, folklore, and literature proceed out of an experience that is unknown to most white Americans; they are products of a culture that white America has chosen to ignore, misrepresent, or deny. Call it black, Afro-American, Negro, the fact remains that this culture has little if anything to do with the white American's culture, or his definition of culture.[21]

Populations of minority cultures are becoming larger proportions of the U.S. work force. While those of us who live in small cities and towns in mid-America have a difficult time visualizing the variety of heritages in this country, those in large metropolitan areas on the east and west coasts will readily acknowledge the rapidly changing population of their cities. In Los Angeles, for example, "117,000 school children speak 104 languages in a city that must constantly adjust to the quirky polygot rhythms of 60,000 Samoans, 30,000 Thais, 200,000 Salvadorans, and 175,000 Armenians."[22] Thus, it is becoming increasingly important that human resource managers and supervisors at all levels understand the concept of culture and the influence it has on individual behavior.

The theory of culture and discussions about the role it plays in human development traditionally have been addressed primarily by anthropologists and sociologists. Culture is not a subject often considered by business and public administration scholars. If you are like most human resource-managers you probably have never studied culture, except in the context of "organizational culture." You may not have given much thought to how the culture of your origin influences how you think and what you believe.

The study of organizations has tended to focus on structure and process inside the organization, or it has examined the economic-environmental trends that provide threats and opportunities. Scholars analyze motivation, leadership, communication, and the impact of informal groups; and we devise and administer policies and procedures for hiring, managing, promoting, and terminating employees. Scholars talk about organizational culture as the "shared things, thoughts, and activities"[23] of workers within the company, or within a department. They encourage you to scan the environment for economic fluctuation; and keep an eye on your competitors and regulators. These managerial activities have served us well, for the work force has been, pretty much, a homogeneous group.

Up until now, women and other minorities who have succeeded in the workplace "have voluntarily abandoned most of their ethnic distinctions at the company door."[24] Their differences have not had measurable effects on the organizational culture. The changing composition of the work force, however, will bring more women and minorities into the workplace, even as existing workers are maturing. The homogeneity of workers is coming to an end. These are environmental trends that most organizations have not yet confronted.[25] As more and more diverse people enter the workplace, their cultural values and beliefs will come with them.

When workers with the cultural norms of one group encounter workers with the cultural norms of another group, people in both groups experience "culture shock"[26] or "cognitive dissonance."[27] This is the normal experience of a person faced with new problems that are not a part of the larger framework of the world as it has been known.[28] It's difficult, often impossible, to articulate what has happened. People only know that they feel discomfort, annoyance, maybe even embarrassment.

In today's world, however, this discomfort, annoyance, and embarrassment may cause someone to file a discrimination complaint. That happened in Omaha, Nebraska. A recently hired human resource manager lost his job after he suggested in a staff meeting that Affirmative Action efforts be directed to "little Africa," because on "Kike hill" there were only whites.[29] These terms were apparently acceptable in his culture. He was totally amazed that anyone would take offense, much less file a complaint.

Education is the key to lessening or removing cultural misunderstanding, and its goals must be threefold: (1) it must explain how culture shapes behavior; (2) it must identify specific cultural values, beliefs, and norms that influence the behavior of the members of a cultural group; and (3) it must facilitate communication across cultures.

UNDERSTANDING CULTURE

Culture is defined as "an organized system of symbols by which persons, things, and events are endowed with rather specific and socially shared meanings and values. Cultures are said to 'create' patterns of shared meaning and feeling which combine to shape the social world of a given group."[30] These patterns occur in six areas: (1) perceiving, (2) feeling, (3) acting, (4) believing, (5) admiring, and (6) striving.[31] These areas each provide a set of cultural cues which determine the values, norms, and beliefs of a given society. The following discussion relates culture and its cues to the real world of people and organizations.

Perceiving provides cues defining how and in what ways any person, thing, or event is to be understood. These cues make up the central, large frames of reference of workers. In the culture from which employees have traditionally come into the organization, competition is generally valued, as is the Horatio Alger notion that anyone who works hard can succeed. Usually, however, these perceptions are those only of the majority, white, Euro-American tradition. Minorities may believe that no matter how hard they work, in a white dominated society, only whites succeed.

To illustrate this point, we would like to tell you a story shared with us by a black woman in her thirties; thus she was born in the 1960s after the March on Washington and the passage of Civil Rights legislation.

As snow blew outside her office window and the strains of "I'm Dreaming of a White Christmas" wafted over the speaker system, the woman smiled wistfully. "When I was a little girl," she said, "I used to think that dreaming of a white Christmas meant I was dreaming I could be white so I'd have it easy like all the white folk do. I thought if I could be white for Christmas, I'd have lots of toys, and no one would ever get angry at me, and I'd never be hungry."

Even though, as an adult, the woman knows her concept of white was not realistic, she explained that she still somehow expected that white people had things easier than she did. Unfortunately, such perceptions still have a basis in reality.

Feeling contains those cues telling us what feelings to have and how we must express feelings in a given situation. For example, in the mainstream United States culture, little boys are usually taught to be stoic, not to express feelings. In contrast, little girls are often socialized to believe that crying is acceptable behavior. In the world of work, then, the male-dominated culture may foster negative reactions to behavior that females have been taught is not only "acceptable," but normal. One supervisor said, "Most of my work force are women. I just keep a box of Kleenex on my desk." Was he being accepting and tolerant, or condescending and judgmental? We weren't certain.

Since the majority culture in most workplaces values competitiveness and success, supervisors and fellow workers may have difficulty accommodating values such as those of the American Indian culture in which "a man's prestige was based traditionally on what he had given away and not on what he was accumulating for himself."[32] Thus, while the traditional employee experiences pride in achievement, the American Indian experiences pride in family and sharing. People of other cultures have learned different attitudes toward work than the dominant culture.

Acting provides those cues about what one must do, or avoid doing, in given situations. It tells members of the culture how to act in an embarrassing situation and when they are being questioned or instructed. People growing up in the United States usually learn early how to act at work. They are socialized in elementary school to arrive on time, sit in assigned seats, ask questions when they don't understand, and complete assignments. Yet children of immigrants may receive mixed messages about what kind of behavior is appropriate.

As one second-generation American explained, "I don't know how to act at work. I'm never sure if I'm supposed to look away when my supervisor talks with me, or if I'm supposed to look him straight in the eye. My mother is Polish. When's she's giving me directions, she says, 'Look at me so I'll know you're paying attention to what I'm saying.' But my dad's Hispanic. To look him in the eye is a sign of disrespect. He slaps me."[33]

Grades in our school systems function much like paychecks in our organizations. Hard work that maximizes use of knowledge, skills, and abilities equals higher grades, higher pay, or more opportunity. Children of employed parents learn how to act in the work force from their significant adults. Children of unemployed parents, or whose parents are from other cultures, often do not. Thus employees from cultures different than mainstream America may need to be taught how to act in U.S. workplaces. Supervisors will need to be taught how to manage employees with diverse cultural heritages.

Believing contains those cues that tell cultural members what to believe. A belief shared by traditional white American employees, for example, is the "work ethic." In this belief, advanced education and hard work lead to greater pay, which equals success. Young people in middle- and upper-class families frequently believe there are two kinds of work. They define their employment activities as either "a job" or "a real job." "A job" is a temporary activity engaged in to earn enough to pay for a car, a trip, or college. A "job" pays a minimum wage and is viewed as temporary and often worthy of contempt. A "real job," on the other hand, is one for which the young people acquire advanced knowledge, skills, and abilities, and for which they earn wages sufficient to support them in the manner to which they are accustomed. Within American subcultures, however, different beliefs about work may be learned.

A young black woman told us that upon completing her college degree, she applied for a supervisory position in the organization where she worked. Recently married, she was obviously several months pregnant. She was excited about her application and told several coworkers about it. "You'll never get that promotion," was the typical response. The young woman was at first disbelieving, then frustrated, then confused. Finally, she said to one of the nay sayers, "Why won't I get promoted? Because I'm black? Because I'm a woman?"

"Oh, no" was the response, "because you're pregnant!"

Think of the cultural messages imbedded in these beliefs.

Admiring contains the cultural messages about who the heroes are, and what characteristics should be admired. In the United States, those who "should" be admired are identified in advertising and other media, as well as in the role models we admired as children. One feminist writer points out:

Every one of our public fields of endeavor—business, government, medicine, law, technology, urban design—have been shaped by the ideals, images, values, and language of the Warrior. The Warrior is the traditional male hero who charges into battle with the aim of dominating and winning.[34]

While the "warrior" and all he implies may be the model for industry and government, the model for women is less dramatic, more personal, more complex—a "siren": a subservient pleaser, concerned with shiny floors, spotless dishes, and intimate talks over coffee. A look at television advertising tells us that "she" should be young, with beautiful hair, thin, free of cellulite and dandruff, and able to be a wife, lover, breadwinner, and friend—without ever getting tired or irritable.

Both the warrior and the siren are cultural images, far from the reality of most lives, but the repetition with which the images have been beamed into American homes shapes values and beliefs. How often you have discounted the competency of an old person or a timid person or an overweight person or a disabled person will tell you how much you have been influenced by the warrior and siren images of competency.

Striving is the final cultural message received in all cultures. It describes the worthwhile goals in life. This message defines success for culture members. In the United States, television plays a major role in defining what striving means in twentieth-century culture. Success has come to be defined by what one has, rather than who one is. Success is equated with financial status and symbols of wealth such as mansions and limousines. Education is often seen as ancillary, of value because of the doors it can open, not as an end in itself.

The preceding pages have introduced you to two concepts important to understanding culture: (1) The way the work force is managed is greatly influenced by the culture of those who manage; and (2) The way work-force participants behave is greatly influenced by their own culture.

Sheer numbers have forced a change in work-force composition. Whether or not to hire a woman or a minority is rapidly becoming a nonissue. Women and cultural minorities are a viable part of a shrinking work force.[35] Successful organizations will welcome the diversity they bring and capitalize on their strengths, while also teaching all workers how to understand and communicate with one another. As Xerox executive David T. Kearns observes, "The company that gets out in front of managing diversity, in my opinion, will have a competitive edge."[36] Advantages of being "out in front" include:

1. The opportunity to hire and keep the best of the new labor pool;
2. Greater innovation;
3. Better performance by female and minority workers;
4. The ability to make the most of ethnic and international markets; and
5. The ability to make the most of mature adult and women's markets.[37]

THE CRITICAL IMPORTANCE OF DIVERSITY MANAGEMENT

Why devote so much space to diversity issues and culture in a book on job satisfaction and performance? We believe that diversity management is essential to maximizing performance and satisfaction for several reasons:

1. Minorities are less likely to be in jobs that lend themselves to worker satisfaction, because minorities tend to cluster in lower-paying, less skill-based positions, in the lower levels of the organization. These jobs are less likely to be enriched and less likely to contain the elements that foster satisfaction: task significance, task identity, skill variety, autonomy, and feedback.[38]
2. Minorities are less likely to report satisfaction with the way supervisors treat them.[39]
3. Opportunities to break through the glass ceiling to higher-paying jobs are not often available to minorities.[40]
4. Even minorities in positions of authority, whose performance is outstanding, report dissatisfaction with the amount of information received from their supervisors or coworkers at a significantly higher rate than do their white male cohorts.[41]

Simply put, minorities want the same job characteristics and opportunities that all workers do, in order to be satisfied performers; minorities, however, are disappointed more often. The workplace has been so long dominated by the European white culture that it may be hostile to minorities, without any deliberate intent to hurt or discriminate. This unconscious hostility interferes with job satisfaction and performance. It also inhibits information sharing, without which promotion opportunities are difficult to find.

Despite the advantages of acquiring and maintaining a diverse work force, the presence of mature workers, women, and racial and ethnic minorities does generate frustration for managers and supervisors. As human resource manager, your concern for the job satisfaction and performance of your employees must be twofold. You do not want to get so focused on facilitating the performance of the rank and file of workers that you forget the humanity of supervisors whose satisfaction and performance may decline as a different breed of worker enters their arena of responsibility.

MANAGING CULTURAL DIVERSITY

Managing diversity is a skill that can be learned. It is a necessary skill in today's organizational world. It is also a skill that managers generally did not learn in school, nor one that they have previously had to develop. As a result they often have difficulties dealing with those in the workplace who are different from them. The three most frequently identified sources of frustration for managers of a multicultural work force have been identified as: (1) the hesitance by minimally English-speaking workers to ask questions or to admit lack of understanding; (2) the reluctance of the foreign born to make negative statements; and (3) the unresponsiveness of those from other cultures to conventional incentives.[42]

We suspect that, in the general scheme of things, managers have a more difficult time learning to look beyond race and culture to see the qualified human within than they have in looking beyond differences in sex or age. Freely offering equal treatment to women and to mature workers of the same race or cultural background seems to come more easily. We believe this occurs for two reasons: (1) the traditional white male manager can identify more readily with the problems of women because he has a mother, maybe a wife or daughter, and they help educate him about women's issues; and (2) everyone is growing older, and it is readily evident that inroads made in opportunities for, and treatment of, mature workers may someday have a personal payoff.

When dealing with those from a different race and culture, understanding and empathy do not come as easily. Because of past experiences, often long forgotten, members of different racial groups may be suspicious of one another, hostile to one another, or afraid of one another. The position and power of a manager can be intimidating to any worker under that manager's supervision. When worker and manager represent different cultures, the feeling of intimidation can intensify, even though no conscious reasons for wariness exist in either person. This may be the same fear of the unknown that one feels when entering any new and different situation.

How will you value cultural and racial diversity? How can you rise to the challenges diversity presents? The following examples and guidelines illustrate the possibilities for improving working conditions, as well as for balancing the job satisfaction and performance of all workers.

One human resource manager with whom we talked, has demonstrated his commitment to minority advancement. He instituted a program that identifies minority workers who want to pursue higher education in order to advance themselves within the organization. In a competitive process, one minority worker a year in each of the past four years has been given a reduced job assignment so that the person can go to college full time. A promise has been made that promotion and salary increase will be forthcoming when the degree is completed. This is the kind of behavior that fosters job satisfaction and performance. It is not a major step, but a small and consistent one. Will it make a difference? We think so. For instance, one study found that those

who see themselves as having opportunities for advancement within the organization will be more satisfied than those with limited opportunities. The presumption that these opportunities do exist provides the basis for developing the kinds of skills that contribute to efficacy . . . and will also increase the likelihood of making an investment in time and energy in the workplace.[43]

How, then, does one manage diversity? Guidelines recently published in the *Personnel Journal* offer these suggestions:

1. Don't avoid the issue of diversity. Bring it out in the open and talk about it.

2. Explore how all employees come to the workplace with a unique combination of background influences. Start with yourself and your own background.

3. Be an intercultural ambassador by being tactful and respecting the rule for discussions of ethnic, cultural, racial, and gender differences.

4. Don't tolerate racist or sexist behaviors. Stay within EEO guidelines.

5. Mediate between personal and professional needs.

6. Explain the unwritten rules of the organization.

7. Refer employees to coworkers so they get a well-rounded perception (about your organization).[44]

Although these guidelines were written as a guide for incorporating
members of differing ethnic cultures into the corporate culture of an
organization, they are as helpful for managing women and mature workers as they are for ethnic minorities. The philosophy is the same. The
message is clear. To promote job satisfaction and performance, treat all
workers in the way that recognizes their individual strengths and skills,
while recognizing that none of us are clones of one another, ready to
march in mindless lock-step. Do not try to make workers from different
backgrounds into your own image, but learn from them and grow with
them.

Benefits of Successful Diversity Management

You can reap substantial long-term benefits from making a commitment to valuing diversity.[45] Today's employees do not want to deny
their cultural identities to fit some organizational mainstream. They want
to maintain their unique ethnic and cultural heritages while receiving
the respect and support of their bosses and their colleagues. In asking
to be valued as diverse people, employees are asserting that they can,
in return, bring added value to the organization.[46] Among the prime
benefits of valuing diversity are full utilization of human capital, reduced
interpersonal conflict, enhanced work relationships, shared organizational vision, and increased employee commitment.[47]

Organizations that do not value diversity, cannot, of course, reap the
benefits that diversity can bring. In addition, organizations that view
diversity as a liability are more likely to be plagued by high turnover,
low employee morale, limited innovation, and lagging productivity.[48]
Clearly, valuing diversity makes good business sense.

The story is told about a white U.S. Commissioner of Indian Affairs
who long ago asked, with earnest intent, "What can we do to Americanize the Indian?" His concern was genuine; his methods, misdirected.
The reply of an Indian spokesman:

You will forgive me if I tell you that my people were Americans for thousands
of years before your people were. The question is not how you can Americanize
us, but how we can Americanize you. We have been working at that for a long
time. Sometimes we are discouraged by the results. But we will keep trying.
And the first thing we want to teach you is that, in the American way of life,
each man has respect for his brother's vision. Because each of us respected his
brother's dream, we enjoyed freedom here in America when your people were
busy killing and enslaving each other across the water. The relatives you left
behind are still trying to kill each other and enslave each other because they

have not learned there that freedom is built on my respect for my brother's vision and his respect for mine. We have a hard trail ahead of us in trying to Americanize you and your white brothers. But we are not afraid of hard trails.[49]

RACIAL AND CULTURAL MINORITIES

As a human resource professional, you are daily challenged to utilize fully the talents and abilities of all the workers in your organization. The increasing numbers of racial and cultural minorities present a special challenge. In spite of the rhetoric about the benefits of managing diversity, racial and cultural minorities still face difficult barriers to success in most organizations. These barriers are often placed unconsciously by members of the majority culture.

Attitudes and statements of some workers, no matter how innocent and nondeliberate, can inflict great harm to those who are the brunt of the remarks. Thoughtless remarks and behaviors exhibited by coworkers can be as personally hurtful as past discrimination has been professionally harmful. As a human resource manager, you need to be aware of the impact of past discriminatory behavior both in the larger community and in your organization and its particular work units.

We personally regret having to write this section. We wish that merely reporting on balancing job satisfaction and performance, and describing how to do that, were adequate. Unfortunately, it is not. We would like to think that people in the workplace—whether red, yellow, black, or white—were treated just the same. Unfortunately, they are not.

Sometimes members of one group are treated worse than members of other groups, with unfair expectations placed on them. Sometimes they are ignored, for lack of skills to manage them. Sometimes they are denied discipline and direction, for fear of costly litigation if the discipline and direction are perceived as illegal discrimination. Sometimes the habits of a lifetime are so ingrained that disparate treatment is not even recognized by those who experience or exhibit it.

An Australian visitor to this country told us this story. She was staying in a hotel that she had been told was near public transportation and went to the front desk to inquire about bus schedules, location of the bus stop, and the fare.

"We don't ride the bus," sneered the desk clerk.

When the visitor persisted in her inquiry, the desk clerk sent for a hotel laundry worker, an elderly black man who came forward reluctantly.

"These people ride the bus," said the desk clerk. "He can give you directions."

Indeed he could, but he was so out of his element, and so bewildered at being summoned to the front office, that he could barely stammer.

The subtle undercurrents of racism were evident to the visitor, and probably to the laundry worker, but apparently not to the desk clerk.

Racism is defined as "the assumption that psycho-cultural traits and capacities are determined by biological race and that races decisively differ from one another, which is usually coupled with a belief in the inherent superiority of a particular race and its right to domination over others."[50] Racism so permeates the culture of the United States that even when it does not exist, it is often suspected. Because of this phenomenon, managers may fear being accused of racism, and workers may see racism when none exists. Thus, they fear openness. They tip-toe around each other in a kind of self-imposed delusion that inhibits the open communication that seems to come more readily between those of the same cultural heritage. Managers sometimes refrain from clearly deserved disciplinary action for fear of cries of discrimination from a minority worker. And, indeed, members of minority cultures sometimes hide behind civil rights legislation when they have failed or have refused to make the contribution to the organization for which they were hired. This is why training for diversity management is so essential, and why your leadership is so important.

Alex Haley, author of *Roots*, wrote in a recent *Time* magazine article:

Mostly we need action. The most shining example of what can be done to diminish racism is the U.S. Armed Forces. As a retired twenty-year veteran, I can personally testify that up until World War II, our military forces, racially, were run like an antebellum plantation. But today, without question, our Armed Forces represent the most nearly fair model of opportunity within American society.

That happened because a Presidential Commander-in-Chief, Harry Truman, issued a policy, supported by military orders, that no further segregation nor discrimination would be permitted—and enforced it. Racism can be radically reduced when that goal is genuinely desired.[51]

The Impact of Discrimination

Despite the Civil Rights legislation of the 1960s and the subsequent Equal Employment Opportunity and Affirmative Action programs, racial and cultural minorities, for the most part, continue to be clustered at the lower levels of the organization. Their jobs provide less pay and less security. They are most likely to be hit the hardest by layoffs brought about by downsizing and the recession. This adversely affects the satisfaction of those who remain employed, because the pall of potential unemployment hangs heavy. Last hired/first fired continues to be a reality. The editors of *Black Enterprise* put it this way:

For Afro-Americans, the Reagan and Bush administrations' 10-year assault on affirmative action has taken its toll. The hard-won gains of the 1970s have been stalled. Although blacks make up 10.1 percent of nation's 112.4 million employed civilians, we represent only 6.2 percent of its nearly 28 million managers and professionals and 8.5 percent of its 3.3 million technical and related support staff.[52]

While the proportion of blacks in white-collar positions between 1966 and 1985 more than tripled, a 1991 survey of Fortune 1,000 companies indicates that only 6 percent of the managers and only 2.6 percent of the chief executives are minorities.[53] Black leaders fear that these numbers will diminish rather than grow.

A 1991 Bureau of Labor Statistics study identifies the percent of blacks employed in various industries as follows[54]:

Agriculture	4.4%
Manufacturing	8.2%
Finance, Insurance, and Real Estate	8.8%
Wholesale and Retail	10.1%
Services	11.4%
Transportation, Communication and Public Utilities	14.0%
Public Administration	15.1%

Despite the representation of African Americans in these industries, they are clustered on the bottom rungs of the corporate ladder, where a very low ceiling blocks their progress.

To identify the percentage of other minority groups employed in these industries is not as easy. For example, census data indicate that the fastest growing group of minorities in the United States are the Hispanics, who are expected to comprise 23.4 percent of the work force by 2010. Hispanics, however, "are a racially mixed group that include Indians, Blacks, Whites, Asians, and their descendants by intermarriage."[55] Most come from Mexico (60 percent) and Puerto Rico (14 percent). Others are from Cuba, the Dominican Republic, Columbia, Chile, and from the Central American countries of El Salvador and Guatemala. They are a diverse people, grouped in this country under the rubric "Hispanic," which a number of scholars decry as a misleading label that masks their differing cultural backgrounds.[56] The minority community, concerned about economic advancement for their own, have reason to worry. What about human resource managers? Why is this relevant to those of us concerned about balancing satisfaction and performance?

Job Satisfaction of Members of Minority Cultures

Opportunity for advancement is one major contributor to job satisfaction and performance for members of all racial and ethnic groups. Job satisfaction is the result of a complex interaction among job characteristics, worker characteristics, and *"the potential to attain valued rewards from work."*[57] One study of black managers concludes that those "who see themselves as having opportunities for advancement within the organization will be more satisfied than those with limited opportunities."[58] Several studies of black and Mexican American Hispanic groups confirm this intuitively correct finding.[59]

You may already know that numerous studies have failed to find a significant difference in job satisfaction based on race or national origin, so long as those in the same job are studied.[60] In fact, a number of researchers have found more difference in satisfaction and performance within groups designated as races than between them.[61] In other words, what is said about maximizing job satisfaction and performance is related to organizational and job characteristics rather than to race or culture. One can generalize about jobs and working conditions. One cannot generalize about people.

In our own job satisfaction studies, the percent of minorities is small, but their responses are telling. No statistically significant difference existed in the job satisfaction of the 13 percent of respondents who were minorities, and that of their white cohorts. Significant differences did, however, exist in areas of concern to those wanting to maximize the value of diversity.

None of the minority respondents expect to be promoted, and 50 percent of the minorities believe good work will not be rewarded. On the other hand, 65 percent of their white cohorts expect promotion, and 85 percent of the white workers expect rewards for good work. Seventy-five percent of the minority respondents report unfair treatment because of age and gender and state that personnel policies are not administered consistently. None of the minorities believe that labor relations between employees and managers are good, and 50 percent do not believe they have an opportunity to use all the knowledge and skills that they have.

Do you know how the minorities in your organization feel about their rewards and opportunities? Do you know if equal rewards and opportunities exist? Human resource professionals bear the burden of ensuring that workers of all races and cultures have the same opportunities for employment and advancement throughout the organization. You are the heart of the system, and you are its conscience. You are also the voice of the organization. Make certain that you speak to, and on behalf of, the racial and cultural minorities who work for you.

Job satisfaction and performance can be greatly enhanced when the managers in your organization can set aside prejudices and fears and learn to deal with each employee, as a human being, not as a representative of a cultural community. Dr. Joseph Mancusi, president of the Center for Organizational Excellence, puts it this way:

Cultural diversity can be a terrible concept the way it is often applied to the work force. The terms Hispanic, Asian, and African American are legal, political terms; but they are often detrimental to meeting the needs and opportunities that individuals provide. There are more differences between three Asians from Thailand, Taiwan, and Korea; or three Hispanics from Cuba, Puerto Rico, and Mexico; or three African-Americans from rural Mississippi, Los Angeles, and Haiti than there are between a Caucasian, an African American, and an Oriental all born in New York's Little Italy.[62]

Mancusi notes that "we are all people of color, sex, and accent,"[63] yet, in the United States, the color, sex, and accent that has been in traditional good currency is white, male, and East Coast, with a twinge of Harvard or Yale. To continue to encourage only this group's advancement is to forget the other 55 percent of the work force, a group whose relative numbers are increasing.[64]

In 1990 top managers at Ortho Pharmaceutical surveyed their black and female employees. They learned that most of them were overqualified for the positions they held, and they found that the overriding reason for this unfortunate condition was bias. In discussing the situation, their human resource manager observed, "It would be the same if we had a piece of equipment that was only producing 80 percent."[65]

Are the knowledge, skills, and abilities of the minority workers in your organization fully utilized? Is their potential for advanced education or for greater responsibilities being cultivated? Are they experiencing satisfaction with their jobs? Do prejudices detract from their performance? Do you know? Have you asked?

MATURE WORKERS

The culture of the United States is not one that values age and maturity. Yet the new supply of highly trained, technologically sophisticated workers is dwindling. Those who are now in jobs that demand significant levels of knowledge, skills, and abilities are more likely (simply because of past practices and work place demographics) to be white, male, mature workers, who cannot be sacrificed on the altar of diversity management, either ethically or legally.

One very young, female human resources manager wanted to do just that. "It seems to me," she said, "that the way to manage responsibly is to get rid of workers who are past fifty. We have to pay them more than we do young people, and their skills are probably out of date, anyway. We could hire more women and minorities, and we'd be more efficient because they'd do the same work for less money."

We were flabbergasted, almost speechless. The tragedy is that she is not alone in her "solution." For instance, a 1988 survey that defined older workers as fifty and older found that the majority of human resource managers see the older worker as different, less competent, and less innovative than younger workers. Two thirds of the respondents reported that older workers are "complacent and lacking in motivation" and "clogging the promotion pipelines."[66]

The findings of that survey, however, may say more regarding stereotypes about older workers than they say about their actual characteristics. Rosen and Jerdee, after extensive research, conclude:

The commonly accepted belief that older employees reach a point in their careers when motivation declines significantly . . . is due in part to organizationally created self-fulfilling prophecies. . . . Lowered motivation may result, *not from aging itself*, but from managerial expectations and treatment of older employees.[67]

A recent Harris poll found that over two million adults between the ages of fifty and sixty-four are "ready and able to work." Of those, 1.1 million, or 55 percent, were identified as "highly qualified and motivated."[68] That's a far cry from the stereotypes of older workers being undermotivated or less-than-competent. These statistics highlight the wisdom of utilizing the capabilities of the existing work force.

The median age of the work force is increasing. In 1970 it was approximately twenty-eight and will climb to nearly forty by the year 2000, with the forty-five-and-over contingent increasing by a whopping 30 percent. . . . By the year 2000, the bulk of the work force will be middle-aged; 51 percent will be between the ages of thirty-five and fifty-four. . . . The senior work force, those over fifty-five years of age, will remain fairly stable—approximately 11 to 13 percent.[69]

Despite these work-force realities, stereotypes that imply that mature workers are not as competent as their younger counterparts abound in the United States today. The stereotypes arise out of a time when most work requirements were physically demanding and medical science was still unsophisticated. They are fueled by television and print advertising that portray young as beautiful and competent, and old as obsolescent and repugnant. They influence the way youth thinks about middle age, and the way the middle aged think about those older than they. Despite the inroads made by such lobbying organizations as the Gray Panthers and the American Association of Retired People (AARP), in which membership can begin at age 50, aging workers are not often viewed as organizational assets.

Perspectives on Adult Development

The perspective about adult development typically held today is based on now-obsolete research conducted prior to and during the 1970s in which the four "eras" or "seasons" of a white man's life (not the life of a woman or a member of a minority group) were identified as: (1) childhood and adolescence—age 0–22; (2) early adulthood—age 17–45; (3) middle adulthood—age 40–65; and (4) late adulthood—age 60–.[70]

The primary task of each stage was identified as creation of a life structure in which to pursue goals and values. The progression through these stages was viewed as linear, in a "fixed sequence." It was believed that no one could skip one life stage, nor was anyone believed to be able to go back and re-negotiate unresolved issues from a previous phase. Life was viewed as ever onward, straight ahead, driven by the aging process, with the developing individual seen as a long-distance traveler, getting more tired and more burned-out as the journey continued. By age forty, one was expected to begin to think about impending death, not upcoming opportunities.

The early development theorists attempted to explain what happens in each life stage. They thought that the sequence of life's "eras" begins around age twenty in an "Early Adult Transition" that has two tasks: to terminate pre-adulthood and to begin early adulthood. To do this required letting go of childhood and one's family of origin while making the initial choices of occupation, love relationship, peer relationships, values, and life-style. This era, between twenty and thirty, is when people used to leave home for college or the military or to strike out on their own.

Life in the 1990s is much different than when these notions of development were first conceived. In a 1987 survey of 27 million families, with both members of the couple employed, 4.9 million were identified as having adult offspring still living at home.[71] The average age of undergraduate students no longer falls within the traditional 18 to 22-year age group. At the University of Nebraska at Omaha, for instance, the average age of an undergraduate student is 26+. This aging of the student population is a trend being documented across the country.

Does that mean that the current generation have become over-aged adolescents, unable for some reason to make the transition into or out of early adulthood? Is that another problem for human resource managers? We don't think so. Rather, young people in the 1990s are frequently "re-cyclers" who leave home and find that the economics of living alone are more than they can manage so they either return temporarily to their parents' home or decide to enter college as a means of improving opportunity.

Today's trends may indicate that middle- and working-class men and

women in early adulthood have a more complex set of developmental
tasks to accomplish than did those in the 1950s and 1960s. The messages
about what to do and how are less clear. People are marrying later. They
are spending more time developing self-responsibility before taking on
responsibility for the lives of others. Clearly, the young people of the
1990s are poles apart from those young men upon which our stereotypes
about adult behavior are based. Clearly the parents of today's "early
adults" have different sets of challenges than did their own parents.

Because of the "re-cyclers," many parents look forward to an "empty
nest" instead of dread it. Traditionally, men in middle adulthood had
generally worked at the same or similar occupations, and established
themselves in job and community. For the subjects in one 1960s study
of adult development, the "primary (male) responsibility of life . . . (was)
to provide for the family's material well-being and community
standing."[72]

The group who matured in the 1960s entered an "Age Thirty Transition" somewhere between the ages of 28 and 33. This is when the men
said, "If I am to change my life . . . I must now make a start for soon it
will be too late."[73] "In the period from age 30 to 40, these men tried to
establish a *niche* in society . . . (and) work at 'making it' "[74] Early adulthood culminated for them with a "Mid-Life Transition," about age 40,
in which they came to terms with their mortality and literally asked
themselves, "Is this all there is?" The literature that has fueled our
stereotypes has been supplemented by countless novels and plays about
midlife defeat, and a preoccupation with bodily decline and impending
death.[75] The reality is substantively different, as any of you who are past
the age of 40 can attest.

We want to debunk the stereotypes about aging. They were fostered
by studies of those who began their development either during or in
the aftermath of the Great Depression. These were studies of white men
(again, not women nor minorities) who grew to adulthood in the 1950s
when the world was much simpler and societal expectations of all much
different than in the 1990s. These were men who had only begun to
experience the excitement of technological advancement. These were
men for whom the expected life span was not the 71.8 years that it is
in 1991.[76] Think about it. From age 20 (the beginning of adulthood) to
age 40 is 20 years. From age 40 to age 71.8 is 31.8 years. Men at age 40
in 1992 can generally expect to have more adult life left to live than they
have lived already. They are not thinking about obsolescence but about
opportunities.

In the 1990s, people change careers an average of seven times over a
life time. People in mid-life return to (or enter) college. Some are seeking
career advancement. Others are seeking self-fulfillment. For example, a
simple count of the numbers of part-time students in accredited Master

of Public Administration programs for the years 1982 through 1985 (the last available data) revealed that 62.5 percent of them are adult students. Percent of adult students in each school ranged from 31 to 92 percent. Personnel literature indicates that those who are upwardly mobile change jobs (and often geographic location) every two years. One of the developmental scholars observed in 1978 that "as a man passes 40, his older children are likely to be in or near adolescence."[77] In 1992 as a man passes 40, he and his wife may just have decided to begin a family.

In short, organizations today may have expectations about older workers grounded in stereotypes that are no longer appropriate for the work force of the twenty-first century. With the effects and potential effects of the rapid technological and societal change that has occurred, adult development can no longer be viewed as linear and egocentric, as in a "ladder" and a "long-distance journey." The reality is markedly different.

With the constraints of cost-cutting, reduced numbers of competent young people, and the restrictions of both anti-discrimination legislation and pension plans, these "older employees" are likely to be the bulk of the work force for the next 15 years. . . . Organizations need to learn how to maximize their continued competence, not wring their collective hands about the graying of the work force.[78]

Managing Mature Workers

How will you successfully assist mature workers to balance job satisfaction and productivity? The same way you do that of workers in any group. The key to effective management of older employees is to treat them exactly the same way you do employees of any age. Age does not equate to any predictable set of attributes. The distinctive characteristic of the adult, at all ages, is diversity. Adults are a heterogeneous group who have widely disparate life roles, styles of learning, prior experience, and patterns of participation.[79]

Rather than the linear progression that has influenced most of the current thinking about adults, begin to think about development as a Jungian mandala symbol, which is a symbol of wholeness, unity, and integrity. David Kolb suggests that adults engage in an "endless circular process of knowing."[80] Barry Sheckley expands this circular process to one of a spiral that is ever twisting back on itself as it moves forward, relying on completed learning and development tasks to support and inform the new.[81]

Mature employees have a store of experiences that they bring to the work place. At the executive levels, this is frequently recognized, with top executives most often beyond middle age. On the shop floor or in the secretarial pool or in middle management, however, workers' skills are often viewed as becoming obsolescent rather than as becoming finely honed.

In the technological core of an organization, mature workers may be viewed as unable or unwilling to learn new skills or adapt to new ways. These workers, however, have the right to the same training and the same promotion opportunities as their younger counterparts.[82] Training and promotion opportunities for older workers are not just good management. They are required by antidiscrimination law.

Age Discrimination in Employment Act

Because of U.S. culture's generally negative view of the aging process, discrimination against those past the age of 40 may be inherent in many organizations. Older workers are not overtly discriminated against, but opportunities may be routinely denied them, without conscious thought. One sure way to lower productivity and reduce job satisfaction in all employees is to treat one group in a disparate manner.[83] Thus, in this section, the requirements of the Age Discrimination in Employment Act (ADEA)[84] are summarized and discussed. Because of this legislation, employees can no longer be forced to retire. The purpose of the ADEA is "to promote the employment of older persons based on their ability rather than age; to prohibit arbitrary age discrimination in employment; to help employers and workers find ways of meeting problems arising from the impact of age on employment."[85]

The ADEA protects all workers age 40 or older; it applies to all private employers with twenty or more employees, to all state and local governments, to all employment agencies, and to all labor unions with 25 or more members. Similar protection is provided for federal employees under Executive Order 11141.[86]

Factors that may be considered a valid basis for discrimination under the ADEA include:

- A bonafide occupational qualification (BFOQ), such as "actors required for youthful or elderly roles"[87]
- A physical fitness requirement
- Employment tests that are specifically related to the job
- Standards of quality or quantity of production.

In other words, older workers can and should be expected to meet the same standards of production that all workers meet. What an employer cannot do is arbitrarily expect that older workers will do less or that they should do more.

Job Satisfaction of Mature Workers

A number of scholars[88] have concluded that older workers (51 + years) are more satisfied than younger colleagues and that the length of time an employee has been on the job directly affects job satisfaction. Mature workers generally tend to be more satisfied than youthful workers.[89] Those who have been in a career long enough to have become established in it are more satisfied with their jobs than are workers in earlier career stages.

In a study of municipal clerks that we conducted in 1988, we found distinct patterns in the relationship of both age and length of time on the job to job satisfaction. One hundred percent of the youngest and oldest respondents (under 30 and over 60) reported being "very satisfied" with their jobs. Eighty-three percent of those between the ages of 41 and 50 were very satisfied, as were 92 percent of those between ages 51 and 60.[90] A 1990 study of 434 employees of a federal agency produced similar results,[91] as did our study of outstanding performers in a major corporation.

In that corporate group, 100 percent of those over age 51 and 86 percent of those over age 41 were very satisfied with their jobs. By definition, these were high performers. No significant difference between their perceptions of working conditions and the perceptions of younger cohorts existed, except in one area. Only 33 percent of those between ages of 41 and 50 believe they are involved in decision making. No one over age 51 felt involved. That particular corporation is denying itself valuable resources by not consulting mature workers. Are you?

This is not to say that mature workers will be satisfied with anything, just because they're getting older. They do often expect fewer quantitative rewards from the workplace, but they want a higher Quality of Work Life (QWL).[92] The ingredients of QWL, in priority order are effective supervision; good relations with coworkers; challenging, interesting, and meaningful job assignments; good relations between work groups; adequate compensation and benefits; and job security.[93] These are job components that you, as a human resource manager are in a position to facilitate.

It seems evident that mature workers are generally satisfied employees. The question of concern for human resources managers however, is, are they also productive workers? The evidence would tend to say "Yes."

A pioneer in recruiting older workers to work its reservations centers, Days Inns of America, Inc., reports many benefits: "Turnover is low (1 percent among seniors, compared with 40 percent among other employees), absenteeism and tardiness are virtually nonexistent, guest satisfaction with service is higher, and health-care costs have not increased.''[94] Other companies that have had similar experiences are identified in the 1991 book *Managing Workforce 2000*.[95]

As we traveled across the Midwest, conducting research for this book, we met mature employees in a number of organizations both public and private. Some were retired from the military and in second careers or pursuing advanced education to prepare for a career change. Several had retired from a company, then returned for special projects or to trouble shoot. Some had taken advantage of the demise of mandatory retirement to stay on in long-held jobs. All showed evidence of high productivity. The following list is representative, providing testimony that older workers can be assets. We met a retired industrial engineer who conducts plant tours and explains manufacturing operations to visitors from around the country and around the world; a seventy-year-old woman who manages the branch office of a dry-cleaning establishment; a retired military officer who directs the computer operations for a bank; a woman who entered the work force for the first time after age 50 and directs a metropolitan Girl Scouts operation; a saleswoman, age 60+, who achieved an award for outstanding production; a septuagenarian who is the municipal clerk of a large city; and a retired city manager who uses his expertise to do consulting for municipalities.

If we included every satisfied and productive mature worker that we met, our list would be longer than the space available. Older workers are an asset on which you can capitalize in the upcoming period of scarce human resources. The American Association of Retired Persons (AARP) has a Business Partnerships program that provides specific advice on how to recruit, manage, and train older workers. It also provides, free to employers, a data base called the National Older Workers Information System, which lists 180 programs concerning older workers. Contact AARP by writing Business Partnerships Program in Washington, D.C.[96]

WOMEN WORKERS

According to United Nations statistics, women make up one-half of the world's population and do 75 percent of the world's work. In the United States, you may remember, that the percent of women in the work force has grown from 43 percent in 1970 to 57 percent in 1990.[97] More than 46 percent of American women are in professional or managerial careers.[98] A college education is the gateway to a career, and more than half of all U.S. college and university students are women.[99] Women in this country in the 1990s are being educated to become self-sufficient and independent. Their presence in professional and managerial positions increased by 77 percent between 1975 and 1985.[100] These figures may, however, be misleading. Women are still occupying managerial and supervisory positions clustered at the lower levels of the organization.

A study released by AT&T in 1985 reveals the percentage of that company's women in management-level positions. The pyramid shape shows from the base: Level 1, managers 38.7 percent; Level 2, managers 22 percent; district managers, 15 percent; division managers, 8.3 percent; directors 2.8 percent; executives 2.5 percent. Fewer than 3 percent of the top 800 executives are female. And this company is typical.[101]

Women are no longer living traditional life-styles. In growing numbers, they have entered the workplace. Our research indicates that the same conditions that foster job satisfaction and performance in men are also crucial to women's job satisfaction. We also found, as have others, that "the job satisfaction of women in general is at least as high as that of men,"[102] and that women have more issues with which to cope than men. The workplace may not yet know how to deal with them, especially when they are in positions of authority and other jobs traditionally occupied by men.

As with the discussions we have presented on diversity and on mature workers, we personally regret feeling a need to write this section. We would like to think that men and women working together can act equally, treating one another as equals. We would like to think that everything that has been written about job satisfaction and performance has been written about people, regardless of sex (or of age or race). We would like to think that women in the workplace, at all levels, are treated the same as their male counterparts.

We believe, however, that our cultural heritage has so far prohibited such androgenous an approach to human resource management. A 1984 analysis of white women's place in contemporary society, asserts that "under the gender system as presently constituted women are subjected to an enormous array of increasingly questioned, but still dominant, norms."[103]

This complex of "gender norms" governs women's presentations of self, marriage, and motherhood, sexuality, criminality, and occupational choice. A "normal" woman is a warm, attractive, fragile, White wife, and willing mother with a decorous sexual image who refrains from permanent participation in the labor force. Any woman who falls outside of this narrow definition suffers from the general devaluation of things female and from the punishment meted out to those who stray beyond these demeaning boundaries of normal womanhood.[104]

We hope that our children and grandchildren will know a world free of sex bias, where both men and women can work productively together. The twenty-first century holds promise. For now, however, we will devote space to women workers whose satisfaction and performance have become a critical part of organizational processes.

Do you know how the women in your organization are treated by their supervisors and coworkers? Most will not complain formally. This reluctance to complain about perceived inappropriate treatment was graphically illustrated in the 1991 confirmation hearings of Supreme Court Justice Clarence Thomas. Anita Hill came forward to testify to incidents she alleged occurred ten years in the past. Why she had not complained ten years previously has been a question worth hours of speculation by many. The issue is that she, like most women, did not complain. As TV personality Vanna White put it, "You just get used to hearing that stuff."

In our culture, we have been carefully taught that a "woman's place is in the home." Despite mounting and powerful evidence to the contrary, cultural messages die hard. These messages have been taught to both men and women and they influence behavior and expectations by both employees and managers. Satisfaction in the workplace and productive performance are as much a part of female employee's desires as they are a male's. Unfortunately, long-held cultural biases can hamper women's achievements.

In discussing performance and job satisfaction of women, we take a two-pronged approach: (1) how female managers and professionals are perceived by, and relate to, employees and peers; and (2) how women who work in the technological core of the organization either along side of men, or in typically female occupations, are perceived by, and relate, to supervisors and peers.

Female Managers and Professionals

Neither scholars nor workers can agree about the effect women managers have in the workplace. Some believe that "Women in general are the greatest detriment to the success of other women.... There is a repeated lack of cooperation by female employees with newly promoted female supervisors and managers."[105] Others conclude:

It is clear that the widespread assumption about "problematic" relations between women bosses and their women subordinates must be re-examined.... Surely, there are women bosses who might be characterized as "bosses from hell," but there are also women bosses who fit the description of "the nicest person I ever met." Like their male counterparts, women bosses represent a wide array of personalities and management styles. There is no prototypic woman boss.[106]

Whether "nice" or "obnoxious" seems hardly relevant, for these terms are, of course, only two very subjective descriptions of behavior. Yet, it has been our experience that when employees (at all levels of organizations) talk about female managers, they focus on personality, rather than on objective performance measures. It seems as though people somehow expect women to sacrifice performance for niceness, and that productive women are viewed as unfeminine rather than as valuable to the organization.

One very competent woman, whom we shall call Lisbeth, said of her boss, "I hate working for her. It seems as if she's constantly got to prove that she's tougher and better than the rest of us. I'd much rather work for a man. With a man, you know where you stand." We were never able to get Lisbeth to describe specific instances in which her female boss acted differently than a male would. We finally concluded that it was not her supervisor's behavior that was different. Rather, Lisbeth had a different set of expectations of a woman than she did of a man. She expected the woman to care about her, to develop a friendship with her. She had no such expectations of previous male bosses, who she was able to categorize as "in charge, having to make tough decisions." Lisbeth's dissatisfaction was based on her own perceptions about how women ought to act, not on any particular characteristics of her job nor of her supervisor.

There, has, indeed, been a great deal of research to determine, how, and if women behave differently in the workplace than do their male counterparts. A leader in this research has been Carol Gilligan, who concludes that most women do indeed have a "different voice" than their male counterparts, though Gilligan has not addressed potential differences between male and female supervisors and managers.[107] As a part of the research conducted for this book, we did address those differences.

That men and women are different seems hardly a revelation until one considers the implications of this difference on managerial decision making. As more and more women enter the work force, and rise through both experience and education into levels of managerial responsibility, the differences in how they make decisions becomes important, especially if what they decide is also different. If how women decide, and what they decide is inherently different than men, then a female presence in upper levels of management will dramatically affect organizational culture, worker satisfaction, and worker performance.

Before you read our description of the differences in how men and women make decisions, consider the "Case of Nurse Night" focusing on an employee's deteriorating performance. After you read the case, answer the two questions that follow it. Then read how the eighteen men and women we asked answered those same questions, compare their answers to your own, and consider the implications of the answers on job satisfaction and performance.

THE CASE OF NURSE NIGHT

You are a human resource manager in a large hospital. The nurses here receive a salary slightly higher than those paid by most medical facilities.

Nurse Night has been with the hospital for ten years, and had an early record of high performance. She was a superb nurse until about two years ago. Thinking back, you remember that it was about then that Nurse Night was caught sleeping in a linen closet by your predecessor who took no formal action. Since then her performance has steadily deteriorated. Her patient records are carelessly done. She is often late for work, but always has a "good" excuse.

The patients seem to like Nurse Night, but you have heard her complaining bitterly about "incompetent managers." You've been told that she refers to you as "that nerd." You have also noticed that she avoids both you and her supervisor whenever possible.

Just this morning, Nurse Night's supervisor brought you a patient record which Nurse Night had turned in late. The report has a make-up smudge in one corner, and mustard and ketchup stains on the cover. It lacks essential patient information, and several clinic visits are described simply as "chit-chat." You have told Nurse Night that you want to talk to her later today. You are planning your interview.

Respondents were asked to read the dilemma and answer the following two questions: (1) "How will you decide what to do?" and (2) "What action will you take?" We presented the above dilemma to eighteen practicing managers, ranging in age from 25 to 50+. Eleven were male, seven were female. All but two were white. Their responses are recorded in Tables 2.1 and 2.2; compare them with your own.

As you can see in the tables, there was a distinct difference between the answers of men and women. Men responded to both questions by using criteria of role-related obligations and organizational rules. Women, on the other hand, were concerned about not severing relationships. This is the difference between males and females that the developmental literature describes. Most women approach decisions in a framework of "caring" and relationship maintenance, while most men are inclined to use "justice" as the main criterion of decision making. Briefly summarized, the differences between the criteria of caring and justice are as follows.

JUSTICE

- Individuals are defined as separate and objective in relation to others
- Morality is equated to justice, which is equated to fairness, with

Table 2.1
Differences in *How* Men and Women Decided

FEMALE	MALE
I'd decide based on her response to me.	I'd give her one more chance.
I'd think about how to treat her so I would not hurt her.	Since we pay her salary, she can be replaced.
I'd worry because she called me a "nerd."	At some point we must be realistic and ask if she fits the organization.
I'd be concerned about the patients, so I'd review the records. If she was just doing a few things wrong, I'd try to help her.	If she won't work, let her go.
	I'd see what she's done in the past.
If she seems genuinely sorry, I'll try to help her.	I would compare her behavior to good work standards.
I'd want to work with her and help her because that's how I'd want to be treated.*	I'd start gathering evidence so I can win.
I'd check the policies and do what I'm supposed to.	I would want to keep her, so I'd explain the rules.

*   Response of African-American

Table 2.2
Differences in *What* Men and Women Decided

FEMALE	MALE
Doesn't anyone care about this woman?	I'd say, "You've done good work in the past. What are you going to do now?"
I'd show her direction and see if she'll work with me.	I'd talk to her, and I'd have a witness.
I'll meet with her and talk back and forth and share our perceptions.	I'd call her in for a disciplinary interview and I'd record the interview for self-defense.
I'd try to get agreement on what we can do.	I would want to act responsibly so the patients wouldn't get hurt by her behavior.
I'm concerned that this employee needs help. I'd get her help.	I want to know if her excuses are valid before I judge her.
I'd want to help her.	I would confront her problems and focus on their effect on other employees.
We'd have to see what was best for her and for the other employees.	I'd get the facts before I decide.
I'll help her decide how to change her behavior so she wouldn't lose her job.*	I'd use positive reinforcement to change her behavior.

*   Response of African-American

relationships seen as reciprocity grounded in duty and role obligations

- Problems are construed as conflicting claims to be resolved by rules
- Problem resolutions are evaluated according to principles or standards, especially of fairness.[108]

CARING

- Individuals are defined as connected in relation to others
- Morality is equated to caring, which rests on an understanding of relationships
- Problems are construed as issues of relationships
- Problem resolutions are evaluated considering how things worked out or whether relationships were maintained or restored.[109]

The managers in our small study gave almost stereotypical solutions to the dilemma about Nurse Night. The women were concerned about building and maintaining relationships, about helping, about treating Nurse Night as they would want to be treated. The men, on the other hand, emphasized being realistic, gathering data, looking at history, enforcing rules. How did you say you would decide?

We believe that there is clearly a difference between how men and women approach managerial problems. What was evident in our research, however, is that while men and women managers approach problem solving differently, successful managers tend to arrive at the same resolution.

A trap that tends to capture those who discuss women managers is the tendency to try to identify whether men or women are better managers and to argue about who has the "advantage."[110] It seems to us that the issue should not be one of "Who has the advantage?" That implies an attempt to create a new stereotype at a time when an increasingly diverse work force is crying for an end to stereotypes and a valuing of diversity.

The research by Gilligan and others indicates areas of similarity between morally mature men and women. While many women grow to an ability to balance self-sufficiency with relationships, many men will, conversely, come to understand that, in seeing others equal to themselves, they can safely develop relationships. In other words, both successful women and successful men learn to balance the demands of, and their commitment to, relationships *and* responsibilities.

If the differences between women and men result in contrasting decision-making styles or in dissimilar end results, then the differences become important. Organization culture and performance will be influenced by the different styles. Personnel decisions will be affected. Performance evaluations will be approached differently. Productivity may even be defined differently. If, however, as our own research as well as that of others indicates, competent men and competent women reach equivalent managerial decisions, then fears about women managers are just that.

We hope this discussion has helped dispel some of the myths. Whether a manager is male or female, the expectations they have for subordinates can be the same. Both subordinates and executives need to be taught this fact so that stereotypes can be dispelled and women managers can get on with doing their jobs.

In our study of men and women who are superstars (as determined by their organizations), no statistically significant difference existed in how they report their performance or their job satisfaction, nor in what they perceive they receive from, and contribute to, their jobs. Women, however, are more likely to describe themselves as "workaholics" than are men, and women were more highly educated than their male counterparts.

Women in Blue-Collar and Pink-Collar Occupations

Approximately 70 percent of employed women work in low-paying service jobs in which many cannot earn enough to keep their families above the poverty level.[111] They are caretakers and helpers. They are the "pink-collar" workers, so called because pink is so often associated with female babies.

Blue is said to be males. Blue-collar workers produce the goods or provide the services for which an organization is established. Their jobs require some form of manual labor and are ones which have traditionally been filled by men. Not many women are currently in blue-collar occupations. Only 8.7 percent of the precision production and craftspersons are women, while about 25 percent of the operators, fabricators, and laborers are female.[112] Because of the opportunity for higher pay, the numbers of women in blue-collar jobs are increasing at a rate that exceeds that of men.[113]

Women in blue-collar occupations have been one of the most taken-for-granted group of employees in organizations. How they are treated, and managerial expectations of them, have, for the most part, been based on "stereotypes and media myths."[114]

What basically occurs is that women employed in a predominantly male workplace are seen as women first, and only secondly as workers. To survive in this environment, the women behave in ways that are in keeping with male expectations about women, but are inappropriate to the work environment.[115]

The worst problem blue-collar women are apt to face is "hostility" that manifests itself in "practical jokes, threats of violence, sexual harassment, and actual violence."[116] The ways blue-collar women are likely to behave have been identified as "sex object," "mother," "little sister," "daughter," and "pet."[117] Men and women growing up in American culture have learned these are the roles that women play. Men and women generally have not been taught that women can be coworkers. Teaching that role becomes the job of the human resource manager who wants to assist the blue-collar work force to balance performance and satisfaction.

One study of what attracts women to blue-collar occupations found that it was "primarily money," with Affirmative Action programs having been the impetus for their obtaining a blue-collar job.[118] Once in the job, however, they are completely vulnerable,[119] facing a work situation for which they have been neither trained nor socialized.

As a human resource manager, you can facilitate their performance, satisfaction, and longevity in the job by taking a few simple steps:

1. Make it known that women are welcome in the rank and file of your organization. Develop, implement, and advertise a policy that clearly articulates opportunities for women at all levels in your organization.

2. Affirmatively seek women to fill vacant blue-collar positions by advertising in-house and by encouraging pink-collar workers to transfer to blue-collar jobs.

3. Introduce women into blue-collar jobs in pairs or trios, which will give them a support system that a woman alone in a crew of men does not have and will make their differences from male coworkers less striking.

4. Prepare the blue-collar workplace by conducting training, such as that presented in Appendix A, for line employees as well as managers.

5. Remember that in actively recruiting and supporting female blue-collar workers, you will be a pioneer and subject to feelings of uncertainty. Although antidiscrimination laws have been in effect some thirty years, women still have a long road ahead to achieve equality of opportunity in the blue collar work force.

6. Be patient and consistent[120]

Clearly, women have become a resource upon which you can capitalize. Collectively they have become a majority of American workers.

Their presence, however, is unevenly spread across different occupational groups. They cluster in the traditional service occupations such as nursing, teaching, and clerical work. Their numbers are sparse in upper levels of management, where many have reached a "glass ceiling" through which they can dimly see opportunities not yet available to them. Their numbers are equally sparse in traditional blue-collar occupations, where cultural stereotypes are still very strong.

One of the tragedies for women workers is that in occupations in which they are in the majority, salaries for both men and women are lower than are salaries in occupations where men represent the majority. In one organization we visited, for example, skilled office workers earned only 63 percent of the wages of illiterate groundskeepers. A secretary with an associate degree, able to word process at over 100 words per minute, and competent in management, was paid $11,000 per year. Those assigned to rake leaves, shovel snow, and mow grass were paid $17,500. Is it any wonder that pink-collar workers are attracted to blue-collar jobs? Is it any wonder that the comparable-worth debates rage?

Another tragedy for women workers is often hidden. That is the tragedy of sexual harassment. Harassment is difficult to address because it is subtle and pervasive. It is a much greater problem than most people realize. Sexual harassment alone costs the average Fortune 500 company over $6,000,000 per year in absenteeism and low productivity![121] Despite what many think, sexual harassment does not occur only between males and females, and it is a major deterrent to performance and satisfaction.

SEXUAL HARASSMENT

Three trends are making sexual harassment a more prevalent issue in the workplace. One is a demographic trend. The others are cultural. First, the increasing proportion of women in the work force provides more opportunities for male/female harassment. The increasing number of women in the work force has introduced more targets for jokes, innuendos, and outright sexual advances. Our culture has not traditionally provided men and women with the skills for dealing with each other as peers or with the expectations that they can do so. What manifests itself as harassment may in fact be an inability to deal with one another as coworkers. The conflict created decreases job satisfaction and performance.

Second, the increasing willingness to express sexual preference provides increased likelihood of homosexual advances. In this last decade of the twentieth century, U.S. culture has become more open to expressions of sexuality. People have not realized that what has become more acceptable in the general culture can be disruptive in the work setting.

This is true of people with both heterosexual and homosexual preferences.

Finally, people are less likely to passively accept sexual harassment and more likely to actively object to unwanted sexual behavior of any kind. The enactment of civil rights legislation and subsequent effects on the workplace has empowered people to speak up for themselves.

It is easy to confuse discrimination with harassment. Discrimination can occur without any direct contact with another individual. Harassment, on the other hand, involves direct interaction. Both kinds of behavior are illegal and have been since 1964; however, people tend to be more knowledgeable about discrimination than they are about harassment.

Harassment comes in many forms and can victimize anybody, including white males. Generally, however, harassment is associated with unwanted words and conduct of a sexual nature, and, therefore, is more often seen as a woman's issue. We believe that it is an issue for everyone.

A 1987 survey of federal employees reports that 42 percent of women and 14 percent of men have experienced some form of sexual harassment. Responses to a magazine survey from 160 Fortune 500 companies indicate that nearly 90 percent have received at least one sexual harassment complaint in the past year, and fully one-third of the companies responding had been sued.[122] This demonstrates that harassment is more prevalent than one might think and more dangerous than seems immediately evident. Harassment is insidious because it is so easily concealed and because the victims are often reluctant to file complaints because of threats to their own job security.

Both men and women alike can be sexually harassed and can sexually harass others of both sexes; but studies of blue-collar women indicate that they are more apt to experience sex discrimination and sexual harassment than are other groups of women employees.[123] Workers who are experiencing sexual harassment are neither satisfied nor performing to the best of their capabilities. Workers who are perpetrating sexual harassment are spending their energies in ways that are counterproductive for themselves and for their coworkers. In fact, research indicates that one of the greatest detriments to performance at all levels of the organization is having to deal with sexual harassment and sex discrimination.[124]

Often people do not understand what constitutes sexual harassment. They may not even be aware of the effects of sexual harassment on satisfaction and performance. Such a lack of awareness was graphically illustrated recently when the Personnel Director of the City of Omaha, Nebraska, resigned in the face of formal complaints that he had made racist, sexist, and religious slurs. Claiming that if he was "guilty of anything, it is not being politically astute and being overly trusting, extremely honest, possibly slightly insensitive, and having an aggressive managerial style," the man described several incidents that others thought offensive.[125]

For example, in response to a male employee who said, "Life's a bitch," the personnel director had said, "Then you marry one. Then you die." A female employee overheard and complained. The defense of the personnel director was, "I tease my wife this way all the time. The employee is too sensitive."

What do you think? Are the remarks distasteful enough to constitute sexual harassment?

Of course, sexual harassment occurs in many forms. Offensive language is only one of them. Offensive behavior is equally repugnant. Most women have learned over the years to discourage a flirtatious man's unwanted advances, but when that man is a supervisor, his organizational power makes many women afraid to resist, much less complain. When that supervisor is a woman, the harassment is equally threatening and repulsive to the recipient.

Most people in this society think of harassment in terms of a heterosexual male harassing a female. However, a female homosexual may make unwanted advances to a woman; and a male homosexual may make unwanted advances to another man. If the person receiving homosexual advances is "straight," then the harassment is considered even more offensive. Not only is it unwanted, the recipient of the attention lacks the social skills to avert it.

A young secretary, whom we will call Linda, told us about being harassed in her office by a lesbian professional, whom we will call Rhea. The situation began innocently enough. Linda had volunteered to work overtime to type and assemble a major project for Rhea. In seeming gratitude, Rhea said, "Let me take you to dinner to pay you back for all the extra effort." Linda readily agreed. Rhea offered to pick up Linda so she would not have to drive, and Linda accepted. Rhea arrived bearing flowers. She took Linda to a luxurious restaurant. They sat in a booth. During after dinner drinks, Rhea moved close to Linda and made a sexual advance. Linda was astounded. She didn't know what to do. She said, "I would have slapped a man, but a woman?" She asked Rhea to take her home. At the door, Rhea tried to kiss Linda. Linda shoved her, and said something like, "I'm not in to this." Rhea replied, "That's all right. I'll give you time."

For weeks after that, Linda tried to dodge Rhea and to repulse her continued advances, which were now occurring on the job. Rhea became so aggressive that Linda started to think maybe she was a latent lesbian and that Rhea recognized that in her; Linda was ashamed to tell her supervisor. She started to call in sick so she wouldn't have to deal with Rhea. Finally, Linda went to a counselor, who identified the situation for the harassment it was, explained Linda's rights to her, and supported her in complaining to her supervisor. The supervisor, untrained in the organization's sexual harassment policy and ill-equipped to deal with the situation, immediately called Rhea into the office, saying she had a right to face her accuser. Rhea said Linda was imagining things, after all she was only a secretary. Linda collapsed in tears. Rhea went back to work.

What would you have done? Would the supervisors in your organization know how to handle the situation of Linda and Rhea? Would they know if such a situation exists? Would you?

When one remembers that most sexual harassment is not even reported, then it is easy to see that a six-million dollar productivity loss is only the tip of the iceberg. Employees frequently do not take the issue seriously, however. For example, in two large organizations, a formal anti-sexual-harassment policy was developed and circulated. Each policy contained the statement, "There is no room in this organization for sexual harassment." In one case, a joking employee said, "Let's find a room." In the other case, a member of the organization circulated a memo that stated, "Anyone who needs a room for sexual harassment can borrow my office."

In the case of sexual harassment, wit is not appropriate. It is incumbent upon you to insure that employees in your organization are free of both discrimination and harassment. Establishing and enforcing policies is the first step. Having a policy is a necessary but insufficient means of preventing harassment. We expect that you already have a formal harassment policy, as do 81 percent of organizations surveyed in 1989.[126] The questions we raise:

- Have you taught the policy to your supervisors?
- Have you established sanctions so the policy can be enforced?
- Do the employees in your organization understand their protection under your policy?
- Have you established a climate where employees feel free to report incidents of sexual discrimination or harassment?

If you can emphatically answer "Yes!" to each of the above questions, then you have accomplished a great deal toward promoting job satisfaction and performance. What typically happens, unfortunately, is that once a policy is established, very little is done to educate people about the policy or about their rights and responsibilities under the policy.

Although the data indicate that 81 percent of companies have established a protective policy, only 57 percent of those same companies train their supervisors to deal with issues of sexual harassment.[127] Even those who do provide what they call "training" may in fact only be providing a speech and a list of "thou shall nots," rather than actual training in the two areas we believe are critical: (1) awareness of the problem and (2) policies to deal with the problem.

Surveys indicate that few employees take advantage of the protection offered by policies that prohibit sexual harassment. Most people simply are reluctant to report sexual harassment, as though being the victim of harassment somehow reflects negatively on them.

For example, in a study that defined sexual harassment as "occurring when a person is subjected to sexually explicit derogatory comments, unwanted physical contact, or sexual advances,"[128] 88 percent of the respondents reported verbal harassment, 28 percent reported being victims of unwanted physical contact, and several reported having been physically assaulted. Yet, only 8 percent reported incidents of sexual harassment to their supervisors, and those who did "got very little support."[129] Indeed, formal policies are often "not implemented at the level of the frontline supervisors."[130]

A climate where job satisfaction and effective performance can flourish must be free of sexual harassment as well as sexual discrimination. Appendix B provides a model anti-sexual-harassment policy. Appendix C contains a series of questions and answers about managing sexual harassment that were developed in 1990 by the law firm of Berens and Tate in Omaha, Nebraska, for distribution to their clients; this material is reproduced with the permission of Berens and Tate. *This information should in no way be construed as substituting for the legal advice of your own attorney.* It is reproduced in its entirety to help you understand EEOC guidelines and the importance of preventing or stopping sexual harassment if it exists. Knowing the law is self-protection for you and for your organization.

SUMMARY

One key to balancing job satisfaction and performance within your own organization is successful diversity management. Such management requires you to embrace the value of diversity while educating the managers and supervisors in your organization to set aside their stereotypes about female, minority, and mature workers. Successful diversity management also requires you to insure that your workplace is one that is free of sexual harassment and sexual innuendo.

NOTES

1. R. Roosevelt Thomas, Jr., "From Affirmative Action to Affirming Diversity," *Harvard Business Review* (March/April 1990): 107–17.

2. Patricia Galagan, "Tapping the Power of a Diverse Workforce," *Training and Development Journal* 45, no. 3 (March 1991): 43.

3. "Specialists Champion Issues Affecting Family," *Omaha World Herald* (November 19, 1990): 1G, 4G.

4. Daphne Spain and Steven Nock, "Two-Career Couples: A Portrait," *American Demographics* (August 1984): 25–27, 45.

5. Fairlee Winfield, *Work and Family Sourcebook* (Greenvale, N.Y.: Panel Publishers, Inc., 1988): 3.

6. Ibid., 5.

7. William Johnston and Arnold Packer, *Workforce 2000* (Indianapolis, Ind., 1987): 79.

8. Ibid., 79.

9. Ibid., 89.

10. "Metropolitan America: Beyond the Transition," *Population Bulletin* 45, no. 2 (July 2, 1990).

11. Marilyn Loden and Judy B. Rosener, *Workforce America! Managing Employee Diversity as a Vital Resource* (Homewood, Ill.: Business One Irwin, 1991).

12. Jaclyn Fierman, "Do Women Manage Differently?" *Fortune* (December 17, 1990): 115–18.

13. Thomas, "From Affirmative Action to Affirming Diversity," 107.

14. Jaemin Kim, "Schools Mandate Diversity Classes," *U. The National College Newspaper* 4, (May 1991): 1.

15. *Training and Development Journal* (March 1991): 43.

16. Ibid.

17. Ibid.

18. Mark Satin, *New Options*, in *Training and Development Journal* (March 1991): 43.

19. Thomas, "From Affirmative Action to Affirming Diversity," 108.

20. Ibid., 109.

21. Houston A. Baker, Jr., "Completely Well: One View of Black American Culture," in Nathan I. Huggins, et al., eds., *Key Issues in Afro-America Experience (New York: Harcourt Brace Jovanovich, Inc., 1971): 20–33.*

22. Nancy Adler, *International Dimensions of Organizational Behavior* (Boston: Kent Publishing Co., 1986): 101.

23. Vijay Sathe. *Culture and Related Corporate Realities* (Homewood, Ill.: R. D. Irwin, 1985).

24. Thomas, "From Affirmative Action to Affirming Diversity," 112.

25. Notable exceptions are Avon, Corning, Digital, Proctor and Gamble, and Xerox.

26. Guy Adams and Virginia Hill Intersoll, "Culture, Technical Rationality and Organizational Culture," *American Review of Public Administration* 20 (December 1990): 285–302.

27. Leon Festinger, "The Motivating Effect of Cognitive Dissonance," in W. Natemeyer, ed., *Classics of Organization Behavior* (Oak Park, Ill.: Moore Publishing, 1978): 58–70.

28. Bruce Malina, *The New Testament World: Insights from Cultural Anthropology* (Louisville, Ky.: John Knox Press, 1981): 13.

29. "Personnel Manager Resigns," *Omaha World Herald*, June, 27, 1990, 1.

30. Malina, *The New Testament World*, 9.

31. Ibid.

32. Joan Ablon, "American Indian Relocation: Problems of Dependency and Management in the City," *Phylon* 26 (1965): 363.

33. This story was originally cited in W. Bruce and D. Olshfski, "The New American Workplace," in M. Holzer, ed., *Public Productivity Handbook* (New York: Marcel Dekker, Inc., 1991): 430.

34. Sally Helgesen, *The Female Advantage* (New York: Doubleday-Currency, 1990): 253.

35. See, Johnston and Packer, *Workforce 2000*.

36. This statement is contained in a series of videos called *Valuing Diversity*, 1987, available from San Francisco training film producers Lennie Copeland and Lewis Griggs.

37. The first four of these statements are found in S. Nelton, "Meet Your New Workforce," *Nation's Business* (July 1988): 11–21. We add the fifth.

38. Steven Tuch and Jack Martin, "Race in the Workplace: Black/White Differences in the Sources of Job Satisfaction," *The Sociological Quarterly* 32, no. 1 (Spring 1991): 103.

39. Leonard Chusmir and Christine Koberg, "Ethnic Differences in the Relationship Between Job Satisfaction and Sex-Role Conflict Among Hispanic and Non-Hispanic White Individuals," *Psychological Reports* 66 (April 1990): 567–78.

40. "Glass Ceiling Remains," *Omaha World Herald*, August 18, 1991: 18G.

41. This is a finding of the research conducted for this book.

42. S. Thiederman, "Managing the Foreign-Born Work Force: Keys to Effective Cross-cultural Motivation," *Manage* (October 1988): 26–29.

43. Roosevelt Wright, Jr., Shirley W. King, William E. Berg, and Robert F. Creecy, "Job Satisfaction Among Black Female Managers: A Causal Approach," *Human Relations* 40, no. 8 (November 8, 1987): 489–506.

44. Jeffrey Goldstein and Marjorie Leopold, "Corporate Culture vs. Ethnic Culture," *Personnel Journal* 69 (November 1990): 83–92.

45. Loden and Rosener, *Workforce America!*, 232.

46. Ibid., 5.

47. Ibid., 232.

48. Ibid.

49. Felix Cohen, "Americanizing the White Man," *The American Scholar* 21, no. 2 (Spring 1952): 172–91.

50. *Webster's Third New International Dictionary of the English Language*, unabridged (Springfield, Mass.: Mirriam-Webster, 1981).

51. Alex Haley, "Ideas with a Payoff for Us All, *Time* 138, no. 2 (July 15, 1991): 44.

52. "Careers and Opportunities, 1991," *Black Enterprise* 21, no. 7 (February 1991): 45+.

53. "Rights Activists Fear Firms Will Backslide on Affirmative Action," *Omaha World Herald*, August 18, 1991: 18G.

54. "Executive Suite Eludes Many Blacks," *Omaha World Herald*, June 23, 1991: 1G, 4G.

55. Margarita Melville, "Hispanics: Race, Class, or Ethnicity?" *The Journal of Ethnic Studies* 16, no. 1 (1988): 67–83.

56. Ibid.

57. Tuch and Martin, "Race in the Workplace," 105.

58. Wright et al., "Job Satisfaction Among Black Female Managers," 503.

59. These studies are cited in Chusmir and Koberg, "Ethnic Differences in the Relationship Between Job Satisfaction and Sex-Role Conflict," 567–78.

60. Tuch and Martin, "Race in the Workplace."

61. Marvin Zuckerman, "Some Dubious Premises in Research and Theory on Racial Differences," *American Psychologist* 45, no. 12 (December 1990): 1297–1302.

62. Joseph Mancusi, "Another View of the Golden Rule," *HRMagazine* 36, no. 4 (April 1991): 102.

63. Ibid., 102.

64. "Past Tokenism," *Newsweek* (May 14, 1990): 37.

65. Ibid.

66. "Innovation Urged to Fully Use Skills of Older People," *Omaha World Herald*, September 11, 1988, 1G, 3G.

67. B. Rosen, and T. Jerdee, *Older Employees: New Roles for Valued Resources* (Homewood, Ill.: Dow Jones-Irwin, 1985).

68. *Omaha World Herald*, January 28, 1990.

69. David Jamieson and Julie O'Mara, *Managing Workforce 2000*, (San Francisco: Jossey-Bass, 1991): 15–16.

70. See Daniel Levinson, *The Seasons of a Man's Life* (New York: Alfred Knopf, 1978): 18. See also Catherine Marienau and Arthur Chickering, "Adult Development and Learning," in B. Memson, ed., *New Directions for Experiential Learning: Building on Experiences in Adult Development*, no. 16 (San Francisco: Jossey-Bass, 1982).

71. Bickley Townsend and Martha Farnsworth, "Two Paychecks and Seven Lifestyles," *American Demographics* 9 (August 1987): 24–29.

72. Levinson, *The Seasons of a Man's Life*, 231.

73. Ibid., 58.

74. Ibid., 59.

75. Ibid., 216.

76. *Omaha World Herald*, February 4, 1991, 25.

77. Ibid., 254.

78. Bruce and Olshfski, "The New American Workplace," 435.

79. Barry Sheckley, "The Adult as Learner," Part I, *CAEL News* 7, no. 1 (1984).

80. David Kolb, *Experiential Learning: Experience as the Source of Learning and Development* (Englewood Cliffs, N.J.: Prentice-Hall, 1984).

81. Sheckley, "The Adult as Learner."

82. B. J. Boelen, *Personal Maturity: The Existential Dimension* (New York: Seabury Press, 1978).

83. Adams and Ingersoll, "Cultural, Technical Rationality and Organizational Culture," 1978.

84. The Age Discrimination in Employment Act (ADEA) was passed in 1967, then amended in 1978 and 1986 (401 Federal Employment Practices Manual 351).

85. Ibid.

86. 401 FEP Manual 615.

87. See Michael Levin-Epstein, *Primer of Equal Employment Opportunity—Fourth Edition* (Washington, D.C.: Bureau of National Affairs, 1987), pages 61–68, for a more detailed discussion of the Age Discrimination in Employment Act.

88. See W. Bruce, *The Relationship Between Quality of Work Life and Job Satisfaction: Study of the Nation's Municipal Clerks* (Ann Arbor, Mich.: School of Education, University of Michigan, ERIC/CAPS, 10/90, text-fiche), ED 318 939; and J. W. Blackburn and W. Bruce, "Rethinking Concepts of Job Satisfaction: The Case of Nebraska Municipal Clerks," *Review of Public Personnel Administration* 10, no. 1 (Fall 1989): 11–28.

89. R. L. Schott, "The Psychological Development of Adults: Implications for Public Administration," *Public Administration Review* 46 (November-December, 1986): 657–67.

90. This research was previously published in J. W. Blackburn and W. Bruce, "Rethinking Concepts of Job Satisfaction: The Case of Nebraska Municipal Clerks," *Review of Public Personnel Administration* 10, no. 1 (Fall 1989): 11–29.

91. Gerald Zeitz, "Age and Work Satisfaction in a Government Agency: A Situational Perspective," *Human Relations* 43, no. 5 (1990): 419–38.

92. B. Boelin, *Personal Maturity: The Existential Dimension*, (New York: Seabury Press, 1978).

93. D. Nachmias, "The Quality of Work Life in the Federal Bureaucracy," *American Review of Public Administration* 18 (June 1988): 166–73.

94. Jamieson and O'Mara, *Managing Workforce 2000*, 76.

95. Ibid., 75–77.

96. Jamieson and O'Mara, *Managing Workforce 2000*, 197.

97. "Specialists Champion Issues Affecting Family," 1G, 4G.

98. Spain and Nock, "Dual Career Couples," 25–27.

99. Winfield, *Work and Family Sourcebook*.

100. R. Selbert, "Women at Work," *Future Scan*, no. 554 (November 16, 1987): 1–3, cited in Jamieson and O'Mara, *Managing Workforce 2000*.

101. Tara Roth Madden, *Women vs. Women: The Uncivil Business War* (New York: AMACOM, 1987): 59.

102. John Smart and Corinna Ethington, "Occupational Sex Segregation and Job Satisfaction of Women," *Research in Higher Education* 26, no. 2 (1987): 202–11.

103. E. M. Schur, *Labeling Women Deviant: Gender, Stigma, and Social Control* (New York: Random House, 1984): 51.

104. Cheryl Gilkes, " 'Liberated to Work Like Dogs!' Labeling Black Women and Their Work," in H. Grossman and N. Chester, *The Experience and Meaning of Work in Women's Lives* (Hillsdale, N.J.: Lawrence Erlbaum Associates, 1990) 165–88.

105. Dr. Kris Moore cited in Madden, *Women vs. Women*, 175. See also, J. Briles, *Woman to Woman: From Sabotage to Support* (Far Hills, N.J.: New Horizons Press, 1987), and S. Hardesty and N. Jacobs, *Success and Betrayal: The Crisis of Women in Corporate America* (New York: Simon and Schuster, 1986), both cited in H. Grossman and N. Chester, eds., *The Experience and Meaning of Work in Women's Lives* (Hillsdale, N.J.: Lawrence Erlbaum Associates, 1990).

106. Virginia O'Leary and Jeannette Ickovics, "Women Supporting Women:

Secretaries and Their Bosses," in Grossman and Chester, *Work in Women's Lives*, 35–56.

107. Carol Gilligan, *In a Different Voice: Psychological Theory and Women's Development* (Cambridge, Mass.: Harvard University Press, 1982).

108. Adapted from Nona Lyons, "Two Perspectives on Self, Relationships, and Morality," in Carol Gilligan, Janie Ward, and Jill Taylor, eds., *Mapping the Moral Domain* (Cambridge, Mass.: Harvard University Press, 1988): 21–48.

109. Ibid.

110. Helgesen, *The Female Advantage*.

111. Kris Kissman, "Women in Blue-Collar Occupations: An Exploration of Constraints and factors," *Journal of Sociology and Social Welfare* 17, no. 3 (September 1990): 139–49.

112. U.S. Department of Commerce, Bureau of the Census. *Statistical Abstract of the United States, 110th ed.* (Washington, D.C.: U.S. Government Printing Office, 1991).

113. Karyn Loscocco, "Reactions to Blue-Collar Work: A Comparison of Women and Men," *Work and Occupations* 17, no. 2 (May 1990): 152–77.

114. Ibid., 152.

115. Jean Reith Schroedel, "Blue-Collar Women: Paying the Price at Home and on the Job," in Grossman and Chester, *Work in Women's Lives*, 242.

116. Nina Colwill and Heather Colwill, "Women with Blue Collars: The Forgotten Minority," *Business Quarterly* 50, no. 4 (Winter 1985): 15–17.

117. See, Rosabeth Kanter, "Some Effects of Proportions on Group Life: Skewed Sex-Roles and Responses to Token Women," *American Journal of Sociology* 82 (1977): 965–90; and E. P. Enarson, *Wood-Working Women* (University, Ala.: University of Alabama Press, 1984).

118. Ibid., 248.

119. Colwill and Colwill, "Women with Blue Collars," 15.

120. Ibid.

121. Thomas Harman, "Sexual Harassment: Employers Should Pay Close Attention to EEOC Guidelines," *Special Focus* 7, no. 1 (February 1990): 1.

122. Ibid.

123. Schroedel, "Blue-Collar Women," 250–51.

124. Harman, "Sexual Harassment," 1.

125. "City Personnel Director Resigns," *Omaha World Herald*, June 27, 1991, 1, 6.

126. Johnson and Packer, *Workforce 2000*.

127. Ibid.

128. Ibid., 252.

129. Ibid.

130. Ibid., 258.

APPENDIX A: TRAINING PLAN

Objectives:

- To discuss feelings and ideas that foster prejudices in the workplace
- To identify and debunk common prejudices
- To demonstrate how stereotypes and prejudices affect the workplace.

Group Size: 7 to 10 triads of supervisors who know one another (or of any equal group of employees such as line workers or clerical workers)

Time Required: Two hours to three hours (depending on the length of your lecturette.)

Materials:

- A set of cards representing 7 to 10 "objects of prejudice" (cards may be adapted to the particular minority groups you wish to address or to issues of sexual harassment; suggestions included at the end of this appendix)
- 7 to 10 letter-size envelopes
- 7 to 10 lists of discussion questions
- Overhead projector and screen
- Overheads of any appropriate cartoons
- Newsprint and felt-tip marker for each triad
- Stopwatch
- Whistle, bell, or buzzer
- Masking tape or push pins
- Copy of your policy on discrimination and harassment for each participant (see Appendix B)
- Copy of your grievance process for each participant

Physical Setting: A room large enough to allow triads to work together without disturbing one another.

Process:

1. Welcome participants and introduce yourself; make comments specific to group assembled in terms of reason for coming together.
2. Divide group into triads and provide each triad with a piece of newsprint and marker.
3. Deliver instructions as follows:
   a. In a few minutes I will distribute an envelope that contains three cards. Each member of your group should take one card without looking at it. Each card will contain the name of a group that has historically been the object of prejudice.
   b. When I tell you, one group member will turn over the card he or she received and announce the word on it.
   c. The other two members will have approximately three minutes to say every disparaging remark they have ever heard about that particular group. The person representing the group should respond in defense of every remark made.
   d. At the end of three minutes, I will ring the bell, ask the second person in the group to announce the name of the card he or she has and

repeat the process; I will ring the bell at the end of three minutes and you will repeat the process one last time.

4. Ask triad members to take about five minutes to share with one another how they felt about being the object of such prejudicial statements.

5. Ask triads to select one member to be a recorder while you provide each group with a list of discussion questions. Ask the recorder to write key ideas on the newsprint already provided and to be prepared to post the newsprint in about fifteen minutes.

6. Distribute these, or similar, questions:

   a. How did you feel when you were defending prejudicial statements?

   b. How did you feel when you were making prejudicial statements?

   c. What did this experience tell you about your own prejudices or lack of prejudice?

   d. What did this experience tell you about the importance of a prejudice-free workplace?

   e. How were prejudices debunked?

7. After fifteen minutes, have each recorder tape notes to a wall and ask each person to walk around the room, read the notes, and generally comment to one another any thoughts or feelings.

8. Spend another fifteen to twenty minutes having participants share what they have learned about prejudices and stereotypes and about themselves.

9. Use overheads or other visual aids and follow an outline similar to the one provided here to highlight why it is important to understand how prejudices affect the workplace. Take about fifteen to twenty minutes to express both the importance of an organization free of prejudice and company policy regarding a prejudice-free workplace.

10. Ask participants how what they learned can improve relations at the work site.

"*Objects of Prejudice*" *Cards*: Use 3-by–5-inch cards and write one word or phrase on each. You may include the same three cards in each envelope, or give each triad a different set. Depending on your unique personnel mix, you might want to utilize any of the following, or some choices of your own:

mother of a small baby	yuppie
newlywed	smoker
old	fat
gay	Asian
Native American	Hispanic
black	woman boss
sexy	parent
hard-of-hearing	bald

Lecturette Outline:

1. Stereotypes and prejudices affect our assumptions about different groups of people. They also affect how we treat others.

2. When we treat people who are different from ourselves disrespectfully, this can be construed as either harassment or discrimination or both. This is illegal, and against this company's policy. (Distribute your policy and review it here. Explain who is a "protected class" and why. Emphasize the rights of employees to grievance and legal redress.)

3. These behaviors can constitute harassment: jokes, innuendos, or abuse.

4. These behaviors can constitute discrimination: denial of employment/promotion/raise; or closer scrutiny of a member of a protected class.

5. Emphasize importance of supervisors when harassment or discrimination occurs; supervisors have responsibility for investigation of complaint and for the grievance process.

6. Emphasize that supervisors must

    a. evaluate themselves and be very aware of their own prejudices;

    b. learn to recognize others' prejudicial comments;

    c. choose words carefully so that no unintended offence is committed;

    d. be aware of others' reactions to what they say;

    e. not tell or repeat derogatory remarks or jokes; and

    f. respect other peoples' feelings and differences.

Note: We suggest that you follow this training workshop with one or more of the several good films that further sensitize people to issues of diversity management: Copeland Griggs Productions. *Valuing Diversity: A 7-Part Film/ Video Series* 302 23rd Avenue, San Francisco, CA 94201: (415) 668–4200; Instructional Technology, University of Maryland. *Still Burning* Baltimore, MD 21228–5398: (301) 455–3686.

APPENDIX B: MODEL POLICY ON WORKPLACE DISCRIMINATION AND HARASSMENT

It is the policy of (your organization) to maintain a workplace that is free from discrimination based on race, creed, color, religion, gender, age, disability, (and any other protected classes that may be included in your state or city legislation). (This organization) will neither condone, permit, nor tolerate harassment of employees in any manner whatsoever. All employees are expected to treat each other with sensitivity and professionalism and avoid any behavior or conduct toward any other employee that could be interpreted as harassment. It shall be considered a violation of the policy for any employee to engage in workplace harassment or discrimination, or for any supervisory personnel knowingly to permit workplace discrimination or harassment.

For the purposes of this policy, "workplace discrimination" shall be defined as any comments or behavior that are directed toward, or expressed about, any person or persons because of race, creed, color, religion, gender, age, disability, (and any other protected classes that may be included in your state or city legislation). It is the express intent of this policy that all employees are guaranteed a workplace free of such discriminatory treatment, both because such conduct is illegal and because such conduct violates the basic human dignity of the employee and his or her right to a work environment conducive to satisfaction and performance.

For the purposes of this policy, "workplace harassment" shall be defined as any inflammatory comments, jokes, printed material and/or innuendo based, in whole or in part, on race, creed, color, religion, gender, age, disability, (and any other protected classes that may be included in your state or city legislation), or any other non-job-related factor when (1) such conduct has the purpose or effect of creating an intimidating, hostile, or offensive working environment; or (2) such conduct interferes unreasonably with a person's work or employment opportunities.

For the purpose of this policy, "sexual harassment" shall be defined as any unwelcome sexual advances, requests for sexual favors, or other verbal or physical conduct of a sexual nature, when (1) submission to such conduct is made—either explicitly or implicitly—a term or condition of an individual's employment; or (2) submission to, or rejection of, such conduct by an individual is used as the basis for employment decisions affecting such individual; or (3) such conduct has the purpose or effect of unreasonably interfering with an individual's work performance or of creating an intimidating, hostile, or offensive work environment.

Observed or experienced violations of this policy should be reported (specify time period, such as "immediately" or "within ten days of the date of the incident") without fear of retaliation to the violating employee's manager or supervisor or the (Human Resource Office) for purposes of prompt investigation. If an allegation of workplace harassment is substantiated, (the organization) shall take appropriate corrective action against the employee or employees responsible for the harassment.

APPENDIX C: SEXUAL HARASSMENT*

Employers Should Pay Close Attention to EEOC Guidelines

Sexual harassment is illegal under Title VII of the Civil Rights Act of 1964. The past decade has spawned substantial litigation over such claims. In response to the developing law in this area, the Equal Employment Opportunity Commission (EEOC), in October of 1988, issued a Guidance Memorandum to its field office personnel defining sexual harassment and establishing employer liability. The issues set forth by the EEOC guidelines are explored in the questions and answers that follow.

*Reprinted from "Sexual Harrassment: Employers Should Pay Close Attention to EEOC Guidelines," by Thomas K. Harman, in *Special Focus* 7, no. 1 (February 1990): 4–6. Used by permission of Berens & Tate, P.C.

1. Is sexual harassment a problem with which all employers should be concerned?

ANSWER: Yes. The EEOC reports that approximately 4,000 sexual harassment cases are filed with that office annually. However, this probably does not accurately reflect the actual number of incidents that take place annually.

2. Is all sexual conduct in the workplace prohibited?

ANSWER: No. Therefore, it is important that employers clearly understand exactly what types of conduct are illegal. The guidelines explain that only unwelcome sexual conduct that is a term or condition of employment constitutes sexual harassment.

3. What is sexual harassment?

ANSWER: Two general forms of sexual harassment exist. "Quid pro quo" harassment occurs where employees are asked for sexual favors in return for job-related benefits (i.e., "your body or your job"). Asking an employee for sex in exchange for a job promotion or salary increase is quid pro quo harassment.

"Hostile environment" harassment exists where conduct of a sexual nature is so frequent as to create an offensive environment for one or more employees, resulting in adverse job performance. Any form of sexual conduct may create hostile environment liability. Reported cases reveal work place behavior which has been found to constitute sexual harassment includes dirty joke telling, posting of obscene photos or drawings, requiring female employees to wear revealing garments, etc.

4. How does an employer determine what sexual conduct is unwelcome?

ANSWER: Sexual conduct is considered unwelcome only if the recipient did not somehow cause or encourage the conduct and the recipient considers it offensive. Even if the alleged victim at one time welcomed sexual advances from the employer, and the consent for the conduct is withdrawn, employers must end the conduct or risk liability. In a landmark case, a bank was held liable for sexual harassment of one of its employees despite the fact that the employee willingly had sex with her supervisor on dozens of occasions. At some point, the employee made known the fact that future sexual advances were unwelcome and when the conduct continued, the employer was found liable.

EEOC investigations of alleged harassment focus on whether the victim "welcomed" the sexual conduct by acting in a sexually aggressive manner, using sexually oriented language, or by soliciting the sexual contact. Alleged victims who participate in "telling dirty jokes, discussing their own sexual behavior, etc." or who make sexual advances themselves will be hard-pressed to claim that they found such conduct offensive. However, in a recent case the courts held that a victim's use of foul language or sexual innuendo in a consensual setting does not waive her legal protection against unwelcome harassment. Therefore, the victim's own past conduct and use of foul language did not prove that she was the kind of person who could not be offended by such comments and therefore welcomed them generally. When she had told the harasser to leave her alone, and the conduct continued, the employer was found liable.

5. How can an employer recognize potential problems?

ANSWER: Recognizing quid pro quo harassment is very simple. Any time a supervisor promises a promotion, salary increase, preferential work schedule, or any other type of job-related benefit in return for sexual favors, quid pro quo harassment exists. By the same token, quid pro quo harassment occurs any time a supervisor threatens to discipline or discharge an employee if the employee refuses to consent to sexual advances.

"Hostile environment" sexual harassment is much more difficult to pigeon-hole. These claims are limited only by the imagination of the victim's attorney.

The critical issue in hostile environment cases is whether or not the conduct creates an atmosphere for any employee which is offensive or repulsive to the extent that it affects the employee's job performance. The alleged harassment will be scrutinized from the standpoint of a "reasonable person." Thus, sexual flirtation or innuendo, the off-hand remark or dirty joke, even overt language that is trivial or merely annoying would probably not establish a hostile environment.

Because hostile environment claims usually require proof of conduct that is severe in nature or a pattern of offensive conduct, a single or rare incident of offensive sexual conduct or remarks generally does not create liability for employers. However, if such a single incident is particularly offensive, as in the manner of intimate physical touching, the employer may be liable. In one such instance, an employer was held liable for an incident in which he slipped his hands under an employee's skirt and squeezed her buttocks.

The EEOC guidelines have listed many factors affecting the strength of hostile environment claims. Some of these factors include: (i) whether the conduct was verbal or physical, or both; (ii) frequency of conduct; (iii) whether the conduct was hostile and patently offensive; (iv) whether the alleged harasser was a co-worker or supervisor; (v) whether others joined in perpetrating the harassment; and (vi) whether the harassment was directed at more than one individual.

6. When will an employer be liable for a supervisor's conduct?

ANSWER: An employer may be liable for sexual harassment by their supervisors at any time, *even when the employer is unaware of such conduct* (italics ours). Although the U.S. Supreme Court has stated that employers are not automatically liable for acts of their supervisors, absence of notice to the employer that the supervisor is sexually harassing an employee does not necessarily protect the employer from liability. The EEOC is much more willing to subject an employer to liability, asserting that "an employer . . . is responsible for its acts and those of its agents and supervisory employees with respect to sexual harassment regardless of whether the specific acts complained of were authorized or even forbidden by the employer and regardless of whether the employer knew or should have known of their occurrence." 29 C. F. R. Section 1604.11(c).

The EEOC will hold employers liable for acts by their supervisors which occur within the scope of the supervisor's authority or which result from authority granted to the supervisor.

In determining employers' liability for the conduct of their supervisors in these cases, the EEOC focuses its inquiry on whether the employer knew or should have known of the alleged harassment. If the employer had knowledge or should have had knowledge (i.e., any investigation at all would have revealed the harassment), and if the employer failed to take immediate and appropriate corrective action, the employer will be liable.

7. Can an employer be liable for harassment by a nonsupervisory co-worker?

ANSWER: Yes. The EEOC guidelines state that with respect to conduct between fellow employees, an employer is responsible for acts of sexual harassment in the workplace when the employer (or its agents or supervisory employees) knows or should have known of the conduct, unless it can show that it took immediate and appropriate corrective action.

Generally, this is not a controversial area, where results in each case simply depend on an interpretation of the facts. If the employer had sufficient notice, did not investigate properly, or discipline offenders, etc., they will be found guilty. Similar to an employer's liability for a supervisory employee, a lack of actual knowledge may not insulate the employer. Knowledge may be imputed if the harassment is so severe and pervasive that a reasonable employer would be expected to investigate and discover the facts.

8. What should an employer do to stop sexual harassment and avoid costly claims?

ANSWER: It is absolutely critical for every employer to implement a program for prevention of sexual harassment. The EEOC guidelines state that employers have a duty to affirmatively and convincingly tell their employees that sexual harassment is illegal. The first step in an effective program is the creation of a clear, written company policy against sexual harassment. The policy should be regularly communicated to employees through employee handbooks, posted company rules, meetings and/or pamphlets or leaflets distributed to the employees.

Second, employers should create and publish the proceedings for voicing complaints of sexual harassment. A critical element of internal complaint procedures should be accuracy and confidentiality of all communications related to every complaint. Care should be taken that these communications are reviewed only by people with a genuine need to know. The EEOC guidelines state that the procedure for resolving sexual harassment complaints should be designed to "encourage victims of harassment to come forward" and should not require a victim to complain first to the offending supervisor.

Finally, a preventive program should not have a "bark that is worse than its bite." To be effective, the program must not only attempt to prevent sexual harassment, but must also provide for quick and effective remedies when and if sexual harassment occurs. Employers must immediately investigate every complaint. Problems should be remedied at once. According to the EEOC guidelines, effective remedial action may include: (i) taking necessary action to end the harassment; (ii) make the victim whole by restoring lost employment benefits or opportunities; (iii) discipline the offending party; and (iv) conduct follow-up investigation to ensure that the problem is not recurring or the victim has not suffered retaliation.

9. Can an employer be liable for investigating a complaint of sexual harassment?

ANSWER: The nature of sexual harassment claims are such that implications to the accused and the accuser outside the workplace may give rise to employer liability in other areas. The unique quality of sexual harassment claims requires that the internal grievance procedure receives different treatment than that of other types of grievances. Harassment claims, especially quid pro quo claims, give rise to potential defamation claims by the accused. Because of these potential risks to the employer, confidentiality is paramount. The restriction of communications to those with a genuine need to know must be observed. Any inquiries of the accused or accuser regarding behavior outside of the work place during non-working hours involve privacy rights. It is recommended that questions of this nature should be reviewed in advance with a lawyer.

Thomas K. Harman

Chapter 3

Environmental Trends Affecting the Workplace

The way technology is used—and its impact on the lives of the workers—depends as much on management ideology as on technology itself.

Tom Forester[1]

Human resource managers are realizing that their organizations face an increasingly complex and turbulent external environment. In this chapter, we will describe environmental trends affecting the workplace and give practical advice to human resource managers for coping with the effects of these trends on their organizations.

In the first section, we will examine forces shaping the American economy. In the next section, we will describe the emerging "Information Society" and examine the impact of the development of information technology upon productivity in goods production and the office. We will then show how new information technologies may flatten the shape of organizations. In the last section, we will suggest how the human resource manager might apply the principles of work design to different kinds of work that are of key importance in the information society's workplace in order to enhance job satisfaction and performance.

FORCES SHAPING THE AMERICAN ECONOMY

A number of economic and demographic forces are reshaping American jobs and industries. In varying degrees, the patterns that will shape the future are visible in recent economic history.

The Integration of the World Economy

The world economy is becoming more and more integrated. Improvements in transportation and communications technologies have woven the world's economic fabric together. Such innovations as container ships, jet airplanes, and satellite and fiber-optic communications have created a new international market.[2] The combined value of imports and exports now constitute one-quarter of the gross national product (GNP) of the United States[3]

The integration of the world economy means that the United States has lost control of its economic destiny. The importance of trade means that no nation can expect sustained growth unless the world economy grows. The United States can no longer unilaterally set its own interest rates or balance its trade accounts. An international network of currency traders, central banks, and corporations now determines relative currency valuations, trade flows, and national interest rates. These now affect rates of economic growth and unemployment.[4] The value of a nation's currency may depend less on its position in international trade than on fiscal or monetary policies of many governments, banking decisions, and other world events that effect foreign investment. Exchange rates can fluctuate by close to 50 percent. The effects of these fluctuations on the relative cost of a product, and a firm's ability to compete in international markets, may dwarf the impact of productivity improvements, or other managerial decisions.[5]

Since the 1950s the U.S. economy has closely mirrored the world economy. The importance of trade has meant that, with few exceptions, when the world has been booming, the United States has been booming, and when the world has been in recession, so too has the United States.[6]

The Shift of Production from Goods to Services

Since World War II, the provision of services has displaced manufacturing as the largest element in the economy of virtually all advanced nations. In the United States, service industries, broadly defined, now account for over 70 percent of GNP and about 75 percent of all jobs.[7]

How do we distinguish the production of goods from services? Services are economic activities whose output is not a physical product or construction, are generally consumed at the time they are produced, and provide added value in forms (such as convenience, amusement, timeliness, comfort, or health) that are essentially intangible. A raw material or manufactured product, in contrast, may retain its value when it is transported, stored, or resold. A simple definition of a "service" is "anything sold that could not be dropped on your foot."[8]

Increases in the productivity and efficiency of manufacturing have meant that it requires fewer people, capital, and energy to produce greater quantities of goods. Part of these productivity gains are passed along to consumers in the form of lower, or more slowly rising, prices. These lower relative prices for manufactured goods are causing them to decline as a share of the GNP, even though the volume of goods is rising.[9]

The Proliferation of Advanced Technologies

Technology is a powerful economic force. During the early twentieth century, the development of electricity, telephones, airplanes, and automobiles fundamentally restructured American cities and brought dramatic changes in the nature of work. The invention of computers, television, and jet aircraft brought more changes.[10]

Five technologies will have especially significant impacts upon the productivity and efficiency of the American economy in the next few years:

Information storing and processing has been characterized by steady improvements in the price/performance ratios of computing devices. Today, many desktop microcomputers are more powerful than the machines that were used to guide the Apollo rockets that carried a man to the moon in 1968. Continuing improvements will continue dramatic increases in data processing and storing capabilities.

Communications improvements parallel and enhance improvements in information storing and processing. Fiber-optics cables provide enormous increases in communications capacity. Electronic communications are a growth industry, with continuing advances in software to integrate, analyze, and present the huge array of electronic information that is becoming available.

Advanced materials are providing industry with many sophisticated and useful synthetics to replace traditional materials. Enhanced hardness, durability, and resilience of materials will extend the life of moving parts and surfaces exposed to weather and extreme conditions and will extend the life of manufactured products. These improvements, coupled with a trend toward less material-intensive products, will substantially reduce the use of raw materials.

Biotechnologies are facilitating the manipulation of life forms at the cellular and subcellular levels. The results are new plant varieties that can withstand extremes in temperature, moisture, and soil conditions, create their own fertilizer, or combine the best features of widely different strains. Super-producing animals grow faster with less feed and have greater disease resistance.

Superconductivity is the potential to carry electric current without energy loss. The discovery in 1986 of a new family of materials that are superconductive at relatively high temperatures created a potential to transform the whole structure of the nation's energy system. Electricity could be generated near coal deposits and then shipped cheaply even thousands of miles to urban areas.

Increased Competition in Product, Service, and Labor Markets

The world economy has become more competitive in recent years, for several reasons. The integration of global markets, excess production capacity, a rapidly growing world labor force, the decline in labor unions, and the general deregulation of industry by many Western governments are all contributing toward this competitive trend. For the United States, increased competition means that maintaining world leadership in any industry or technology is a ceaseless struggle. Great changes in America's economic power could come in a matter of decades or even years, depending on how well the nation continues to innovate, adapt, and grow.

Economies are operating at increasing speeds. Their pace is determined by the speed of transactions, the time needed to make decisions (especially about investment), the speed with which new ideas are created in laboratories, the rate at which they are brought to market, the velocity of capital flows, and above all the speed with which data, information, and knowledge pulse through the economic system. The speedup of economic change makes our knowledge perishable—about technology, markets, suppliers, distributors, currencies, interest rates, consumer preferences, and all other business variables.[11]

American producers are challenged to meet new competitive standards. National competitiveness is no longer based primarily upon productivity, but also upon the quality, variety, customization, convenience, and timeliness of goods and services offered. Consumers are richer than they used to be and they are demanding high-quality goods and services that are competitively priced, available in a variety of forms, customized to specific needs, and conveniently accessible. In addition, people do not want to wait patiently for state-of-the-art goods and services. In the global economy, if American firms do not meet these standards, someone else will.[12]

Changes in the Supply of Labor

Projecting the future supply of labor is very tricky because so many variables can change in unexpected ways. For example, trends in the rate of participation of women in the labor force in recent decades took many demographers by surprise.

The rate of American population growth during the 1980s was 1.0 percent, and it dropped to .75 percent during the 1990s. In the 1990s, population growth will be lower than any time during the nation's history except during the decade of the Great Depression. Changes in fertility and death rates and in immigration can have significant impacts on the size of the population in the next ten to fifteen years. Technological advances in birth control, new means of treating the AIDs virus, and changes in social values that influence family size could substantially influence population growth.[13]

The slowing growth of the population will be mirrored in a reduced growth in the labor force. Immigration and changes in labor-force-participation rates will have the greatest impact on the size of the labor force. A strong economy could pull more workers into the labor market, or international unrest could swell the supply of immigrants. A weak economy, growing desires for early retirement, restrictive changes in immigration legislation, or renewed emphasis on child care by stay-at-home parents, could reduce the size of the labor force. Different assumptions about immigration and labor-force participation indicate that the labor force could be as great as 147 million by 2000, or as small as 129 million, reflecting labor-force-growth rates as high as the low-twenties, or as low as a little above 10 percent.

Experts expect the most likely scenario to be slow growth in the population and labor force. They suggest several possible consequences of an aging population and work force, and a smaller supply of younger workers:[14]

1. A more experienced, stable, reliable, and generally healthy work force should improve productivity.

2. The national savings rate may rise, as the "baby boomers" reach middle age.

3. Labor markets for younger workers could tighten.

4. An aging work force may increase the rigidity of the economy.

5. A dearth of young workers may hamper the ability of companies to grow rapidly or respond to change.

6. Many companies with older work forces may find that their aging, higher-paid workers make them uncompetitive.

7. The job squeeze among middle-aged workers may become intense.

8. Many industries that depend on young people for market growth may retrench.

Impending shifts in the population and labor force will challenge employers to do some serious thinking about traditional approaches to hiring and keeping employees.[15]

THE INFORMATION SOCIETY AND PRODUCTIVITY

A number of analyses of the American economy suggest that we are becoming an "Information Society." Information is becoming an increasingly important component of economic activity, and this has led to extraordinary developments in information technology (IT). In this section we trace the emergence of the information society, and examine the nature and extent of the information revolution. Next, we explore the impact of the development of information technology upon productivity in goods production and in the office. We then examine how new information technologies may flatten the shape of organizations.

The Emergence of the Information Society

The idea that the United States is becoming an "Information Society" is controversial. A leading proponent of the concept claims that in 1956, for the first time in American history, white-collar workers in technical, managerial, and clerical positions outnumbered blue-collar workers. Now, well over 65 percent of us work with information as programmers, teachers, clerks, secretaries, accountants, stock brokers, managers, insurance people, bureaucrats, lawyers, bankers, and technicians. Many more hold information jobs within manufacturing companies. "Most Americans spend their time creating, processing, or distributing information."[16] A similar analysis used the U.S. census to create six occupational categories. The results indicate that information workers increased from 48.8 percent to 62.1 percent of total employment between 1960 and 1980. More important, the rate of growth was 24.5 percent. The researchers concluded that knowledge production contributes strongly to productivity growth in the sectors in which the activity is located.[17]

Another leading proponent of the Information Society concept argues that while in an industrial society the strategic resource was capital, now the strategic resource is information—it is not the only resource, but it is the most important. The creation of the Intel Corporation, which developed the microprocessor, is an example. The company was launched with an investment of $2.5 million in 1968. It was the brainpower behind the financial resource that led to the technological breakthroughs that brought the firm annual sales of $900 million by 1982.[18]

Two economists have estimated that two-thirds of recent growth in U.S. industrial productivity resulted from advances in knowledge. The nation's productivity grew because of the increased education of the work force, the greater pool of knowledge available, and the use of that knowledge by better-educated workers. It is knowledge, not cheap labor and symbols, not raw materials, that embody and add value.[19] Wealth is increasingly dependent on brainpower. It is claimed that the advanced economy could not run for thirty seconds without computers. The new complexities of production, the integration of many diverse (and constantly changing) technologies, and the de-massification of markets, continue to increase, by vast leaps, the amount and quality of information needed to make the system produce wealth.[20]

Knowledge is inherently different from capital as a productive resource. Two people can use the same knowledge without using it up, and can create new knowledge in the process. The most revolutionary characteristic of knowledge is that it can be used by anyone, while capital and wealth are available only to the rich.

Knowledge is a new form of capital. It is inherently inexhaustible and nonexclusive. It exists in paper form symbolizing tangible assets, in paper form capturing the knowledge workers use to create more knowledge, and in electronic blips symbolizing knowledge on paper. Our economy is now based on a key resource that is infinitely renewable, and self-generating.

Peter Drucker, a business expert, supports these arguments: "The productivity of knowledge has already become the key to productivity, competitive strength, and economic achievement. Knowledge has already become the primary industry, the industry that supplies the economy with the essential and central resources of production."[21]

The importance of knowledge in the U.S. economy is reflected by the fact that information companies have emerged as some of the nation's largest. AT&T grossed $65 billion in 1982, far surpassing the GNP of many nations. Other information companies include IBM, ITT, Xerox, RCA, all banks and insurance companies, broadcasters, publishers, and computer companies. Almost all of the people in these companies and industries spend their time processing information in one way or another and generating value that is purchased in domestic and global markets.[22] In the smokestack era, any list of the richest people in the world would have been dominated by car makers, steel barons, rail magnates, oil moguls, and financiers, whose collective wealth ultimately came from the organization of cheap labor, raw materials, and the manufacture of hardware. In contrast, a recent list of *Forbes* magazine's ten richest American billionaires includes fully seven whose fortunes were based on media, communications, or computers—software and services rather than hardware and manufacturing.[23]

A contrasting perspective argues that the "knowledge" sector of the U.S. economy, "Education, Research and Development, Communications, Information Services, etc." already accounted for 29 percent of the U.S. economy in 1958. By 1980, it accounted for 34 percent—in two decades not a dramatic enough increase to suggest that we are becoming an information society.[24]

The argument about whether we are becoming an information society hinges upon how "information work" is defined and upon estimates of how much of any particular type of work involves the manipulation of information. We take the position that the U.S. economy is indeed in a transition from muscle work to mental work, or work requiring psychological and human skills. This shift is occurring in both manufacturing and services. This trend has important implications for human resource professionals, which we shall explore.

A key factor in the productivity of workers, then, is the "information revolution." It has had important effects upon the workplace, job satisfaction, and productivity. Human resource managers need to understand both the information revolution and its impact upon job satisfaction and performance.

The Nature and Extent of the Information Revolution

The information revolution is simply the extent to which new and more efficient means of acquiring, manipulating and transmitting information are developing, the extent to which these new means are changing the workplace, the way organizations are managed, and how business is conducted.

It is generally agreed that the computer is the most important technological innovation of this century and that information technology (IT) is a pervasive technology at least as important as electricity or steam power. The revolutionary importance of IT stems from the fact that decreases in the cost and size of computers have been accompanied by increases in their power, speed, and sophistication. Recent improvements in technology have, in addition, brought about the convergence of voice, image and data transmission, and of the electronics, telecommunications, and computing industries based upon them.[25] Consequently, we stand at the threshold of a mammoth communications revolution. The combined technology of the telephone, computer, and television have merged into an integrated information and communications system that transmits data and permits instantaneous interactions between persons and computers. This new integrated communications system fuels the information society.[26]

Some comparisons that have appeared in the popular media suggest the impact of the computer. Whereas the multiplication of two ten-digit numbers required five seconds for an early mainframe computer, now sophisticated computers can accomplish a billion such computations in one second. If the automobile had changed to the extent that the computer has changed since the 1940s, a Rolls Royce would cost about $3 and would travel three million miles on one gallon of gasoline. The price of storing data on memory chips has been decreasing about 35 percent each year. The microchip has put cheap computing power on the desks of millions.[27]

Changes in telecommunications have greatly increased the utility of computers by enabling them to communicate directly with each other. Fiber-optic cables have vastly multiplied the amount of information that can be communicated, thus enabling computers to communicate the enormous amount of data needed to transmit color computer screen graphics images. Conversely, changes in computer technologies have contributed to changes in communications technologies.[28] These changes may be as significant for society as the building of railroads and highway networks.[29]

Due to the availability of cheap and compact computing power, the information revolution is affecting a tremendous variety of activities. Its impact is often visible in familiar places. People taking inventory in grocery stores punch data into tiny computers hanging on their belts. Checkout registers collect data from bar codes on the products we buy. Some retailers transmit this information almost immediately to warehouses and suppliers. Many functions in our automobiles are controlled by tiny computers.

Mechanics use computer systems to conduct automobile checkups and to diagnose problems. Cabbies use computers on their dashboards to find the quickest routes to their destinations. Airlines instantly reserve specific seats on particular flights. Sales clerks communicate with distant computers to quickly check the status of our credit card accounts before we can complete a purchase. Computers and telecommunications complete electronic fund transfers between our employer and our bank. Automatic teller machines allow us to withdraw money from our bank account at any hour of the day or night. Computers may control the temperature and light in the offices where we work. Computers make familiar machines such as office copiers much more versatile. Computers even assist these machines to "self-diagnose" problems when lights flash and indicators suggest what needs to be done to make the machine function again.

Computers have had a pervasive impact upon industries such as banking and insurance, which manipulate vast quantities of information. Financial transactions are particularly amenable to electronic processing. Even agriculture is benefiting from the information revolution. Computerized irrigation systems use sensors to calculate different water and fertilizer needs on different areas of a field. Satellites may soon provide the information needed for farmers to decide which areas of fields need specific types of fertilization. Electronic ID tags record an animal's life history. Automated chicken houses and packaging stations are appearing.[30] Biotechnologies that manipulate genes to produce organisms with new characteristics no doubt use computerized information extensively.

Speech recognition, voice processing or "talkwriters" are still in a relatively primitive state, but have tremendous potential to revolutionize the interactions of humans with machines. Developments in liquid crystal displays are making laptop computers smaller and more portable.

Information Technology and Productivity in Goods Production

The application of information technology to goods production has produced some of the most dramatic and highly visible improvements in productivity of any economic sector. Cheap, reliable and sophisticated control systems based on the computer are bringing about a revolution in manufacturing. Machine tools can store data and designs in a computer memory, making it possible to produce a variety of goods on one machine. Labor costs have been greatly reduced because one operator can control several machines. The microchip in computers has made computers cheaper and less space consuming in robots. Their use is ideal in noisy, dirty, dangerous, and repetitive jobs, or tasks that require great exertion to achieve precise results in awkward positions. The automobile industry has greatly enhanced productivity through the application of robots.[31]

On a research tour of a tractor assembly plant we saw robots in action. One machine extruded a sealing material precisely around the perimeter of a window assembly to seal it snugly into its frame. The material hardened into a heavy, rubbery caulking material. A robotic arm placed the material in a very smooth layer that would have been almost impossible to duplicate by hand. The physical exertion needed to make a smooth seal would have been substantial. Another function carried out by robots is painting tractors. Robots can spread the paint very evenly to assure complete coverage while minimizing the time needed to complete the job and the amount of paint used. A major advantage of using robots for this task, of course, is to avoid the problems caused when humans breathe the paint spray that fills the air.

We witnessed another dramatic demonstration of the contribution and sophistication of computer technology on the tractor assembly plant tour. At the end of the engine assembly line an enormous overhead moveable crane picked up each completed engine and placed it, ever so gently, on another assembly line conveyor, or placed it precisely on blocks in a storage area if it needed certain parts for completion. The dramatic aspect was that no human operator was present to control the crane nor direct it where to pick up or where to place the engines. A computer gave exact instructions.

Computers have made possible flexible manufacturing systems in which a set of machines is linked so that parts are passed automatically from one to another for different manufacturing processes. Product specifications can be varied, or small batches of components can be produced with the same efficiency and economy as with traditional mass production methods. Savings in labor costs and plant space are achieved because a single set of versatile machines replaces several conventional, less adaptable machines. Employees who control these machines can replace several workers who simply operated one or two of the older types of equipment. This versatility helps to produce economies by reducing the amount of work in progress and plant inventory.

More precise control of machines by computers decreases the amount of waste from less precise machining in the old machines, or the need to correct problems in the products produced. Plant utilization is increased because the machines can be kept running most of the time and reprogrammed quickly. Reduced lead times to develop new products or initiate the production of particular items enable firms to react much more quickly to market trends, which often makes the difference between profit and loss.[32] This decreases costs also by reducing the amount of finished goods sitting in warehouses and railroad sidings.

Computer-driven manufacturing technologies make endless variety possible. In 1972 Philips made one hundred different models of color TV, but with modernization five hundred models are produced. A shoe company offers semicustomized women's shoes—32 designs for each size—depending on the individual customer's feet as measured by computer in the store. A Japanese company synchronized its production lines to those of its customers so perfectly that it reduced its inventories drastically, thus lowering real estate costs, taxes, insurance, and overhead.[33]

During our visit to the tractor assembly plant, we were told that most tractors are now customized for particular customers. This saves the costs of storing large numbers of identical tractors on lots, deteriorating while waiting until a customer finds the particular model with the right combinations of features. Customers now have a great variety of options that were not previously available. They do not pay for options or features they do not need.

Computer-aided design (CAD) has greatly increased the productivity of expensive design staff, eliminated boring and repetitive tasks, cut the lead time from the design stage to final product, reduced design and manufacturing errors, increased product quality, and cut the cost of updating and modifying products. In computer-aided engineering (CAE), three dimensional designs can be examined, analyzed and even tested to simulated destruction without ever having been made.[34]

Improvements in computing have made simultaneous engineering possible. The unprecedented precision and coordination achievable through the use of the computer makes is possible to design the manufacturing process while the product is being designed, which decreases the time between conception of the product and its appearance on the market. The precision possible with computers facilitates the design of products with fewer components. Elements of products can be assembled into modules to further reduce manufacturing costs. By redesigning a component, IBM cut costs from $5.95 to $1.81, and reduced manufacturing time from three minutes to seconds. Intelligent organization and sophisticated electronic information exchange at a new Motorola plant increased the probability of perfection to 99.99997 percent. Twenty-seven robots do the physical work of forty employees—only one person touches the product.[35]

The cost savings and labor-saving contribution of computer technology were also evident during our tour of the tractor assembly plant. A large section of shelves, rising many feet toward the high ceiling, were mostly empty. This was the storage area for tractor parts. A computer-controlled mechanical device knew exactly where each part was stored and would retrieve it and deliver it without any human operator present. A just-in-time inventory system used a sophisticated computer and telecommunications system to obtain delivery just shortly prior to when parts were scheduled for installation. This system created substantial cost reductions by keeping the size of inventory down, which accounts for the empty shelves.

Electronic data interchange between producers and customers, and between producers and suppliers, can help to reduce the amount of inventory kept on hand, and facilitate moving materials more quickly to where they are needed. Burlington sends customers free software that communicates directly with the mainframe to find a particular batch of fabric and exchange data on invoices, specifications, and inventory. Some auto firms refuse to deal with suppliers not equipped with electronic interaction capability. To reduce paperwork, and facilitate quicker and more flexible responses, fifty-seven parts plants that supply Ford have been told they must exchange shipping schedules, material requisitions, releases and receipts with both customers and suppliers. The use of advanced information processing and communications to link with suppliers has enabled the General Electric division which builds locomotives to turn over its inventory twelve times faster and save a full acre of warehouse space.[36]

The need to bring new products to market quickly has made it necessary to integrate firms through greater communication of information through the use of computers. Production used to be a series of disconnected steps—raise capital, acquire raw materials, recruit workers, deploy technology, advertise, sell, and distribute—either sequentially or in isolation. Now production is increasingly simultaneous and synthesized. Information gained by sales and marketing people feeds to engineers, whose innovations need to be understood by the financial people, whose ability to raise capital depends on how satisfied the customers are, which depends on how well scheduled the company's trucks are. The integration of these phases through the application of information technology speeds up production and helps to make these firms more competitive in an increasingly dynamic and demanding marketplace.

Toyota uses computer technology to accomplish simultaneous engineering, apply advanced information systems, and share information with suppliers at an early stage to achieve faster development cycles, frequent new product introduction, and a constant flow of major and minor innovations on existing models.[37]

Information Technology and Productivity in the Office

Interest in increasing the productivity of office operations is great for two reasons. First, more people now work in offices than in farms, factories, shops, and services combined. Over 50 percent of the U.S. labor force are now white-collar workers. Second, labor costs are about four-fifths of office operation costs.[38] Improvements in office productivity have a potential for substantial reduction in the costs of operations.

Efforts to improve office productivity are not new. A great variety of devices have been created to improve office operations. Such creations as dictation equipment, duplicating machines, ticker tape, offset printing, calculators, automatic telephone switches and photocopiers have made regular appearances through this century. Their cumulative impact upon productivity, however, has not been great. The emergence of the electronic computer and high-speed data processing brought dramatic changes. By the 1960s most large organizations had data-processing centers handling payrolls, issuing checks, controlling inventory, and sending out bills.

Advances in computing and telecommunications have brought the costs of information processing down, with dramatic increases in the use of information processing technology. In 1990 there was roughly 1,000 times as much computing power in offices as in 1970. The population of keyboards—electronic typewriters, wordprocessors, desktop personal computers, and computer terminals—has grown to over 50 million. The "desktop revolution" brought 8 to 10 million personal computers in the United States just four years after IBM's PC was launched in 1981.[39] The versatility of these machines meant that they could be used for word processing, number crunching, and spreadsheet analysis, and they could be hooked up to mainframe computers, facsimile machines, printers, and data bases. They become "workstations" that could be communications hubs enabling professionals to keep in touch with other people and vital sources of information. Most new integrated office networks are being built around workstations.

Productivity gains in office work, however, are not easy to demonstrate. White-collar productivity is not amenable to precise measurement as in manufacturing productivity, and therefore assessing gains is difficult. There is no clear link between spending money and seeing results. Even measuring the output of word processors is difficult. Effectiveness in office work may be much more important than efficiency. For example, projects that are completed on time, or very "efficiently," but with poor quality and excessive costs are not considered to be successful.[40]

Although evaluating the productivity of information technology is difficult, new office technologies generally allow more work to be done by the same number or fewer people and enhance job satisfaction. In several studies, it was found that the introduction of information technology resulted in a restructuring of office work. The proportion of workers requiring technical training and higher skills increased, and other workers in routine or semiskilled office jobs decreased sharply. Secretaries were able to spend more time using more creative skills and devoting less effort to routine typing. The jobs needing greater training and technical skills, and requiring broader responsibilities and knowledge of organizational operations, provided greater job satisfaction.[41]

The Impact of Information Technology on Organizational Hierarchy

The development and use of information technologies widely in organizations may have an impact upon the hierarchy and shape of the organization. In many organizations much of the work of middle managers consists of collecting information from subordinates, synthesizing it, and passing it up the line to their own superiors. Group executives, corporate directors, and assistant vice presidents whose primary functions are either to filter information or to manipulate data being passed up from lower levels, or to make routine decisions, are vulnerable to replacement through the introduction of information technology. Routine decisions can be preprogrammed in software, through the application of artificial intelligence, so that line employees do not need to go to managers or specialists when questions arise.[42]

In an economy that is speeding up, in part due to improvements in communications and information technologies, timely reporting of information is becoming more critical in maintaining an organization's competitive position. New information technology is often the key to capturing new markets, creating new products, and entering new fields. A key to success often is getting a new product to market before competitors do, or before they copy a product. Entire reporting systems are becoming overloaded, and top managers can no longer wait for messages to move up the chain of command in the traditional manner. They have set up systems in which computers can communicate with other computers, and in which they can retrieve data directly from information systems themselves. Electronic networks speed up communications— up, down, sideways. New ideas and problems make an end run around hierarchies. The traditional channels of information are being bypassed, and organizations are doing away with many middle-management positions. This often leads to changes in the shape and mission of the organization, and sometimes to a flattening of the organizational hierarchy.[43]

During our tour of the tractor assembly plant, our guide pointed out a number of empty rooms. These had once been occupied by a large operations staff. The installation of sophisticated computer and information technology had reduced the need for many staff positions.

To use expensive new computers and networks effectively, reorganization is sometimes needed. "Chief Information Officers" are often in the middle of fights over information. Conflicts arise over who gets what kind of information, who has access to main data bases, who can add to that data base, what assumptions are built into accounting, which department or division owns which data, and who dictates assumptions or models built into data bases. These decisions affect money, status, and power.

At IBM the "PROFS" sub-net replaced the work of 40,000 middle mangers and white-collar workers. Such developments are changing the information infrastructure and structure of power. Communications ignore rank. Desktop computers are making organizations less monolithic.[44] Increasing numbers of business problems require cross-disciplinary information that is broken out from traditional "cubbyholes and channels." New horizontal networks help the organization to reconfigure quickly to meet changed conditions. Leadership is based on competence and personality rather than on social or organizational rank. In leading-edge industries, the old authoritarian command structure is being replaced by a new, more egalitarian or collegial work-style.

BALANCING JOB SATISFACTION AND PERFORMANCE IN THE INFORMATION SOCIETY WORKPLACE

In an "information society," the management and manipulation of information is becoming an increasingly important dimension of work.

Classifying jobs according to their information content and the way information is used is helpful to managers in understanding what they can do to enhance job satisfaction and performance. In this section we introduce a classification of jobs according to the kinds of skills employed and the kinds of information that are important.

"Work Design" is emerging as one of the most powerful means for enhancing both job satisfaction and performance. We review the principles of work design, and suggest how they can be applied to the three skill categories introduced in the new classification in order to enhance job satisfaction and performance.

A New Skills Classification for the Information Society

In thinking about balancing job satisfaction and performance in the information society, it is useful to examine jobs in terms of a "mind-work spectrum." While an enormous range of jobs involve the manipulation and management of information, they differ greatly in the way information is used, the kind of data processed, the skills that are employed to handle the information, the purposes and outcomes of these efforts, and the organizational context of the activities. The mind-work spectrum can be viewed in terms of how much of a job entails information processing, how routine or programmable it is, what level of abstraction is involved, what access the person has to the central data bank and management information system, and how much autonomy and responsibility the person enjoys.[45] A new skills classification provides three categories that are distinctly different in the way in which information is used and the kinds of data that are processed.

In the scheme used by the census—which made sense in an economy focussed on high-volume, standardized production—jobs were categorized into "Managerial and Professional," "Technical, Sales, and Administrative Support," "Service Occupation," or "Operator, Fabricator, and Laborer." A new classification uses just three groupings, which are "Routine Production Services," "In-Person Services," and "Symbolic-Analytic Services."[46] We shall refer to the workers in the first two categories as "Routine Producers," and "In-Person Servers." Instead of using the term "Symbolic-Analysts," we shall refer to "gold-collar workers" as the third kind of workers. These categories encompass almost all of the jobs that are important in organizations in the information society.

The jobs of Routine Producers involve repetitive tasks. Routine supervisory positions in which low- and mid-level managers make repetitive checks of subordinates' work and enforce standard operating procedures fit this category, as well as the traditional blue-collar workers. Job titles such as foreman, line manager, clerical supervisor, and section chief describe this kind of jobholder. Even workers in high-technology industries, doing such activities as assembling circuit boards or devising routine coding for computer software, fit here.

In the information society, vast quantities of raw data must be processed. Employees who routinely enter or retrieve data from computers are Routine Producers. Their work includes handling such data as records of credit card purchases and payments, credit reports, checks that have cleared, customer accounts, customer correspondence, payrolls, hospital billings, patient records, medical claims, court decisions, subscriber lists, personnel records, and library catalogue holdings.

In-Person Servers carry out simple and repetitive tasks. A major difference from Routine Producers is that In-Person Servers have contact with the beneficiaries of their work. This category includes retail sales workers, waiters and waitresses, hotel workers, janitors, childcare workers, cashiers, hospital attendants and orderlies, nursing home–aides, house cleaners, home-health-care aides, taxi drivers, secretaries, hairdressers and barbers, auto mechanics, flight attendants, and security guards. These people must be pleasant, cheerful, courteous and helpful, and put others at ease.

Gold-collar workers solve, identify, and broker problems by manipulating symbols. They are often imaginative and original. They simplify reality into abstract symbols that can be rearranged, juggled, experimented with, communicated to other specialists, and then, eventually, transformed back into reality. Their tools may include mathematical formulas, legal arguments, financial gimmicks, scientific principles, psychological insights about how to amuse or persuade, or any other set of techniques for doing conceptual puzzles. They devise means to shift financial assets, or create new inventions or innovative legal arguments, new advertising ploys, or new sounds, words, or pictures in order to entertain or to provoke people to reflect on the human condition.

Gold-collar workers include many who call themselves research scientists, public relations managers, software engineers, civil engineers, financial analysts and managers, lawyers, marketing managers, auditors, and accountants. Also included are management consultants, management information specialists, organization development specialists, strategic planners, and systems analysts. Advertising managers, art directors, architects, production designers, publishers, writers and editors, journalists, musicians, and television and film producers fit this category.

Many of the traditional census categories overlap all of the these categories. For example, as Routine Producers, secretaries perform strictly routine tasks, such as entering and retrieving data, taking dictation, filing, making photocopies, or getting out mailings. Others perform In-Person Services such as making appointments, screening visitors, or serving coffee. Others are gold-collar workers who must assist their superiors in editing letters, planning meetings, or keeping track of vital information. Similarly, workers in sales may simply fill orders or quotas, as Routine Producers, or may perform In-Person services such as maintaining machinery or demonstrating products to customers. They may help potential or current customers to solve sophisticated problems, as gold-collar workers. The work of computer programmers ranges from routine coding, to In-Person troubleshooting for clients, to translating complex functional specifications into software.

Some lawyers simply crank out wills and contracts in monotonous fashion, others may provide personal counsel as In-Person Servers, while others prepare complex legal arguments as gold-collar workers. Many managers take no more responsibility than noting who shows up for work, making sure they stay put, and locking the place at night. Others spend most of their time making work assignments and training new workers. Managers who devise strategies for enhancing the effectiveness of their organization are gold-collar workers.

Very different management principles and methods are needed to enhance the job satisfaction and performance of employees who use these different kinds of skills. Job titles and job descriptions are not as relevant in the Information Society as they once were when mass production was the major mode of operations in the nation's premier enterprises.

Work Design as a Means of Enhancing Job Satisfaction and Performance

"Work Design" or "Work Re-Design" refers to any activities that involve the alteration of specific jobs, or interdependent systems of jobs, with the intention of increasing both the quality of the employees' work experience and their on-the-job productivity.[47] It subsumes such means as "Job Rotation," "Job Enrichment," and "Sociotechnical Systems Design."

A set of action principles have been developed for redesigning jobs to enhance job satisfaction and performance. These are (1) forming natural work units; (2) combining tasks; (3) vertical loading; (4) establishing client relationships; and (5) opening feedback channels.

Forming natural work units involves creating tasks that are identifiable and meaningful wholes. Workers see the results of their work in completed products, elements of products, or sections of work, rather than working continuously on one small component or fragment of a task.

Combining tasks often contributes to forming natural work units. For example, instead of assembling just one part of a coffee percolator, when tasks are combined each worker would put together all of the major elements for the complete product.

Vertical loading gives workers the responsibilities for tasks that are ordinarily divided among different levels of an organizational hierarchy. These may include planning, organizing, directing, and controlling functions. Workers might choose among different work methods, advise and train less experienced workers, organize their time, and do their own troubleshooting and manage crises instead of relying on a supervisor. Managing financial aspects of a job could be included.

Establishing client relationships provides workers with feedback on their performance. They are challenged to use their interpersonal skills in these interactions and take responsibility for translating this feedback into improved performance.

Opening feedback channels helps workers learn how well they are performing, and whether their work is improving, deteriorating, or remaining at a constant level. When workers are responsible for quality control, this greatly increases the quantity and quality of feedback on work performance. Computers can be programmed to provide regular feedback on performance.

Similar principles have been developed for the design of work for interacting teams to increase the quality of the work experience of the people involved, and simultaneously to increase the quality and quantity of the work produced. The principles are these: (1) work is assigned as a whole task to produce an identifiable and significant task that is meaningful to the group; (2) workers in the group each have several skills needed for the task to facilitate flexibility in carrying out the task; (3) the group has autonomy to make decisions about scheduling, job assignments, and how the work is carried out. Sometimes groups select new group members; and (4) compensation is based upon group performance.

Managing Routine Producers to Balance Job Satisfaction and Performance

In this section, we examine some of the challenges to balancing job satisfaction and performance for routine producers. We then provide a number of examples of the application of the principles of work design to specific jobs as a means of balancing job satisfaction and performance. We give advice for meeting the challenges of using new technologies in the workplace.

Routine Producers have repetitive tasks, jobs such as assembly line work as well as information processing. The productivity, performance, or direct output of the Routine Producer is often determined by the movement of an assembly line, by compensation for the amount of work performed, and by standards for the units of work performed. What is often hidden, however, are the costs to productivity from excessive turnover, absenteeism, sick leave, or inaccurate performance of tasks. The costs appear in the expense of training new workers, the cost of health insurance, the need to correct errors, or the annoyance of customers whose orders, bills, or payments have been inaccurately processed, lost, or delayed.

While the number of traditional assembly line jobs in the United States is decreasing, great numbers of workers process the immense amounts of information circulating in our information society. These workers enter and retrieve data from computers using video display terminals (VDTs). In some ways this kind of work can be even more monotonous and demanding than the traditional assembly line, although lacking the heavy lifting and sometimes dirty and dangerous working conditions once prevalent on the assembly line. In many modern assembly lines, robots, and ergonomic engineering have eliminated most of the arduous, strenuous, dirty, repetitive and dangerous tasks. In many manufacturing firms, efforts have been made to design jobs to increase job satisfaction and performance.

Data processing workers are tied to a video display terminal (VDT) and keyboard that can be physically confining. While assembly-line work was often very monotonous, the workers could move around physically, talk or sing to themselves, and sometimes talk with each other when noise was not a barrier. Data-processing workers, however, may sit in one position, hour after hour. For workers who process information coming in on a telephone, relieving the monotony by visiting with others is often impossible when calls are coming in rapidly and workers must complete quotas every hour. The VDTs restrict movement much more than the traditional typewriter. The typist had to insert the paper, and move around to set up a new typing project. With information coming in or calls going out constantly, there is little opportunity for a VDT operator to move around or visit with others. Highly repetitive jobs diminish worker alertness, decrease sensitivity to sensory input, and in some situations impair muscular coordination.[48] It is argued that computers have downgraded traditional clerical jobs to lower-pay categories, made them subject to automatic pacing and oversupervision, reduced worker interaction with work mates, and lowered the sense of accomplishment, freedom, and prestige of these workers.[49]

Workers who must process a certain number of orders per hour often complain of back pain, eye strain, and an extremely low quality of work-life.[50] Repetitive motion disorders are a health problem that plagues data-processing workers. Computer technology may be responsible for everything from physical impairment in hands, arms, and shoulders to visual problems. Attention to keyboard placement and illumination contrasts is important.

High levels of stress are often caused by the work environment, however, rather than solely by the VDT. Stress is created by high work demands, tight deadlines and/or lack of control over jobs. A report by the Occupational Safety and Health Administration (OSHA) in 1980 identified possible psychological hazards from the use of the VDT over long periods.[51]

The contribution of ergonomics to easing work on an assembly line was apparent during our tractor assembly plant tour. A hydraulic lift mounts a heavy tractor wheel on an axle, saving the workers much heavy lifting. On the assembly line, pieces of machinery receiving parts are positioned at a height that minimizes bending down for placing components and tightening fittings. This firm has developed its own ergonomics manual.

The application of the action principles for redesigning jobs can do much to enhance the job satisfaction and performance of Routine Producers and reduce some of the health hazards of this kind of work. The following examples illustrate how these principles have been applied to a great variety of jobs of Routine Producers. They range from applications to the work of typists in a communications firm to their use in sophisticated manufacturing facilities. Even in computer operated manufacturing processes there is wide scope for the application of these principles, as is illustrated. Increasingly sophisticated technologies may benefit from greater worker involvement to gain the maximum benefit from these investments.

In a manufacturing facility producing circuit chips, the action principles of using natural work groups, combining tasks, vertical loading, and opening feedback channels were applied. The manufacturing processes were organized in product-related groups rather than the technology-based or functional groups typical for the industry: groups were arranged to produce an identifiable part of the complete circuit chip and to control technical variances in the product, in contrast to being grouped merely around a type of machine or technical function. This application proved to be so successful that the company used redesign in other areas of company. The facility was much more productive, quality exceeded by 15 to 20 percent the results of other organizations in the United States that build similar products, and the turnover rate of 10 percent or less was drastically lower than industry figures, which range from 50 to 100 percent annually.[52]

The application of the principles in a banking organization helped to resolve problems of high turnover, absenteeism, and poor quality and quantity of work due to the boredom of typists engaged in the critical task of stock transfers. The following changes were made: (1) groups of customers were designated; (2) individuals whose work was accurate and reliable were no longer required to have their work verified by checkers; (3) other typists and checkers became teams, and these teams were responsible for a particular group of customers; and (4) typists would correct their own mistakes, and feedback from checkers for those whose work was still required verification was immediate. As a result, errors were greatly reduced, and for the group of typists as a whole, the processing time was reduced. The speed of typists who worked without checkers and verified their own work was slightly reduced, but there was an overall increase in productivity.[53]

Another example of using these principles comes from a department of AT&T that contacts shareholders. Each correspondent must deal appropriately with customer complaint letters or telephone calls. High employee turnover and poor work quality existed as problems in a context of excellent salary, security, and employee benefits. There was no indication of significant employee dissatisfaction other than the poor quality of work. Three changes were instituted. First, the employee signed the reply letters instead of the supervisor. Second, supervisory checking of work was reduced to a 10 percent sampling. Third, members of the workers' peer group with special expertise were designated as consultants as opposed to using the supervisors as such. The supervisors were doing less, and each employee was doing more. After the introduction of changes, turnover came close to zero, already acceptable productivity increased slightly, and formerly troublesome quality issues showed noticeable improvement.[54]

Applications of the principles are found in well-known manufacturing corporations. In an example from a General Electric plant, teams make production, scheduling, and even some hiring decisions. Hours per unit of production were cut by two-thirds, time to customer delivery was slashed by 90 percent, and turnover fell from 15 percent to 6 percent.[55] In a Volvo plant, employees attained new job skills when tasks were rotated between members, and when budget, quality control and maintenance duties were managed by the group.[56]

In manufacturing facilities with advanced computer technologies, the systems are supposed to require little involvement from workers. In practice, however, the need for the application of the principles of work design is often evident. Combining tasks and vertical loading are often necessary due to the way the system operates, and feedback is often immediate. An example is a computer-controlled machine shop that produces transmission cases and clutch housings for a line of heavy-duty tractors. At one end, workers load a large iron casting onto a chain-driven cart. Guided by computer, the cart carries this workpiece to one of 12 computer-controlled machine tools. Here it is unloaded, machined, reloaded, and shuttled off to another work station. A complex formula ensures that the various operations are scheduled efficiently. Although theoretically the pieces are supposed to be completed untouched by human hands, experience has shown that much worker involvement is needed to administer the "tender loving care" needed to keep the system operating. A tool may wear in such a way that it fails to cut accurately, or the boring head, which turns and maneuvers the cutting tool, may be slightly out of alignment. In both cases the operator has to make sensitive adjustments. A cart may jam and have to be unstuck, or the carts drift slightly and the computer loses track of their exact locations. A malfunction of the air conditioning may cause a machine to overheat. A whole shift may be canceled due to problems with software. Because the system is so highly interdependent, problems at one workstation can cause the shutdown of the whole system. Consequently, the application of the principles of work design are highly desirable. The workers do much more than simply load the castings and remove the complete products.[57]

Some firms have invested in extensive employee training in skills that go far beyond the physical tasks of production. At GenCorp Automotive in a new $65 million plant which makes plastic body parts, each worker receives $8,000 to $10,000 worth of training. In addition to learning physical tasks, workers are trained in problem solving, leadership skills, role playing, and organization processes. Workers are divided into teams. Supported by a computer, they will learn statistical process control methods. Each team will learn many different tasks so they can switch jobs and minimize boredom. Leaders receive a full year of training.[58]

The competitive mastery of new technology rests on the successful use of employees' skills in ways which are highly compatible with the principles of work design. Workers often must play a critical role in debugging software programs or intervening when a process goes awry. One manager observed "The higher the operator's skill, the more we get out of the machine." Operators who have responsibility for writing the software programs can look at a readout and understand what the machine is doing. Their jobs become more creative and this increases productivity.[59]

Robots have the capacity to provide consistency and quality as well as flexibility. The ability to realize this potential, however, depends partly on the extent to which employees understand the new technology and are motivated to utilize it to its full potential, as well as organizational arrangements that support the technology.[60] In factories that are highly automated and roboticized, an emphasis on both worker-management interaction and technical systems will enable workers and managers to respond to unique events, opportunities, and failures.[61]

Product innovation requires skilled worker knowledge of production. Broad skills are necessary to help master new responsibilities caused by ever-changing product lines.[62] To maximize the power of microprocessor based instrumentation, workers have to monitor, analyze, and intervene in the continual flow of electronic data in continuous processing plants. In white-collar contexts, clerical workers can assume functions formerly reserved for professionals if they are skilled in the use of new technology and sufficiently educated to understand the new functions.

Metal workers using computer-controlled machinery need to rely on a reservoir of craft skills to prevent disastrous breakdowns and bottle-necks in the production process.[63] It is often appropriate for them to write and debug computer software programs.[64] The speed of change places new demands on the work force, requiring workers to adapt continually to new products and new processes.

While the development of new computer-based control technologies may promise possibilities for downgrading the skill requirements of workers and enhancing control in the hands of engineers and computer programmers, which would result in short-run saving in labor costs, this approach decreases opportunities for future productivity enhancement. In contrast, the application of the principles of work design reduces central control and increases workstation responsibility and skill requirements. This allows greater scope for handling shifts in the flow or specifications of work, troubleshooting production problems, and developing innovative improvements on the shop floor, and contributes to improved quality of working life. One scholar attributes part of Japanese industrial success to wider application of flexible job design principles.[65]

One authority estimates that in the United States as many as one thousand plants may be using novel principles of work design. In these facilities: (1) workers are organized into teams; (2) they are paid salaries based on how many skill clusters they master; (3) a worker rotates into different parts of the plant by temporarily joining other teams; (4) team members frequently evaluate one another's skills; (5) the first-line supervisor develops a facilitating rather than a commanding style; and (6) an elaborate system of committees and task forces is used to solve recurrent problems, accomplish specific projects, and "govern" the plant.[66] Research on these plants suggests that product quality is higher than in conventional plants, and that workers respond efficiently and quickly to the introduction of new product lines.

New technology can be used to increase or decrease the quality of working life. Methods of work organization, the pace of work, and methods of employee control can be used to decentralize work, to give employees greater autonomy, discretion and responsibility, or to deskill, fragment tasks and increase monitoring and control. It is up to the employer whether jobs become computer-aided or computer-degraded.[67]

Research has shown that the way technology is used depends as much upon management ideology as on the technology itself. Beliefs about human nature guide how automated systems are designed. In order to create workplaces that are productive as well as satisfying places to work, several means are available. Extensive user-participation in planning and making decisions about the installation of new technology is helpful. More and better training in the use of technology is often appropriate. Managers should anticipate and prepare for future changes and create an adaptable and flexible work environment.

Involving Routine Producers in Redesigning Their Work

One approach to job design is to involve entire departments in implementing the process. An executive of a firm built on printing technology and direct mail marketing reports on his experience in his own business with involving workers in redesigning their own work. As a result of the redesign effort, order processing capability went from under 300 to more than 400 orders per day. Absenteeism and turnover among production workers went down nearly to zero. Teams finished work early and prowled the office looking for new things to do.[68]

The executive concluded that the quickest way to increase dignity, meaning, and community in a workplace is to involve people in redesigning their own work. This is also the shortest route—in the long run—to lower costs, to improve quality, and to have more satisfied customers.

The redesign effort started with a department vulnerable to absenteeism. Departmental teams identified work problems and each sent a representative to weekly meetings of teams to discuss long lists of problems. The executive discovered that workers knew little about what they were doing. He became discouraged with the number of problems being identified, and was on the verge of discontinuing the effort when the workers found that they had no problems to report one week.

The executive concluded that the essence of effective organization is learning, not coercing and controlling output. The effort took time and required real problems to be solved. The process involved trial, error, give and take, and experimentation. He realized, however, that good managers involve people in setting important goals, structure their chances to learn, offer feedback and support, provide tools and ideas, and stay out of the way. He found that the previous style of management had been "antilearning," with no tolerance for mistakes. He had not understood the subtle connections among learning, self-esteem, and productivity. Team members had learned how to be self-correcting. Until they knew that was what they had learned, it was not really usable knowledge.

In a learning situation, when everybody has a chance to learn, grow, and achieve, when mistakes are accepted, and when a lot of people are in on the action, there is a great deal more control in the system—self-control. It is the strongest kind, but it cannot be bought, legislated, or achieved through behavior modification.

As part of the redesign, the executive instituted a system of pay-for-knowledge through which workers were rewarded for learning new skills. He concluded that as a solution for equitable compensation, pay-for-knowledge is best in any system where multiskilling is feasible. When everybody does everything, not as many people are needed, including direct supervisors, middle managers, and staff specialists.

The social system of the organization altered in dramatic ways. People spent more time together. Spontaneous parties sprang up at lunch and after work. People began celebrating coworkers' birthdays during coffee breaks, and started visiting one another's homes. The organization had become productive. Now it became a community. There were casualties, however. Two supervisors left in search of more traditional workplaces they understood. The executive states that morality and practicality dictate that all those involved in this kind of change be offered jobs at their former pay. What cannot be offered, however, is jobs that are no longer needed. It is irresponsible for managers knowingly to maintain work systems that punish, diminish, or even injure many of the work force simply to preserve status and perks for a handful who, it often turns out, do not get much job satisfaction anyway.

A redesign effort may not necessarily involve all employees. In the Shipping Department, there was an excellent worker who was not interested in participating in the redesign effort. He had advanced as far as he wanted, but he never missed a day of work.

The executive repeated this experience in factories and offices, large and small, union and nonunion, in chemical, pharmaceutical, steel, banking, and many other businesses, and is dedicated to this mode of workplace improvement. The simplest way to get started is to have workers, technical experts, and managers sit down together and look at how the whole system works. If they listen to each other and stay involved long enough, they can create satisfying and effective workplaces beyond Frederick Taylor's most extravagant dreams.

Perhaps five hundred factories have been designed in North America by these principles since 1975. They integrate work and learning, pay skill-based salaries, are organized around natural production segments, include maintenance, safety, and clerical tasks in work teams, have workers train one another and rotate jobs to acquire skills, have joint team-manager evaluations for pay raises, and coordinate through a committee or task-force system. The most successful ones treat their own culture as a unique feature requiring constant attention. Many install a process review board to keep their norms and principles intact.

A report on America's one hundred best companies to work for noted a dramatic change in corporate life. Many firms are moving away from high-pressure motivational strategies. They have transcended that manipulative framework and achieved a sense that "we are all in it together." To achieve that goal, this executive believes we need people concentrating on core economic and technical dilemmas of their own work. Those who believe in dignity, meaning, and community must somehow try to involve everybody. Though this is not always practical, it is the "right melody to play."[69]

Managing In-Person Servers to Balance Job Satisfaction and Performance

Few examples are available to illustrate the application of the action principles for redesigning the jobs of In-Person Servers. The following illustration, however, indicates that the application of these principles can be extremely effective in enhancing the job satisfaction and performance of In-Person Servers.

The manufacturing firm, Texas Instruments, had become dissatisfied with the performance of contracted cleaning services. It took over cleaning in one building on an experimental basis. Eight supervisors were selected from among the former employees of the cleaning subcontractor after a seven-day program, which doubled as a training and selection mechanism. Each of the supervisors was placed in charge of a team, which was given responsibility for setting its own goals, objectives, and schedules. Each team was given responsibility for a well-defined area of work. Prior to the experiment, turnover had been 100 percent per quarter. After the intervention, job performance in the experimental building increased markedly—ratings were up by about 25 percent, and turnover dropped from 100 percent to 9.8 percent. In addition, a waiting list developed for jobs on the cleaning crew.[70]

Managing Gold-Collar Workers to Balance Job Satisfaction and Performance

Gold-collar workers are a key to the innovation and productivity needed to help organizations face an increasingly turbulent environment. Employees are needed who will ask critical questions, tolerate ambiguity, enjoy challenge, bring diverse perspectives into the corporation and engage in strategic thinking on their employers' behalf. Gold-collar workers can spearhead success in the exciting, promising, and often confusing Information Age.[71]

The prevalence of gold-collar workers is evident in the fact that in an industrial giant such as Exxon, highly educated employees hold the top 45,000 posts in the company—about 30 percent of the jobs. When a major Japanese steel company replaced 2,000 blue-collar factory workers with robots, the technical staff at the site went from 20 to 200. Investors now place a high premium on a company's gold-collar work force. They examine depth, quality, and tenure of gold-collar engineers and technical people in rating companies. They use turnover as a crucial indicator to assess performance.

Innovative organizations realize that gold-collar workers are a key to achieving the changes needed to help organizations keep up with the demands of the information age. They design new contracts that are less adversarial and more mutually advantageous to attract and retain this valuable type of worker.

In organizations in which knowledge is the key to innovation and productivity, managers must recognize that many management practices that evolved during the Industrial Age are undermining the value of brainpower. New management practices are in order. It almost goes without saying that the application of such principles as forming natural work units, combining tasks, and vertical loading are imperative in designing the work of gold-collar workers. Gold-collar workers must have the autonomy they feel they deserve. They reject repetition, tedium, boring supervision, boring management pep talks, boring control systems, boring-looking offices, and boring memoranda. Their work must be stimulating, challenging, meaningful and rewarding, and provide a significant level of responsibility. Challenging work is more important than pay to some gold-collar employees. One researcher found that in one group surveyed, salary increases were valued less than obtaining a more interesting and challenging job or than having more influence in the company's policies.[72]

Gold-collar employees expect to participate in decisions that affect them and their work. Over 84 percent of college graduates indicate that they will be more satisfied, and therefore more productive, if they are allowed active participation in decisions that affect their work. When gold-collar workers take an active part in shaping the organizational vision, they will support it. When they have a part in making decisions affecting their work, they will work diligently to be more productive and effective. To achieve this may require training for both management and their gold-collar subordinates in participative decision making, strategic thinking, and conflict resolution. The organization will benefit from better performance and increased job satisfaction of the work force.

The work design principle of opening feedback channels is critically important in managing gold-collar workers. Managers must praise their gold-collar employees when it is merited. They need variety, association with creative colleagues, respect for their competence, recognition for their contributions, and a supportive environment conducive to high-quality work. They value their individuality and distrust mindless conformity to organizational norms.

Managers need to realize how important work is to the self-image of gold-collar workers. Their employment helps to define who they are, what they know, with whom they interact, and their position in the community. Their work offers them the opportunity to exercise their creativity and intelligence and gain psychic, social, and economic rewards.

Managers must recognize that the primary reference groups for many gold-collar workers are professional associations, alumni groups, or entrepreneurial mentors, from which they derive their values, work standards, criteria of success, and sense of self-worth. To win their allegiance it is often helpful for managers to become attuned to their professional and personal standards of performance. Managers can no longer rely solely on company promotions, loyalty, or directives to influence gold-collar workers.[73]

The social environment of the workplace is often extremely important to gold-collar workers. Many of their projects require collaboration, and a cooperative work atmosphere is a key to productivity. Gold-collar workers often accept jobs based on the presence of certain peers in the organization. They often rely upon networks of fellow professionals for creative stimulation, support, and assistance. The quality of the staff is the single most common reason that research-and-development professionals give for joining a firm.

The gold-collar worker has much to offer the modern organization: general knowledge, professional reputation, expertise, a roster of industry contacts, personal spirit, interpersonal skills, and even good health. Organizations offer equipment and facilities, working contact with professional colleagues, a market reputation and contacts, positive working conditions, training, and benefits.

Employers must give attention to the general health of their gold-collar workers. Long hours, high pressure, unending deadlines and a produce-or-perish atmosphere may create great stress. This kind of pressure has been called the "black lung" of professional workers. Too much stress may reduce the capacity and motivation to work. A fine line separates stress from the creative tension that inspires high-quality performance. Gold-collar workers expect employers to reduce sources of stress while providing mechanisms for coping with it. Progressive organizations realize that good health makes good business sense. They offer stress-control classes, compensatory time off to reward overtime, and pleasant settings in which to relax. Some companies offer Olympic-style recreational facilities and access to mental health professionals.[74]

SUMMARY

A variety of environmental trends are affecting the workplace. Economic and demographic forces affecting the American economy are reshaping American jobs and industries. An information society is emerging in the United States, and is producing an information revolution. Information technology is having an impact on the productivity of goods production and on offices. New information technologies may flatten organizational hierarchies.

It is a challenge to balance job satisfaction and performance in the information society workplace. Jobs can be classified into three skill categories—Routine Producers, In-Person Servers, and Gold-Collar Workers—according to their information content and how information is used. The principles of work design can be applied to the three job skill categories. Human resource managers can help to balance job satisfaction and performance by assisting their organization to design jobs that will use the skills and abilities of workers to a greater extent. A more involved work force can contribute to the better adaptation of your organization to the demands of an increasingly demanding and turbulent economic environment.

NOTES

1. Tom Forester, *High-Tech Society: The Story of the Information Technology Revolution* (Cambridge, Mass.: The MIT Press, 1987): 217.

2. William B. Johnston and Arnold Packer, *Workforce 2000: Work and Workers for the Twenty-first Century* (Indianapolis, Ind.: Hudson Institute, 1987).

3. Anthony Patrick Carnevale, *America and the New Economy: How New Competitive Standards are Radically Changing American Workplaces* (San Francisco: Jossey-Bass, 1991).

4. Johnston and Packer, *Workforce 2000*.

5. J.B. Quinn, Jordan J. Baruch, and Penny Cushman Paquette, "Technology in Services," in Tom Forester, ed., *Computers in The Human Context: Information Technology, Productivity, and People* (Cambridge, Mass.: The MIT Press, 1989).

6. Johnston and Packer, *Workforce 2000*.

7. Quinn, Baruch, and Paquette, "Technology in Services."

8. Ibid., 104.

9. Johnston, *Workforce 2000*.

10. Ibid.

11. Alvin Toffler, *Powershift: Knowledge, Wealth and Violence at the Edge of the 21st Century* (New York: Bantam Books, 1990).

12. Carnevale, *America and the New Economy*.

13. Johnston and Packer, *Workforce 2000.*

14. Ibid.

15. Carl McDaniels, *The Changing Workplace: Career Counseling Strategies for the 1990s and Beyond* (San Francisco: Jossey-Bass, 1990).

16. John Naisbitt, *Megatrends: Ten New Directions Transforming Our Lives* (New York: Warner Books, 1984): 4–5.

17. The census categories were (1) Knowledge Production; (2) Data Processing; (3) Supply of Services; (4) Goods Production; (5) a hybrid class including both knowledge and data activities; and (6) a hybrid class including both data and service activities. By allocating portions of the two hybrid classes to either Knowledge Production or Data Processing, the authors conclude that between 1960 and 1980 Knowledge Workers (those who produce information) increased from 6.8 to 9.1 percent of total employment. In the same period, Data Processing workers (those who use information) increased from 42 to 53 percent of total employment. Thus, information workers increased from 48.8 to 62.1 percent of total employment in two decades. Even more significant is the rate of growth of these two sectors in this period. Knowledge Workers increased at a rate of 33.2 percent, while Data Processing workers increased at a rate of 22.8 percent, for an overall rate of increase of information workers of 24.5 percent, while noninformation workers decreased by –17.8 percent. William J. Baumol, Sue Anne Batey Blackman, and Edward N. Wolff, *Productivity and American Leadership: A Long View* (Cambridge, Mass.: MIT Press): 144–145, 148, 158–159.

18. Toffler, *Powershift.*

19. Robert E. Kelley, *The Gold-Collar Worker: Harnessing the Brainpower of the New Work Force* (Reading, Mass.: Addison-Wesley, 1985).

20. Toffler, *Powershift.*

21. Kelley, *The Gold-Collar Worker,* 16–17.

22. Naisbitt, *Megatrends.*

23. Toffler, *Powershift.*

24. Tom Forester, *Computers in the Human Context: Information Technology, Productivity, and People* (Cambridge, Mass.: MIT Press, 1989): 6–7.

25. Ibid.

26. Naisbitt, *Megatrends.*

27. Forester, *High-Tech Society.*

28. John W. Sewell and Stuart K. Tucker, eds., *Growth, Exports, & Jobs in a Changing World Economy: Agenda 1988* (New Brunswick, N.J.: Transaction Books, 1988).

29. Forester, *High-Tech Society.*

30. Ibid.

31. Ibid.

32. Ibid.

33. Toffler, *Powershift.*

34. Forester, *High-Tech Society.*

35. Toffler, *Powershift.*

36. Ibid.

37. Ibid.

38. Forester, *High-Tech Society.*

39. Ibid.

40. Joseph H. Boyett and Henry P. Conn, *Workplace 2000: The Revolution Reshaping American Business* (New York: Dutton, 1991).

41. Forester, *High-Tech Society*.

42. Boyett and Conn, *Workplace 2000*.

43. Toffler, *Powershift*.

44. Ibid.

45. Ibid.

46. Robert Reich, *The Work of Nations: Preparing Ourselves for 21st Century Capitalism* (New York: Alfred A. Knopf, 1991): 173–74.

47. J. Richard Hackman, "Work Design," in J. Richard Hackman and J. Lloyd Suttle, *Improving Life At Work: Behavioral Science Approaches to Organizational Change* (Santa Monica, Cal.: Goodyear Publishing Co., 1977): 96–162.

48. Ibid.

49. Charles L. Harper, *Exploring Social Change: Second Edition* (Englewood Cliffs, N.J.: Prentice-Hall, in press).

50. Urs Gattiker, *Technology Management in Organizations* (Newbury Park, Cal.: Sage, 1990).

51. Forester, *High-Tech Society*.

52. Donald D. Davis and Associates, *Managing Technological Innovation: Organizational Strategies for Implementing Advanced Manufacturing Technologies* (San Francisco: Jossey-Bass, 1986).

53. Ibid.

54. R. Bruce McAfee and William Poffenberger, *Productivity Strategies: Enhancing Employee Job Performance* (Englewood Cliffs, N.J.: Prentice-Hall, 1982).

55. Toffler, *Powershift*.

56. Gattiker, *Technology Management*.

57. Harley Shaiken, "The Automated Factory: Vision and Reality," in Forester, ed., *Computers in the Human Context: Information Technology, Productivity, and People* (Cambridge, Mass.: The MIT Press, 1989) 291–300.

58. Toffler, *Powershift*.

59. Shaiken, "The Automated Factory."

60. Davis and Associates, *Managing Technological Innovation*.

61. McDaniels, *The Changing Workplace*.

62. Gattiker, *Technology Management*.

63. Stephen S. Cohen and John Zysman, *Manufacturing Matters: The Myth of the Post-Industrial Economy* (New York: Basic Books, 1987).

64. Shaiken, "The Automated Factory."

65. Eileen L. Collins, *American Jobs and the Changing Industrial Base* (Cambridge, Mass.: Ballinger, 1984).

66. Larry Hirshorn, "Robots Can't Run Factories," in Forester, ed., *Computers in the Human Context*, 301–7.

67. Forester, *High-Tech Society*.

68. Marvin R. Weisbord, *Productive Workplaces: Organizing and Managing for Dignity, Meaning and Community* (San Francisco: Jossey-Bass, 1987).

69. Ibid., 1.

70. McAfee and Poffenberger, *Productivity Strategies*.

71. Kelley, *The Gold-Collar Worker*.

72. Gattiker, *Technology Management*.

73. Kelley, *The Gold-Collar Worker*.

74. Ibid.

_____ **Chapter 4** _____

The Impact of Family Responsibilities

> Work and community are connected in important ways we are only just beginning to understand.
>
> Richard Price[1]

This chapter is about family: the families of workers, and the workplace as a surrogate family. Both faces of family affect workers' satisfaction and performance. If the employee has problems and pressures at home or if the atmosphere at the work site is oppressive, performance and satisfaction suffer at home and at work. This chapter explains why traditional management has not taken family issues into consideration but has relegated them to some faraway place called home, separate and distinct from work. It offers some practical suggestions for assisting employees to balance satisfaction and performance while also juggling the myriad demands that home responsibilities can make. It proposes that when the workplace is viewed as a place where one experiences the community of "family," worker loyalty, performance, and satisfaction are enhanced.

As more and more women enter the workplace with plans to stay and advance, personal family demands on both men and women spill over into organizational life. These are not just demands made by children. They are demands made by aging parents, and they are demands made by career-oriented spouses or significant others.

Family problems also take their toll on more workers than one realizes. For example, about one-half of all couples experience at least one incident of domestic violence, and in one-fourth of those couples, domestic violence is a common occurrence.[2] From 3 to 25 percent of American workers are substance abusers.[3] How can a worker, at any level, devote full energies to the organization, if he or she is a victim, or has a spouse or child at home who is troubled by drug- or alcohol-related activities?

In this chapter we will offer insights into how to assist workers to balance the competing demands of work and family. We specifically discuss what to do for victims of domestic violence and those living in troubled families. We will also suggest some family-friendly actions that workers want, and we will encourage you to assess your organization's responsibilities and resources for accommodating employee needs.

We believe that the ways in which life away from work affects the workplace are not just women's issues, as some think. They are human resource management issues. They are performance issues. As one scholar observes, "individuals' nonwork commitments and obligations can have tremendous impacts on employees at their workplaces. Successful managers will recognize the impact of key nonwork factors on their efforts to recruit, retain and motivate a high quality workforce."[4]

INADEQUACIES IN THEORIES ABOUT WORK

Because some inadequacies exist in current theories about people at work, a discussion of family and the workplace is needed, as is a new way of thinking about your employees. The inadequacies arise from the changed composition of the work force, which was identified in the Hudson Institute's *Workforce 2000*.[5] They exist because the very real interface of family with the workplace is rarely addressed by current theories of motivation, leadership, attendance, retention, productivity, job satisfaction, or promotion. This work-family interface represents a shift from the traditional focus on the worker as an independent entity, unencumbered by the roles and responsibilities that are a part of life outside the organization.

Any considerations of job satisfaction and performance must view the worker as an integral part of a family, both away from work and at the work site. Whether the employee is married or not, has children or aging parents or a dual-earner spouse, or some combination of these situations, we believe that family can no longer be ignored in managing behavior in the workplace. Cognizance of the work-family interface has been articulated in personnel law,[6] and each of us individually is very much aware of how family can affect our ability to perform on any given day. Yet the effect family can have on the organization is apt to be viewed as a hindrance to human resource management or an obstacle that requires policies and procedures to overcome it. This effect may also be seen as innocuous or irrelevant.

Most often family has either been assumed away in organizational decisions, or employees have been expected to deal with family problems alone. As more and more companies are downsizing, organizations are "putting pressure, explicit and implicit, on employees to put in more time, stay late at night, come in on weekends, take work home, and so on to help the firm improve its competitive position."[7]

Conventional thinking about organizational roles has emerged from the traditional emphasis on functional rationally espoused by Weber.[8] Here the tendency has been to separate work and private roles "and to create a demarcation" between them.[9] The assumption that this demarcation is a necessary part of organizational life has long affected human resource management.

We believe, however, that ignoring that part of the worker that is a family member in attempts to be "lean and mean . . . will be counter-productive in the long run because it leads to burnout and turnover."[10] The changing nature of the work force and the concomitant effect of family on work (and the effect of work on family) is forcing change in human resource management thinking and practices. Traditional thinking attempts to separate the roles of worker and family member, as though their incumbents were two different people. Trying to live as though these roles can be separate has caused an unknown number of employees to give up some measure of their humanity. In doing so, their job satisfaction and performance has suffered. In doing so, they have exchanged what might be good work for instrumental work.

Good work has been defined (see Chapter 1) as: (1) work that allows people to be themselves as they use the skills that are unique and special to them; (2) work that allows people to be in relationship with one another at the work place; and (3) work that allows people to produce something that is "good," something to which they can look with pride, something that has social relevance.

Traditionally employees have been viewed as bearers of knowledge, skills, and abilities that enable the organization to produce goods and services. For the most part, membership in a family has been assumed away. The "good" employee has been expected to establish priorities with organization first, and family second. Yet the changing composition of the work force no longer makes such prioritization possible for many. For the growing numbers of workers who must balance job and family, the work-family interface is a fact of life that cannot be assumed away. Simply put, the presence of great numbers of women in the work force is forcing a reassessment of the relation of organization and family.

FAMILY RESPONSIBILITIES

Data about the composition of the work force in this latter part of the twentieth century indicate the existence of an interface between family and organizations. More and more women are entering the work force. Their numbers have grown from 43 percent in 1970 to 57 percent in

1990. More than 46 percent are in professional or managerial careers.[11] A college education is the gateway to a career, and more than half of all college and university students are women.[12] Women in the 1990s are being educated to become self-sufficient and independent. Most women are no longer living "traditional" life-styles. In growing numbers, they have entered the workplace. With them has come the concomitant effect of employee/family responsibilities on the organization.

Terms have been coined to characterize the new family relationships: "single parent," "dual career," "dual earner," "domestic partners," and "the sandwich generation."

One futurist predicts that by the year 1995 nine out of every ten married couples will be dual-earner families.[13] *Dual-earner couples* are those in which both husband and wife are employed, although she would stay at home if she could. Their organizational priority is the husband's job; she works to supplement his salary, not because she wants a career. She perceives her role in the home to be more important than her role at her job. She may spend as much as double the number of hours per week dealing with both home and work-related responsibilities as he does dealing with career responsibilities. The remaining hours may be as little as half those left for "traditional" families.[14]

Current estimates indicate that over 20 percent of working couples are dual-career.[15] A *dual-career couple* is a special type of dual-earner family. The dual-career couple is composed of two professional people in a marital or significant relationship in which both partners pursue a career characterized by strong commitment, personal growth, and increasing levels of responsibility. In this relationship, both couple members spend about equal time each week dealing with both home and work-related responsibilities. The remaining free time may be as little as half that available to "traditional" families, and even less than that enjoyed by dual-earner families.

At the same time, the *traditional family*, the one most of us remember from childhood,—with a male breadwinner, female helpmate, and assorted small children—is rapidly becoming obsolete, since only approximately 7 percent of the working population live in traditional families.[16]

Despite the growing numbers of women in the work force, many of whom are single parents, American culture puts unrealistic expectations on those with careers outside of homemaking. A 1977 study found that a major problem for professional women (even when they are single parents) is the assumption by society that they "should have as large a social community oriented life as a non-working housewife, e.g., being a Girl Scout Leader or a fund raiser."[17] In 1990 these expectations had not changed.[18] They cannot help but make the female employee's efforts to balance home and work difficult.

Men, as the twenty-first century approaches, are also having to reassess who they are and what they expect from women, from themselves, and from the organization. The United States tradition still implies that men shoulder the burden of being the major decisionmakers and bread-winners and that they have the support of a wife whose schedule and efforts are directed toward their mutual well-being and designed to protect them from family crises.

In the 1990s this tradition is not reality. A study done in 1985 indicates that from 1975 to 1985 men married to traditional housewives increased their contributions to housework almost as much as husbands of work-ing wives.[19] Family places demands on employees, whether or not a wife works.

Although a woman has been typically (and stereotypically) the family's crisis manager, in the 1990s fathers and mothers are equally affected by a home crisis and often take turns in responding. One study of five-thousand employees with children under the age of 18 found that 77 percent of women and 73 percent of men had dealt with family problems during working hours.[20] A 1987 study of 1,600 employees in two cor-porations found that men and women are about equally affected by family responsibilities: 36 percent of the fathers and 37 percent of the mothers reported "a lot of stress" in trying to balance home and work responsibilities.[21]

Although we usually think of children as being the "family respon-sibilities" a worker tries to balance, that is not necessarily the case. For example, a study found that 7.4 percent of parents with children under the age of 15 are also responsible for caring for their own disabled parents, and usually these caretakers are also employed outside their home.[22] Workers have parents too.

Because of the concern of both mothers and fathers about the well-being of kids as they return home from school, a new term has entered work vocabulary: "three-o'clock syndrome." This is a phenomenon of "reduced productivity and higher error and accident rates as employees' minds turn to their children around the time that school lets out."[23] The syndrome occurs whether the kids are 7 or 17 and it occurs in both fathers and mothers when both parents are employed.

Of women working, 66.7 percent have children who are under 18.[24] One out of every five children and more than half of all black children will grow up in *single-parent families*.[25] Single parents are mostly women. Their home responsibilities and life roles are even more complex and demanding than those of workers in any other type of family. Single parents must successfully survive in the spheres of both work and fam-ily. They have access to none of the emotional, moral, and financial support that their married colleagues do. Yet they too must compete successfully in the world of work.

Single parents and employed women have two commitments and two priorities: (1) home and job or (2) job and home. A traditional wife, the wife in the myth of separate worlds, has a single priority; her home. Within the home of most traditional women are husbands and children, and sometimes aging parents, and these women can devote themselves completely to them. Career women sometimes have husbands, children, and aging parents, but they must divide their time among them. Husbands of working women do not have the luxury of a full-time caretaker in the home. They too must divide their time among competing responsibilities.[26]

Traditional North American values, however, deny that a woman prizes her own ability to contribute in the workplace as much as she values her roles as mother and or wife: "Even when a woman makes all of the personal accommodations needed to continue to work at the same pace she did before she became a parent, she is often perceived as a mommy tracker."[27] Traditional values and the myths that support them determine what people think constitutes appropriate behavior for women and men, and what they think is the appropriate relation of family and work. These values demonstrate why it is only now becoming possible to see inadequacies in the way we address human resource management. They also point to the reasons why acknowledging and affirming the interface between family and work is so difficult for most.

TRADITIONAL AMERICAN VALUES

"Traditional" American values literally set family and work in two separate and distinct spheres that do not impact nor interact with one another. Rosabeth Kanter calls this perceptual separation the "myth of separate worlds."[28] These "separate worlds" represent the traditional way of thinking about work and family, which assumes a husband-wife team who each take responsibility for one sphere of the family's responsibilities. In this now mythical, nearly obsolete relationship, a wife spends about the same number of hours per week dealing with home-related responsibilities as a husband does dealing with career responsibilities. She provides "backstage wealth,"[29] which contains the support services that enable him to devote full time energies to the organizational arena.

As stated above, however, data indicate that in 1990 only 7 percent of the employed population live traditional lives in which a wife stays at home while a husband sallies forth to work.[30] The rest of the women, married and single, work outside the home. Yet the myth persists. Its persistence may be caused by fears that a way of life that Americans had come to embrace and understand is vanishing. Operating as though work and family are completely separated is somehow reassuring, an affirmation that women are good at, and take responsibility for, familial relationships.

Some scholars identify still another myth. It is the myth that family life in the United States is (or should and can be) like that depicted in the television situation comedies of the 1950s and '60s. Whether "Leave it to Beaver" or "I Love Lucy," the "ideal home" was supposed to be the antithesis of the workplace, a retreat from the world of work, to and from which a male breadwinner commuted.

In this myth, work relationships are assumed to be rational, instrumental, and devoid of emotion. Family matters are under control, managed by a woman who insures that family life does not infringe on organizational life. Organizational life is under control too with its demands given priority.

In the myths, *Good Woman* maintains home and hearth, reproduces, and nourishes *Good Man* who sallies forth into the world of industry and commerce. The myths are grounded in the post-Industrial-Revolution nineteenth century, when pampered middle- and upper-class women were more valued as proof of a man's economic success than for any marketable knowledge, skills, abilities, or aptitudes. The myths are perpetuated in the 1990s, even though reality is substantively different.

In this traditional construct, human resource managers have dealt with the family in one of three ways: (1) as a non-issue because family is treated as separate and distinct from the workplace; (2) as a support that provides a respite from workplace responsibilities; or (3) as a detraction to, and an imposition on, workplace performance.

Traditional families are rapidly becoming obsolete. So are human resource management policies and practices that ignore work-family interface. "Evidence indicates that investments in family-responsive programs positively affect productivity."[31] Some companies have recognized the value of providing benefit programs that assist employees to manage family issues and to exhibit high productivity and satisfaction. For example, a 1990 survey conducted by Hewitt Associates found that of the companies surveyed, 50 percent provide some sort of child-care assistance.[32]

The changing demographics of the U.S. work force speak to the necessity of recognizing that family associated problems do affect job satisfaction and performance of both men and women. Women's entry into the work force is forcing reassessment of how family is accommodated in the organization and of the kinds of benefits that are appropriate. We must remember, however, that what an organization does about family benefits is not a women's issue; it is a "legitimate business concern."[33]

Implications

The information presented thus far has led us to the premise that whether one studies an organization or works in one, *family can no longer be assumed away.* Workers are part of families. Family affects worker behavior. Research has documented the impact of family and marital arrangements on the workplace.[34] In fact, a recent study in Spain of two-hundred business managers, concluded that "the study of the family-work relationship came out as one of the four or five most important subjects that must be taught in the business ethics courses.[35] Our research found that the highest correlation with job satisfaction (for both men and women) is the ability to balance home and work. Implications seem clear: family must be considered in any attempts to assist workers to balance job satisfaction and performance. The family and the organization affect one another, whether or not we believe they should.

This relationship calls for serious attention although it has also been trivialized. A recent "In/Out List for Those in the Know," includes the information that "TINKS" (two incomes, no kids) are "out," and "DINKS" (declining income, noisy kids) are "in."[36] We sometimes joke about what is near and dear and of real concern.

WORK-FAMILY PARADIGM

There is a lot of talk about paradigms today. Paradigms, defined simply, are the set of assumptions that guide one's actions and from which one develops a worldview. They are powerful influences on behavior, not readily changed. The traditional assumptions about the impact of family on work, however, must change, if we are to deal with new workforce realities.

Some of the unwritten assumptions that have governed organizational expectations of employees are that workers will put in long hours regardless of family responsibilities, never bring family concerns to the office, travel when and where the organization dictates, relocate without concern for family needs, and if married, expect that one member of the dual-career couple will have to sacrifice advancement.[37]

Once upon a time people believed that the earth was flat, the center of the universe around which the sun revolved. Sailors feared falling off the edge of the world. While no one had actually seen the four corners of the earth, scholars were certain they existed. Decisions were made based on these premises. Then one day Isaac Newton began to wonder why, if the earth was flat, the horizon looked round. A new reality came into being. Scholarship, government, business, and the professions had to change to accommodate it.

One can liken how the employee has been understood with the view that the sun revolved around the earth. The ancient belief about the sun seemed sensible until someone questioned it and began to think about a different reality. In the past the employee has been viewed much like the revolving sun—as the center of a universe around which an organization or a family may orbit. As the universe center, the employee became the focus of study by organizational scholars.[38]

The center of the universe has shifted. It is no longer the employee and his separate, discrete roles. The center has become an interdependence of the employee, the employee's family, and the organizational processes. The employees' role is no longer confined to development and demonstration of knowledge, skills, and abilities. Rather, employees, as family members, must also balance their responsibilities to children, spouses, parents, and community organizations with their obligations to the organization. They must deal with problems at home and at work. "It will be imprudent, indeed costly, for organizations to assume that nonwork roles and interests of their employees have no bearing on worker productivity."[39]

It is both easy and erroneous to accuse these jugglers of having misplaced priorities, or of trying unnecessarily to be "Superman" or "Superwoman." It is irresponsible to relegate their concerns to a niche called "women's issues." People in this decade of the twentieth century are living a new reality for which rules and understanding are emerging. We can be likened to the pioneers and the explorers because there is little to inform us on how to behave and even less to explain behavior.

Employees who leave work promptly at five o'clock or a little before may not have "misplaced priorities"; they may be attempting to juggle responsibilities to organization and to spouse, child, parents, or community. Employees who don't want to work sixty hour weeks may not be "undermotivated"; they may be acting responsibly in family roles. Thinking about organizational behavior, which views family and work as competitors, simply does not account for those in the work force struggling to maintain a dynamic balance between home and work.

Because of the strong interaction of work with family life, and the potential of work's demands to undermine it, both national and international scholars have reached consensus on the necessity to underscore the value of family. They worry that certain intrinsic rights will be "infringed upon as a result of the organizational work within the company."[40] Those rights are

1. The right to find the necessary social support to consolidate the unity and stability of the family so that it may carry out its specific task.

2. The right to socioeconomic conditions that enable a family to carry out its duties with respect to the procreation and upbringing of children.

3. The right to working hours and periods necessary to devote to the other spouse, the children, and to just being together.

4. The right to a quality of work-life that does not affect the workers' genetic heritage nor their physical or mental health nor the necessary attention to their respective families.

5. The right to sufficient compensation to start and maintain a family.[41]

Research indicates that "personal and company concerns interact on how the organization can and will function in the future. Corporate efforts to select, recruit, develop, train, relocate, and promote are all directly affected."[42] Day to day performance and satisfaction are also affected by personal duties. A number of people are concerned about the "escalating conflict between work and family life."[43]

This conflict is prompting the paradigm shift, just as it is prompting scholars to call for family rights, and for companies to act to assist employees as they balance responsibilities at work and at home. "Family-friendly" benefits are one way that companies are responding to employee needs. These benefits are discussed in the next section.

FAMILY-FRIENDLY BENEFITS

Many of you reading this chapter are already employed in organizations that have "family-friendly benefits." If you are one of these people, this section affirms the wisdom of these benefits. If you are a human resource manager in an organization without family-friendly benefits, then this section urges you to consider and implement such assistance. In either event, it is important to remember that work and family programs help employees to balance their responsibilities, while benefiting companies by reducing lost productivity.[44]

Specific programs that assist workers to balance home and family can be grouped under the titles, "flex-time," "child-care assistance," "parental leave," and "elder care." These are programs that strengthen both family-life and work-life. They are not all wanted or needed by all employees, so many companies offer a "cafeteria" benefit package in which employees can choose what they need at different points in their lives. Many organizations also offer training workshops on such issues as "time management," "parenting," "managing in a single-parent household," and "balancing career and family."

A program that can be family-friendly, but which is not generally included in considerations of benefits that help workers balance family and work is home-based employment (HBE). A study conducted in 1987 by Electronic Services Unlimited estimates that 500 United States companies have some type of HBE program.[45]

As with many other innovative ideas, HBE has both advantages and disadvantages. HBE can only be utilized by workers whose job entails long hours at a desk, usually with a computer. Advantages to employers include "workers put in more hours, are more productive, are easier to manage, exhibit increased loyalty, and are less distracted by 'administrivia.' "[46] Advantages for workers include more personal control over time and personal productivity peaks, easier balancing of child-care between parents, no commuting, and relief from office politics.[47]

Disadvantages of HBE programs are many. Managers fear that they cannot control workers they cannot see. Unions are concerned that managers will take advantage of home-based workers. Workers themselves report feelings of isolation, loneliness, and loss of company identity.[48] They lose their sense of being part of a family of workers.

Numerous books and articles have been written on these topics, and on the value of family-friendly benefits. If you are interested in learning more about what other companies are doing about family-friendly benefits, we refer you to two recent journal issues: *HRMagazine*, August, 1990 and *Human Resource Planning*, no. 2, 1990, and to *The Work and Family Sourcebook* by Fairlee Winfield. Guidelines for developing a successful HBE program are provided in the Spring 1991 issue of *Public Personnel Management*. Our purpose here is not to be a source book on family-friendly benefits, but rather to alert you to their affect on job satisfaction and performance, an affect that is profound.

HELP FOR TROUBLED FAMILIES

Workers who live in troubled families may need more assistance than family friendly-benefits can offer. They often need counseling and support services. When a worker is suffering from family imposed worries, it is tempting to look the other way or to become very task oriented. Neither you nor supervisors nor coworkers generally want to "get involved." Yet, in today's workplace, a troubled employee is your problem too.

Labor arbitrators have developed rules to help you determine if an employee's life away from work is an issue with which you must deal. They suggest you ask yourself the following questions:

1. Is job performance affected?
2. Is the performance of coworkers or supervisors affected?
3. Does the behavior directly hurt the organization?
4. Does the behavior indirectly hurt the organization?
5. Is there clear and convincing proof that what's happening off the job is having a negative effect on the workplace?[49]

If you answer "yes" to any of these questions, you would be neglecting your responsibility to not act. How to act, however, is often the question that is difficult to answer. We hope that your organization already has in place support services for employees who are experiencing trauma away from the workplace.

What kinds of troubles might affect performance? The most likely have been identified as: social (marital and personal—37 percent; mental health—14 percent; alcohol-related—9 percent; job related—8 percent; financial—6 percent; health—14 percent; and other—2 percent.[50]

What symptoms of a troubled family life might you see in your employees? Excessive absences, tardiness and early departures, negligence, poor judgment, unusual on-the-job accidents, involvements with the law, deteriorating personal appearance, and mood shifts are some signs of trouble.[51] If the troubles have exploded into violence, you may see bruises or what appears to be extreme fatigue.

A source of help for troubled employees is an Employee Assistance Program (EAP). Large corporations and large government installations are likely to already have an EAP. Generally speaking, an organization with three thousand employees can support one full-time employee assistance counselor.[52] Most of you, however, work for much smaller companies. For you it is more realistic to contract for services with an independent provider. The important thing for those of you concerned with maximizing satisfaction and performance is to have access to employee assistance services that assist employees whose personal problems are interfering with performance.

Two sources of trouble that very negatively affect worker performance are domestic violence and substance abuse. These two sources of distress are discussed below.

Domestic Violence

We take special note of the problem of domestic violence because it is pervasive yet so often hidden. In the United States, it is estimated that a woman is battered every fifteen seconds[53] and that there is a 32 percent chance that a woman who is battered once, will be victimized again within six months.[54] Do you know which of these women are employed in your company? Are you doing anything to help them?

Unfortunately, what is often evident is frequently ignored by fellow workers as well as by human resource departments. One woman, whom we will call Claire, told this story: "My husband beats me a lot. Last week I went to work with a black eye. The whole side of my face was bruised, and the pain was so strong I was half sick to my stomach all day. The hardest part of being at work was that nobody seemed to notice. People just didn't look at me. I began to wonder if I was imagining the bruises."

Claire needed help. Coworkers were embarrassed and talked among themselves. Not much work got done that day by anyone. Performance was literally at a standstill, but Claire thought that no one cared, a thought that sent her back to her abusive situation.

Workers experiencing such pain need help. They also need their problem acknowledged. Counselors suggest that simply letting a victim know that you see the wounds can give courage where none existed. They also suggest that information on services for victims of domestic violence be posted in every workplace. You need to know what a legal aid group can do to help, and, for example, to find the phone numbers for shelters for battered women. You need to encourage supervisors to assist obvious victims of violence to seek help.

Substance Abuse

Another frequent problem that detracts from job performance is substance abuse, which is practiced by from 3 to 25 percent of American workers.[55] A substance abuser consistently functions at about 67 percent of potential.[56] Generally speaking in the private sector, if you discover that an employee has possessed or used alcohol or drugs while at work, you can discharge that employee.[57] In the public sector, you may be forced to assist the substance abuser. Federal employers, for example, are required to "exert substantial affirmative efforts to assist alcoholic employees toward overcoming their handicap before firing them for performance deficiencies related to drinking."[58]

We hope you would assist a substance abuser, as well as all troubled employees, because you care about them. You may already know that such assistance is also good for business. Providing services that help employees manage their personal lives will result in better customer service, a better managed business, and long-term employee loyalty.[59]

THE WORKPLACE FAMILY

The employee's family of origin is not the only family that impacts performance and satisfaction. The workplace itself is a surrogate family for those who interact in it day in and day out.

The 100 Best Companies to Work for in America identifies the number one characteristic of the "best" as a sense of belonging, of identity, of being a member of a work place family.[60]

Where once workers were members of an extended family, living near their place of employment, many in the latter half of the twentieth century have been shifted from place to place. The joke among IBM employees that those initials stand for "I've Been Moved" speaks to the transient nature of workplaces. So does the notion that the mark of success in today's corporate world is a job change every two years.

We have been called a "nation of strangers." We often do not know our neighbors' names. Our social lives as well as our work lives are integrated with the family of the workplace.

Martin Yate, author of *Keeping the Best*, puts it this way, "People are our only reason for coming to work in the morning."[61] What about money, prestige, economic necessity? Oh, yes, that too. As Yate points out, "Headhunters use the mnemonic CLAMPERS to define key areas of dissatisfaction common to most workers. . . . CLAMPERS stands for challenge, location, advancement, money, prestige and pride, equal treatment for equal competence, respect and recognition, and security.[62] However, as one executive put it, "Nothing is worth more than feeling that you belong, that you matter, that people care about you as a person."[63] This feeling of belonging, this sense of being cared for, this awareness of "we" are what can be called a feeling of family. Psychologists are now recognizing that "work is a potential source of psychological well-being, identity, and psychological sense of community."[64] Whether the term one uses is "family" or "community," the concept is the same: this is a place of belonging and mutuality and support.

Work as a Covenant

A family can be viewed as a covenant. Members say to one another, "I will *be* for you and you will *be* for me" even when one of us does not quite meet the other's expectations. *Covenant* implies loyalty and mutual support. "When I am troubled, you will help." "If I make a mistake, you will show compassion." Covenant implies long-term commitment. "We're in this life together." "We are a gift for one another."

The traditional workplace arrangement, on the other hand, has been viewed as a contract. The difference between contract and covenant is profound. A contract is quid pro quo. "I will *do* for you *if* you will *do* for me." Violation of the contract is grounds for separation. A *contract* gives one person power over another. "If you make a mistake, you will be replaced." "If I don't like it here, I'll go somewhere else." A contract is not about commitment or compassion. "I'm in this relationship for what I can get from it." "I'll use you so long as it suits my purpose."

Covenant is the heart of family. It is also the heart of successful organizations. "If one were to draw a composite picture of the ideal company," it would be "Number 1, make people feel that they are part of . . . a family."[65] Listen to what has been said about the best companies to work for:

- Anheuser-Busch: This is a magical place. People who walk through here are amazed at the spirit. The interest, involvement, and feeling of belonging are apparent.[66]

- Armstrong: Promotion from within is gospel. . . . Few people at Armstrong have worked elsewhere. . . . They . . . live and die for Armstrong. . . . My boss and my boss's boss know something about me as a person.[67]
- Baxter Travenol: [It] works hard to maintain a family feeling, which is not easy when you have facilities all over the place. [It] takes good care of its people.[68]
- Celestial Seasonings: What is important is creating a condition in which the work force feels better about their lives.[69]
- Delta: A large number of employees genuinely love their company. They continually talk about the "Delta family feeling."[70]
- Exxon: Exxon rewards employees for loyalty. Most people who work here consider themselves "womb to tombers."[71]

At Hallmark, workers are "like a family."[72] General Mills even named its in-house magazine *Family*. Many similarly run companies value their employees and keep them. Employees who feel valued experience job satisfaction, and, yes, they perform well.

Unfortunately, now, because companies are being faced with the realities of a declining number of skilled workers, the corporate climate is one of disloyalty:

There was once an implied contract: "You give us your loyalty, we'll give you security." That's not true anymore.

Instead . . . as corporate America shrinks, consolidates, and otherwise cuts costs, it is squeezing more people out of work—and more work out of people.

There's been a corporate shift of values. It used to be a sign of failure to cut those people. Now it's a sign of corporate machismo.[73]

Just as machismo has never been behavior that maintains a covenant, corporate machismo is not a way to foster job satisfaction and performance of your employees. In their recent book, *Companies That Care*, Hal Morgan and Kerry Tucker note that as finding good workers becomes more difficult, keeping the good ones becomes more important. In 1991, Morgan and Tucker found 124 companies that do "care," and they believe the numbers are growing.[74]

Some might erroneously think that caring means "taking care of," and is therefore paternalistic and outmoded. We, however, see caring as a covenant, a covenant in which no one is better than the other, or makes decisions for the other. Rather, there is a sense of "we," and decisions are made with the other in the best interest of each, and of the organization.

Some people call this process "participation," and, indeed, we devote

Chapter 6 to the role of participation in fostering satisfaction and performance. Others see a philosophy reminiscent of Total Quality Management (TQM), and indeed we do think covenant fosters communication and cooperation and the production of quality through one's best efforts. Participation, communication, and cooperation are all necessary parts of a covenant but they are insufficient to define the concept.

Covenant generates a culture of belonging, creates a place where one finds identity and meaning. At one author's university, people speak of the "Creighton family." At John Deere Manufacturing Company, we were told that "people who work here have green blood." Sociologists have long known that cohesiveness and loyalty are built by shared activities, interactions, and sentiments. An organization's "culture" is built on this sharing, as well as on the shared sayings and beliefs that knit people into that whole known as organization.

The covenant relationship places requirements on both organization and employee that are not present in an implied contract. Both company and employees are free to grow and change. When one is troubled, the other helps. The organization in covenant provides training and opportunities for professional development. The organization in covenant assists the troubled employee with an Employee Assistance Program or referrals to counseling services. The organization in covenant provides family-friendly benefits. The organization in covenant can expect commitment, loyalty, and performance from its employees. There is a sense in covenant of being together for the long haul—in good times and in bad.

Unfortunately, few organizations and few employees operate under a covenant with one another. They could. Worker and organization can come together: the one to provide good work, the other to perform it, and when they do, work will be satisfying. People will produce. When a covenant is absent, work can be alienating—a treadmill of continuing frustration and quiet desperation.[75]

Work as a Sanctuary

Work is instrumental to our identity. Think about the times you meet new people in social settings. Almost the first question you ask or are asked is something like, "What do you do?" "Where do you work?" In the coal fields of West Virginia, where one of the authors was raised, and unemployment is in double digits, the question is less optimistic, "Are you workin' these days?" Work confers identity on each of us.[76]

When people ask that most self-identifying of questions—Who am I?—they answer in terms of their occupation: tool maker, press operator, typist, doctor,

construction worker, teacher. Even people who are not working identify themselves by their former work or their present wish for it, describe themselves as
retired or unemployed.[77]

We all tend to view ourselves by the roles we play: human resource
manager, author, word processor, parent, neighbor. When one of those
roles to which we have become accustomed is gone, a part of the self
seems torn away. Work is the place where we act out the role of employee. At work we can find sanctuary even when something is amiss
in roles away from work. At work we make a contribution to this world;
we are able to make a difference. This difference contributes to feelings
of safety and security.

Job satisfaction literature indicates that when employees believe their
work is meaningful, their absenteeism and turnover are reduced. The
notion of good work calls for jobs to be ones in which employees can
make a difference for the better. Yet frequently jobs are designed for
efficiency, and workers do not see nor can they conceive the final product
of their efforts.

The task before us is no longer that of "managing workers" as though they were
static and simple things, but rather to establish, nurture, and maintain productive relationships with all of our people, understanding that each of the relationships is going to be in a constant state of flux.[78]

The task before us is also one of recognizing that the workplace and
the jobs in it are the source of pride and personhood of all workers—
from top executive to the assembly line, including you and the authors
of this book. At work, people develop sustaining relationships. They
feel as if they belong and are a meaningful part of a larger collectivity.

The psychological sense of community at work has multiple referents, and . . .
each of them may play a role in our own sense of belongingness. These referents
include: (a) the friendship network, (b) the functional work group, (c) the organization as a whole, (d) the job class or profession, and finally (e) the worksite
itself. Each of these referents is a potentially potent source of the psychological
sense of community.[79]

Think back over your life, and remember the numbers of friends you
have made in the workplace. Think of the interactions, activities, and
sentiments you have shared. Think of the places where you have been
most satisfied, and you will probably remember that great contributors
to that satisfaction were the relationships you had developed. In the
interviews conducted for this book, we learned that the greatest source
of satisfaction were the friendships, not the job's design. People appreciated belonging. Even those who disliked their job would stay in it

because, as one person said, "I wouldn't want to let my supervisor down. She really cares about us."

Such mutual caring creates the sense of belonging that encourages workers to go to work and to perform. Work, as the place where one finds meaning, can be a sanctuary. There one can find respite from the pressures of family and personal responsibilities and disappointments. There one becomes important, needed, and appreciated.

A workplace that provides an Employee Assistance Program can also provide a sanctuary from a troubled family. Victims of domestic violence can escape for eight hours and find a source of support. Victims of substance abusers can find assistance. Those who have mismanaged money, made mistakes, or experienced grief may find help.

A workplace that provides opportunities for training and professional development can be a sanctuary as well. Those whose trades are becoming obsolete will be valued and taught new skills. Those who want to grow receive encouragement and assistance. Those whose talents have not been fully utilized are given new opportunity.

The workplace that treats all employees equally regardless of age, handicap, race, sex, or national origin is a sanctuary. In the world away from work, equal treatment and equal opportunity do not as readily exist. A workplace where workers are free to be themselves, without sexual harassment and without denigrating attitudes and remarks because of age or size is a sanctuary. A workplace where persons with physical disabilities are accorded the same respect as their colleagues is a sanctuary.

Is the organization in which you manage a sanctuary? Is it one where the interface of work and family are embraced and accommodated? Is it one where workers become a part of a surrogate family, with the covenant and all the loyalties that covenant entails? Is it a place where people are treated with respect? Is it a place where the rights of families are respected? Is it a place where people have found good work?

SUMMARY

Work and family are interfacing, interacting spheres that both affect performance and worker satisfaction. This chapter has offered suggestions for accommodating family demands and assisting workers in troubled families. The workplace is a psychological community, a surrogate family, and the workplace has value as a community in a covenant, a place of sanctuary. Carry with you a vision of an organization operating as a covenant with its employees. Think of how, together, with the other workers in your organization, you can engage in planning and training that could better the lives of employees while also contributing to the bottom line—the financial success of your organization.

NOTES

1. Richard Price, "Work and Community," *American Journal of Community Psychology* 13, no. 1 (1985): 1.

2. "Domestic Violence: It's Against the Law," compiled by ASSIST (Kansas City, Mo. Legal Aid of Western Mo., 1991).

3. Paul Cary, "Drugs and Drug Testing in the Workplace," in John Matzer, ed., *Personnel Practices for the 90s* (Washington, D.C.: International City Manager's Association, 1989).

4. Barbara Romzek, "Balancing Work and Nonwork Obligations," in C. Ban and N. Riccucci, eds., *Public Personnel Management: Current Concerns, Future Challenges* (White Plains, N.Y.: Longman, 1991): 1.

5. Ibid.

6. The work-family interface has been articulated by the U.S. Family and Medical Leave Act of 1987, which was designed "to balance the demands of the workplace with the needs of families."

7. Douglas Hall, "Promoting Work/Family Balance: An Organization-Change Approach," *Organizational Dynamics* 18 (Winter 1990): 11.

8. Terry Cooper, *The Responsible Administrator*, 3d ed. (San Francisco: Jossey-Bass, 1990).

9. Ibid., 40.

10. Ibid.

11. D. Spain and S. Nock, "Dual Career Couples: A Portrait," *American Demographics* 45 (August 1984): 25–27.

12. Willa Bruce and Christine Reed. *Dual-Career Couples in the Public Sector* (Westport, Conn.: Quorum, 1991): 30.

13. Fairlee E. Winfield, *The Work and Family Sourcebook* (Greenvale NY: Panel Publishers, 1988).

14. Willa Bruce and Christine Reed, *Dual-Career Couples in the Public Sector*, 27.

15. Christine Reed and Linda Cohen, "Anti-Nepotism Rules: The Legal Rights of Married Co-workers," *Public Personnel Management* 18, no. 1 (1989): 37–44.

16. Joseph Meiseheimer II, "Employer Provisions for Parental Leave," *Monthly Labor Review* (October 1989): 20–24.

17. Norma Heckman, Rebecca Bryson, and Jeff Bryson, "Problems of Professional Couples: A Content Analysis," *Journal of Marriage and the Family* 39 (May 1977): 323–30.

18. Bruce and Reed, *Dual-Career Couples in the Public Sector*.

19. Joseph Pleck, *Working Wives, Working Husbands* (Beverly Hills, Cal.: Sage, 1985).

20. See John Fernandez, *Child Care and Corporate Productivity* (Lexington, Mass.: D.C. Heath and Company, 1986).

21. Hall, "Promoting Work/Family Balance," 8.

22. Barbara Vobejda, "Generation Faces Dual Responsibilities," *Sunday World Herald*, January 13, 1991, 2E.

23. Dana Friedman, "Child Care for Employees' Kids," *Harvard Business Review* 64 (March-April, 1986): 28–34.

24. "Specialists Champion Issues Affecting Family," *Omaha World Herald* (November 18, 1990): 1G, 4G.

25. Ibid.

26. Bruce and Reed, *Dual-Career Couples in the Public Sector*, 27–32.

27. Hall, "Promoting Work/Family Balance," 10.

28. Rosabeth Kanter, *Work and Family in the United States* (Beverly Hills: Sage, 1977).

29. See, Bruce and Reed, *Dual-Career Couples in the Public Sector*, 22–23.

30. Ibid.

31. Ray Collins and Renee Magid, "Work and Family: How Managers Can Make a Difference," *Personnel* 67 (July 1990): 14–19.

32. Lori Miller, "New Benefits Aimed at Work and Family," *Pensions and Investments* 19 (March 18, 1991): 23.

33. Evelyn Gilbert, "Benefits No Soft Issue: J. J. Official," *National Underwriter* 94 (Property and Casuality/Risk and Benefits Management Edition), December 10, 1990: 15+.

34. See, T. Bickley and M. Riche, "Two Careers and Seven Lifestyles," *American Demographics* 9 (August 1987): 24–29; N. Colwell and L. Temple, "Three Jobs and Two People," *Business Quarterly* 5d2 (Winter 1987–88): 12–15; C. Leinster, "The Young Exec as Super-Dad," *Fortune* 117 (April 25, 1988): 233–42; A. Hochschild, *The Second Shift* (New York: Viking, 1989); Bruce and Reed, *Dual-Career Couples in the Public Sector*.

35. Domenec Mele, "Organization of Work in the Company and Family Rights of the Employees," *Journal of Business Ethics* 8 (1989): 647–55.

36. David Grimes, "An In/Out List for Folks Out of the Know," *Omaha World Herald*, December 30, 1991, 7.

37. Renee Magid, "When Mothers and Fathers Work—How Employers Can Help," *Personnel* (December 1986): 50–56.

38. Dr. Christine Reed, Personal conversation, 1991.

39. Carolyn Ban, Sue Faerman, and Norma Riccucci, "Productivity and the Personnel Process," in Marc Holzer, ed., *Public Productivity Handbook* (New York: Marcel Dekker, 1991): 418.

40. Mele, "Organization of Work and Family Rights," 648.

41. Ibid.

42. Francine Hall and Douglas Hall, "Dual Careers—How Do Couples and Companies Cope with the Problems?" *Organizational Dynamics* 4, no.6 (Spring 1978): 59.

43. Lorraine Duskey, "Companies That Care: What the Best Employers Offer Families," *Family Circle* 25 (April 1989): 105–9.

44. Gilbert, "Benefits No Soft Issue," 15.

45. Wendell Joyce, "Home-Based Employment—A Consideration for Public Personnel Management," *Public Personnel Management* 20, no. 1 (Spring 1991):49–60.

46. Ibid., 54.

47. Ibid., 55.

48. Ibid.

49. Ronald Sylvia, *Critical Issues in Public Personnel Policy* (Pacific Grove, Cal.: Brooks-Cole, 1989).

50. Dale Masi, in W. Bruce, *Problem Employee Management* (Westport, Conn.: Quorum, 1990): 80.

51. Bruce, *Problem Employee*, 5.

52. Bruce, *Problem Employee*, 123.

53. "On the Legislative Front," *Ms.* (September/October 1990).

54. Information from a U.S. Senate Committee analysis published in "Crime and Women," *New Woman* (April 1991).

55. Cary, "Drugs and Drug Testing in the Work Place."

56. Ibid.

57. Jennifer Adams, "At Work While Under the Influence," *Marquette Law Review* 70 (Fall 1986): 88–119.

58. Ibid., 110.

59. Donna Klein, "Quality of Life: Mariott," *Personnel Journal* 70 (January 1991): 50. Two resources for learning how to assist workers from troubled families are *Problem Employment Management* by Willa Bruce and *Establishing and Building Employee Assistance Programs* by Donald Myers. Both books are available from Quorum Books, Westport, Conn.

60. Robert Levering, Milton Moskowitz, and Michael Katz, *The 100 Best Companies to Work for in America* (Reading, Mass.: Addison-Wesley, 1987).

61. Martin Yate, *Keeping the Best* (Holbrook, Mass.: Bob Adams, Inc., 1991): 41.

62. Ibid., 27–28.

63. Ibid., 88.

64. Price, "Work and Community," 1.

65. Levering et al., *The 100 Best Companies*, ix.

66. Ibid., 8.

67. Ibid., 16, 18.

68. Ibid., 24–25.

69. Ibid., 41.

70. Ibid., 74.

71. Ibid., 109.

72. Ibid., 132.

73. Gary Blonston, "Some Feel a Chill in Corporate Culture," *Omaha World Herald*, September 29, 1991, G1.

74. Renee Tawa, "Warming to Families Can Pay Dividends," *Omaha World Herald*, September 29, 1991, G1.

75. Dorothy Soelle, *To Love and to Work*.

76. Price, "Work and Community," 2.

77. R. L. Kahn, *Work and Health* (New York: Wiley, 1981): 11.

78. *Yate, Keeping the Best*, 98.

79. T. A. D'Aunno and R. H. Price, in Richard Price "Work and Community," 4.

Chapter 5

The Power of Training and Education

A training program is a vital element in the achievement of productivity.

Sarah Pennefather[1]

The purpose of this chapter is to talk about how job-related and career-development training influence employee satisfaction and performance. The word *power* in the chapter title emphasizes that the influence of these factors is neither innocuous nor incidental, but dramatic and necessary. In fact, experts say that people working today will need to be retrained six to ten times in the course of their working lives.[2]

People thrive on the challenge of new training opportunities. People are motivated when they can learn new ways to perform their job and when they can improve their current skills. They are also motivated by the promise of training and education as mechanisms of career advancement. Training and educational opportunities are what Fredrick Herzberg calls "motivational factors" and "satisfiers." They are occasions on the job that inspire people to feel good about who they are and where they are.

Training is also an essential tool in the implementation of new programs or the creation of new products or the establishment of new processes. Training has been identified as a key area in which the human resource manager will be vital to the success of implementing "Total Quality Management."[3] Training and education have been listed by the National Center for Education and the Economy as necessary to the development of a high-productivity work force.[4] Training and development have been called "important competitive tools."[5] In that balancing act that puts satisfaction and performance in equilibrium, training and development are real resources.

This chapter is about how employees respond to opportunities for education and training. It will not instruct you how to proceed, but it will tell you what employees want and need from different types of training. Without attempting to teach you to teach, it will explain how different teaching styles elicit different employee responses.

This chapter is also about arranging for training by consultants. We will comment on what to look for and what to avoid. We will also talk about some of the resources available and how to capitalize on them, and we will address the need to direct different types of training and education to different audiences. The chapter concludes with information on planning and coordinating a training event.

LEARNING

Educators generally agree that three types of learning can take place: cognitive, affective, and kinesthetic. *Cognitive* learning is rational, left-brain-oriented. *Affective* learning brings about behavioral changes, and *kinesthetic* learning provides new or improved motor skills. All types of learning are necessary, and each can be facilitated by a different type of educational environment and teaching tactics.

Cognitive learning occurs when a learner is presented the facts, memorizes them, and is able to repeat them. Cognitive learning occurs when someone acquires new information and, as a result of the information, is able to accomplish new and different tasks. Examples of cognitive learning are the successful memorization of new policies and procedures, a list of new customers, or an expanded delivery route. Cognitive learning also occurs with interactive computer programs. Sometimes cognitive learning is all that is required; often it is not.

Affective learning builds upon cognitive learning. With affective learning, attitudes and behavior change. Learners move beyond facts to feelings. They do not just get information, they gain understanding. Affective learning is better explained by example than by rhetoric. Consider equal employment and Affirmative Action legislation and policies. Learning what these Equal Employment Opportunity laws and policies are requires cognitive learning. That's knowing the letter of the law. To go beyond the letter of the law to its intent—equality of treatment, empathy, sharing, and understanding requires affective learning.

Consider anti-sexual-harassment policies as an example. In one organization, in order to "train" employees to avoid even the appearance of harassment, the chief executive officer (CEO) had a video prepared in which he spends fifteen minutes lecturing and emphasizing the "Thou shall nots" of harassment. Every employee in the organization was required to view the video, which concluded with the statement, "There is no room in this organization for sexual harassment." The CEO was proud of the video and congratulated himself on training employees about sexual harassment.

"Is that all?" was the response of one senior-level manager. "Well, anyone who wants to commit sexual harassment can have my room." Affective learning had not occurred. Behavior and attitudes had not changed; it was business as usual.

For change to occur, affective learning must happen. Skilled trainers can facilitate affective learning. Training-session members participate in series of activities, even games, in which they are provided experiential opportunities designed to generate feelings and identification. A skilled trainer creates an environment where trainees feel the emotions that their inappropriate behavior creates in others.

A bridge from cognitive to affective learning is sometimes provided by training films in which participants can watch examples of appropriate and inappropriate behavior, then discuss them, and apply them to personal, in-house situations. As you probably know these videos typically address issues relevant to managerial or supervisory behavior in specific areas such as communication, performance appraisal, and, of course, sexual harassment.

Kinesthetic learning occurs when a person develops the motor skills necessary to perform a particular task or array of tasks. Kinesthetic skills are more likely to be needed by employees in the technological core who operate machinery. Training that develops kinesthetic skills must provide opportunities for experience, for trial and error, for doing and re-doing. Folk wisdom has typically said, "experience is the best teacher." A training situation that simulates experience goes a long way toward teaching.

A simple example that demonstrates the difference between cognitive, affective, and kinesthetic learning is that of swimming. Someone can look at pictures of swimmers, memorize the movements of different types of strokes, and practice by swinging his or her arms in the air. However, a person can neither learn to swim, nor learn how the water affects swimming (and breathing), until he or she gets into the water. Yet simply getting in the water, placing one's face in it, and paddling one's arms about, is no way to learn either. Despite its implications, "sink or swim" is simply not the way to learn to swim, or to do anything else.

The literature on adult education indicates that traditional methods of teaching are not always appropriate for adults. As Barry Sheckley says:[6]

The distinctive characteristic of the adult learner is diversity. The adult learner represents a heterogeneous group of learners who are widely diverse in learning styles, methods of learning, life transitions, life roles, learning goals, developmental tasks, prior experience, and patterns of participation in formal education programs.

Nevertheless, organizations contracting for trainers will often assume that adult learners are all alike, and that expecting someone to spout great quantities of information is sufficient, even absolutely necessary. The literature on learning and on adult development would indicate otherwise.

Gail Sheehy's book *Passages* describes the predictable stages of adult life in terms of age. While the ages at which any one individual passes through these stages may differ according to the age a career is begun, the stages still provide helpful information about what each person wants from each career stage. The stages, in roughly ten- to fifteen-year segments of time are, in order: establishment, advancement, maintenance, and withdrawal.[7]

It makes sense to expect that what a person wants from a career at any point in time influences what that same person, as a student, wants from an educational training opportunity. Thus persons in the establishment phase will want education to assist them in beginning a career, while those in the advancement phase are likely to see education as a means of promotion or movement upward or outward. Training and education opportunities, then, it seems, should provide the knowledge, skills, and abilities necessary to assist adult students to meet their professional needs at the point in time they are participating in training. That, however, is easier said than done. It also is a goal not often addressed by training programs.

A number of scholars have developed theories to assist educators in meeting the needs of adult learners.[8] They all see adult life as a progression toward self-directedness and self-evaluation. During this progression, individuals gradually assume increasing responsibility for creating meaning in their educational experiences. Lasker and DeWindt used the work of Loevinger to categorize this progression of "Stages of Ego Development" in relation to the kind of role persons in each stage want a teacher to play:

STAGES OF EGO DEVELOPMENT:	ROLE OF TEACHER:
Self-protective	Enforcer
Conformist	Expert Entertainer
Conscientious	Coach
Autonomous	Counselor

In each of these stages, the adult learner will want something different from the educational experience, something different from the educator.

TEACHING

Richard Brostrom has developed a parallel typology of teaching styles that fit Lasker and DeWindt's Stages of Adult Ego Development and roles of the teacher. These are

- Behaviorism, based on the work of Skinner;
- Structuralism, based on the work of Major;
- Functionalism, based on the work of McClelland; and
- Humanism, based on the work of Rogers.[9]

Behaviorism

The Behaviorist is the Enforcer desired by those in the Self-Protective stage of development. The Behaviorist views people as responding to forces outside themselves, as people who need guidance and direction. This is the typical professor who is confident that he/she knows what material is necessary for the student to learn and constructs a set of rewards and punishments to ensure the student learns what is necessary.

Those who design training or prepare training specifications as part of bid solicitation are frequently behaviorists. They require prospective trainers to submit both credentials and evidence of an ability to speak at great and dynamic length before large groups. One human resource officer insisted that trainers read policy and procedure manuals to training participants "to make sure they get it." Most of the trainees did not. Most employees are no longer in need of an "enforcer" who "makes" them learn. In fact, most will resist such training tactics, not learn from them.

Structuralism

The Structuralist is the Expert Entertainer preferred by those in the Conformist stage of ego development. We all love an entertainer, and a Structuralist is usually popular. Motivational speakers such as Lou Holtz and humorist C. W. Metcalf are examples. The Structuralists view people as intellectual analyzers who will only learn from information presented in a dramatic, entertaining way. They are great in a crowd and can inspire audiences to cheers and sobs.

Structuralists are often popular with trainees. They can command large fees, and people feel good when the presentation ends. The question to be asked, however, is the one often overlooked, what have participants learned? Do participants have different facts? Improved understanding? New skills? Structuralists are cognitive educators. They are extremely valuable when you want to communicate facts.

One of the authors recently received an invitation to bid on conducting a series of workshops on such subjects as motivation, diversity management, and balancing home and work. Since these are subjects in which she has expertise, she carefully read the Request for Proposal (RFP). One of the requirements for bidding was to send a fifteen-to-thirty-minute videotape demonstrating presentation and platform skills.

Presentation and platform skills are not those needed to conduct a workshop of that kind. Workshops on motivation and diversity should facilitate affective learning. Behavioral change should be the goal. Behavioral change occurs with interaction and experience, not from wit and pizzaz. Trainers who conduct behavioral-change workshops tend to be skilled facilitators, experts in process as well as in substantive information. To capture how they work with, and within, a group requires the presence of the group and opportunities for dialogue and participation.

Platform skills will not often create affective learning. To have someone talk about motivation will not teach supervisors how to motivate employees, nor will it teach employees how to motivate themselves. The Structuralist can tell them how. The teacher makes certain they can demonstrate new skills.

Functionalism

The Functionalist is the Evaluator, Role Model, and Coach preferred by adults in the conscientious stage of ego development. The Functionalist believes that people learn best when challenged and assisted. This educator interacts with and inspires participants, giving them opportunities to take risks, to learn by doing, and take responsibility for their own learning. A Functionalist is a teacher as well as a trainer, but not an entertainer.

A Functionalist can facilitate both affective and kinesthetic learning. A functionalist presumes that training participants want opportunities to build on their own experiences, and that one learns by doing, making mistakes, then trying again. The Functionalist sees no need to make participants learn, believing rather that they want to learn and, given the opportunity, will learn.

A Functionalist may use simulations and games as learning tools. A Functionalist will work with individuals and with small groups, never a crowd. Believing in the value of dialogue and interaction, the Functionalist encourages participation and sharing of prior learning and new information and new skills as well. Recognizing the importance of practice, the Functionalist encourages training participants to teach one another so that each is able both to learn and to grow.

Humanism

The Humanist is the Counselor valued by those in the autonomous stage of ego development. The Humanist views people as intuitive, emotional, physical wholes who are in a constant state of growing and becoming. The Humanist is frequently more process consultant than provider of facts and figures, providing training participants with opportunities to discover through self-direction. The classroom is unstructured and student growth is valued more highly than is the acquisition of specific information.

Humanists have often come under attack from contracting organizations and trainees alike. Some of them are so casual and nondirective that they have been taken advantage of by trainees who would rather be somewhere else. When students truly are not self-motivated, the Humanist can be ineffective. Probably experiences in which a Humanist dealt with lackadaisical participants prompted the above-described request for a video of presentation skills.

The story is told that a Humanist once went into a training session and asked participants what they wanted to do, and someone pulled out a deck of cards and said they wanted to play poker. The Humanist, taken aback, felt helpless and was of course, rated as ineffective, even incompetent. Indeed that trainer was incompetent—not because of the values he brought to the training session, but because he did not know how to implement those values into a learning opportunity.

Using the Teaching Styles

Each educator will have a preferred educational style that is based as much on a personal view of human nature as it is on any theory of education. If students are viewed as extrinsically motivated, then the educator is usually a Behaviorist or a Structuralist who takes responsibility for the amount of learning that goes on in the classroom. Functionalists and Humanists view people as intrinsically motivated and allow the responsibility for learning to rest with the students themselves.

An example of how each of the four styles can be used in a training situation will serve to illustrate their differences. An occasion for training that occurs in every organization is orientation—presenting employees with the information they need and want to begin their employee-employer relationship. Think with us how the different training approaches manifest themselves in employee orientation.

No matter which training style is used, certain parameters will apply.

These are: the problem to be addressed, the training style to be used, the goals for this training, and the training procedure and activities to be used. All trainers will address the same problem, to wit: new employees lack information about the organization. All trainers will have similar goals organized around insuring that new workers learn essential organizational policies, understand benefits, and know the location of various administrative offices important to them. What will differ among trainers is the training style to be used, that is, the way participants will be taught, and the setting of goals for orientation.

A Behaviorist will require that all new employees report to a specified place, usually an auditorium or large classroom where organizational information is to be delivered. The trainer, and sometimes various department heads, will talk about the organization. An organizational chart and possibly policy and procedure manuals will be distributed, and participants will be told they are responsible for knowing what is in them. This orientation is a classroom lecture.

A Structuralist will use the same or similar facilities, but make the session an entertaining one. The Structuralist will want people to have a good time so they will have positive expectations of the company. The Structuralist will use humor, perhaps provide a skit. Policies may be illustrated with cartoons. A motivational speech may be included. Here orientation is more like a pep rally.

The Functionalist will assume that every participant in orientation is different and has different kinds of questions. The Functionalist will also assume that employees want to be involved in the learning process. This orientation session will likely be one in which various puzzles or scenarios are developed and given to groups of participants who sit at round tables in order jointly to arrive at solutions or to develop questions. Several trainers will move among the employees providing individual help and instruction.

The Humanist will assume that the new employees know what they need to learn better than the trainer can know. A Humanist's orientation session will be like a job fair. It may occur in a large room with tables, each occupied by an expert from a particular area about which new employees might have questions. It may be a room full of interactive exhibits. Participants will be encouraged to wander about, getting the information they think they will need.

Another example of training style differences can be clearly seen in approaches that might be taken to prepare employees for the changes necessary to meet the requirements of the new laws requiring an affirmative approach to hiring and accommodating the disabled. The Behavioralist will lecture on the details of the law and remind participants of the sanctions that will be applied if it is not implemented. The Structuralist will give an inspiring speech. The Functionalist will explain how the law will affect both employees with disabilities and other employees, and encourage discussion and expression of fears and misunderstandings. The Humanist will provide training aids such as blindfolds or a wheelchair, and give participants the opportunity to feel what it is like to be a disabled worker in your organization.

The participants, of course, are the flip side of this educational coin. Those in the Self-Protective and Conformist stages of ego development tend to be extrinsically motivated. They need Behaviorist or Structuralist training. The conscientious and autonomous are intrinsically motivated. They prefer Functionalists and Humanists. Classes will have a mix. We believe that employee education must meet each student where he or she is. The trick is to figure out how.

We suggest two responses: (1) insure that each training opportunity provides a mix of teaching styles; and (2) find out the kind of teaching styles preferred.

We gathered data on preferred teaching styles. While all groups of adult students are, of course, different, for information purposes, data was collected on 119 practicing managers who have returned to school to earn a graduate degree.[10] We would not attempt to say that these people are representative of anyone's work force. We think, however, that their differences are indicative of the mix of preferred training styles that your employees will have.

In our survey, 38 percent of the respondents preferred that the teacher be an Enforcer, 11 percent wanted an Expert Entertainer, 23 percent wanted a Coach, and 25 percent wanted a Counselor.

We analyzed the managers' responses to see if any significant relationships existed between age, sex, position level in the organization, or policy-making responsibilities and preferred teacher role.[11] Not surprisingly, in light of work-force diversity, no significant difference was found. Adults are a diverse group with diverse needs.

An interesting trend had to do with age. More respondents (46 percent) between the ages of 40 and 49 preferred that the trainer be an "Enforcer" than did those in other age groups. These mid-career adults wanted someone to decide what information they needed and then to take responsibility for their learning.

We wonder if this evidence of a Conformist stage of ego development can be explained by "mid-life crisis." Is the employees' return to school a last chance effort to get what they have not so far acquired? Do they not trust themselves to decide what is best? Are they expecting their teachers to decide for them then "make" them learn the new information? Or is the variance random? We are not certain.

Also, more respondents in upper management (58%) and middle management (50 percent) preferred that the educator be an Enforcer than did those in either supervisory or staff positions. We wonder if, at these levels of responsibility, people are so accustomed to giving and taking orders or to following policies and procedures that they have lost faith in their own ability to take initiative. The existence of a large group of mature and successful people who want to be treated like children in the educational process did, however, surprise us.

The problem, however, is how to meet the diverse needs of your own employees. While trainers cannot be "all things to all people," we do believe that your own assumptions about human nature will govern the process by which you hire trainers or conduct training. Certainly the organization discussed above that required a videotape of presentation skills valued the Structuralist approach and effectively eliminated potential applicants with other styles.

Experiential Learning Model

David Kolb has developed a model of adult education that offers a solution to the dilemma of meeting diverse student needs in a way that maximizes education. Kolb has concluded that the most effective way to teach adults is to emphasize adult learning *process* as much as subject matter content. Kolb has developed an adult education model that he has demonstrated both facilitates learning and allows the instructor to appeal to all levels of ego development. The model is called the "Experiential Learning Model."[12]

Folk wisdom has always said that "experience is the best teacher." Kolb builds on that notion by suggesting that any training session be structured so that participants can work together with the trainer from the base of a shared experience. In an organization, participants may well have a common experience. Or they may not.

For example, if diversity training is being conducted, the white men in the training session probably will not know what is it like to be a minority group member. Healthy participants likely will not have experienced disability. Young people without children may not know the kinds of demands a family can make on energies and time for work. In fact, one newly married young woman who participated in our survey asked, "What do you mean by family responsibilities?" Another participant responded, "If you had them, you'd know what they mean."

If training participants do not have a common experience as a base of departure, then a structured classroom experience can be used as the starting place. Numerous books, particularly from University Associates Publishers, provide samples of experiences that facilitate the development of new interpersonal or intrapersonal skills. The trainer might also design a game or an instrument or a video or an unexpected event. Participants are then asked to reflect upon the experience, to discuss what they observed, what they learned, and what more they need to know. At this point, they become ready for the trainer to present the facts (the laws and policies or the particular skill information) that they have gathered to learn. Then they are ready to try out what they have learned. This tryout might be back at the work site or it might be a simulation.

In addition to its ability to meet the diverse needs of adults in the classroom, the experiential learning model has other advantages. Research has consistently demonstrated that in a typical lecture situation students pay attention only 25 percent of the time. When they are actively involved in learning, however, they pay attention 75 percent of the time.[13] The Experiential Learning Model encourages and facilitates participation to maximize learning. We highly recommend it.

WHAT EMPLOYEES WANT FROM TRAINING AND EDUCATION

In our survey of top achievers,[14] we hoped to find out what facilitated the high-performance levels of this group of people. We believed that their identification of training needs would suggest areas that their own and other organizations would want to consider seriously.[15] We discovered that those responsible for evaluating these performers need general supervision training and specific training in conducting performance appraisals. Supervisors rated employees higher than they rated themselves, and higher than they think their coworkers would rate them. Thirteen percent of these people who were rated by their supervisors as the very best admitted that they could do a better job. Eighteen percent said their coworkers would not rate them as productive.

Even more telling was their perception of the supervisor's fairness. Regarding administration of personnel policies, only 15 percent thought these policies were administered consistently. These superstars seemed to be accomplishing in spite of supervision, not because of it. They wanted those to whom they report to be more knowledgeable about the organization's policies, and they wanted to see those policies administered more fairly. In other words, employees wanted their supervisors to receive training in supervision.

Employees also wanted training themselves. Forty-seven percent agreed that they "need training." This was validated by the 40 percent who stated, "I wish I had more training." They wanted training in job skills so they could advance. They also wanted to know how to balance home and work.

Ninety-one percent of respondents said that their personal life interfered with their performance, but only 47 percent believed that employer services helped them balance personal and work time. They would like some training in time management and in how to balance family responsibilities with workplace demands. They would not ask for this kind of help for fear of being labeled a marginal worker. Rather they stood alone between competing worlds, rarely even sharing their stress with coworkers who might have been in the same situation, but who also preferred to keep their personal stressors secret.

Family demands were only one set of stressors experienced by our survey respondents. Forty-five percent believed their health had been affected because they worked so hard, and forty-four percent said their job has created undue stress. Fifty-one percent were bothered by others smoking in the workplace.

Do you know what kinds of stress your own employees are under? Whether stressors are personal or professional, training and education can assist employees to feel and to be healthier. Programs to teach time management or assist with stress reduction, smoking cessation, or weight control can improve physical and mental health. The first step is establishing the programs. The second step is making it socially acceptable to participate, and the third is to teach supervisors to refer employees to helpful resources.

Frequently, with all good intentions, organizations will establish an assortment of helpful programs for employee family concerns, then discover that people do not attend. To encourage attendance requires that helpful programs be advertised. Supervisors must have training in how to refer employees to them. Never assume that just because a supervisor knows that a training program has been established, employees will be referred. Supervisors often negate the value of training and education—their own as well as others.

In our survey, 80 percent of the respondents thought that management could do more to improve relations between themselves and labor. Fifty percent of the computer programmers, 60 percent of the salespeople, and 30 percent of the department heads said their supervisor's behavior did not facilitate their productivity.

These findings, coupled with the inconsistencies respondents perceived in policy administration and personnel appraisal, raised the following question: Do supervisors have training in motivation, communication, and leadership skills? Often they do not. Sometimes they have been preached to by a Behaviorist or entertained by a Structuralist, but they still do not understand affectively the processes of communication, motivation, and leadership.

Although there were no statistically significant differences between job satisfaction and sex, nor between performance and sex, significant differences between the responses of men and women occurred in the following areas:

- 43 percent of women believed too much work is expected of them; only 12 percent of the men did.

- 85 percent of women believed they have adequate training for their job; only 39 percent of the men did.
- 71 percent of the women reported they have sometimes worked so hard it has affected their health; only 32 percent of the men reported that they have worked this hard.
- 93 percent of the women reported they were well-informed about personnel policies; only 61 percent of the men said they were.
- 93 percent of the women said they knew where they stood with their supervisor, while 52 percent of the men knew.
- 79 percent of the women stated that their supervisor actively encouraged them to seek higher education; only 36 percent of the men had received this encouragement.
- 29 percent of the women were satisfied with the amount of free time they have, and 36 percent were able to comfortably balance the demands of work and home; 55 percent of the men were satisfied with free time, and 71 percent were able to balance home and work comfortably.

These findings led us to question whether supervisors were pushing women harder than they were men. Did they have different expectations? Did they understand diversity management? We were amazed that a simple job satisfaction questionnaire could unearth so many training and education concerns. It was clear that women were treated differently than men, yet we would speculate that supervisors think that they are helping the women get ahead. We strongly recommended diversity training to this organization. To you, we suggest that you find out if women or other minorities perceive disparate treatment, then establish training programs to effect change.

Although there were no statistically significant differences between job satisfaction and age, nor between performance and age, significant differences between the responses of older and younger workers occurred in the following areas:

- 100 percent of those under 30 said they were informed about personnel policies, and 73 percent between ages 31 and 40 were.
- Older workers were not as informed—84 percent of workers between 41 and 50, and 66 percent over age 50 were not well-informed about personnel policies.

There should not be a difference here. All workers of all ages and at all organizational levels need to know what organizational policies are and how they are affected by them. This is not something you can assume that supervisors will communicate. Making policies known is the role of training and development.

- Younger respondents often thought they worked so hard their health was at risk: 67 percent under age 30, and 54 percent between ages 30 and 40, reported overwork, while 23 percent between 40 and 50, and 33 percent over 50 did.
- Those between 31 and 40 reported the most stress (54 percent).
- 30 percent of those between 41 and 50 feared job opportunities were not available for those over age 50, while 100 percent of those actually aged 50 and over believed the opportunities were still there.

Those respondents between ages 31 and 50 were working hard, experiencing stress, and worrying that opportunities decline with age. Maybe they feared a mid-life crisis, or were experiencing it. Here is where both training and an Employee Assistance Program can help. Supervisors need to be trained to communicate and administer policies related to mid-life and older workers. These responses suggested the need for training for dealing with the stresses of aging in a youth-oriented culture and for training about adult growth and development. Significant differences between the responses of minority-group and white respondents to this survey occurred in the following areas:

- Minorities did not expect to be promoted, even if they did well.
- 50 percent of the African Americans and 16 percent of the white respondents believed that their differing cultural backgrounds hindered communication; and 18 percent of those who had been with the organization more than six years thought different cultures were a problem for the work force.
- 18 percent of the total respondents believed people were not treated fairly because of gender (44 percent of the professionals, but only 20 percent of the salespersons held this view).

It took no expert to see that diversity training was strongly indicated. This training needs to be at the mid- and lower-levels of the organization, where people from different cultures regularly interact with each other. What about your organization? What would your employees say about relating with coworkers from different cultural backgrounds? The African American respondents stated they had no input into decisions, did not have adequate authority, did not believe hard work was rewarded, and had inadequate supervisory assistance. Despite this, the respondents believed that they had job security. Again, the issue of training in diversity management for supervisors arose, as did the issue of training employees for working with those different from themselves.

By looking at employee responses to the questionnaire reproduced in Chapter 1, Appendix A: Research Methodology, training needs were readily identified. Even when issues were not overtly addressed, it was easy to see them lurking beneath the surface.

When we asked specifically about job training, the respondents indicated that they wanted more: 43 percent of the executive and 40 percent of the salespersons stated they did not have adequate training for their jobs.

A great many people did not believe they were respected because of their position: 14 percent of the executives, 80 percent of the department heads, 40 percent of sales, 30 percent of professionals, and none of the computer programmers reported feeling respected. These responses confirmed the need for supervisory training in this organization. Only 11 percent of the respondents believed relations between labor and management did not need improvement.

Based on the data from this survey, we recommended to the employing organization that all employees, even the superstars, be provided the opportunity for training that would

1. enable them to perform their jobs even better;
2. help them see what opportunities are available;
3. educate them in time management, stress reduction, healthy work habits, smoking cessation, and balancing work and family; and
4. facilitate cross-cultural communication.

We especially recommended that supervisors at all levels receive training in the following areas:

- diversity management;
- performance evaluation; and
- interpersonal skills of communication, leadership, motivation, and productivity enhancement.

We take the time and space to provide you with this discussion of our research for, and recommendations to, one corporate giant because of its implications and the education and training of your employees. We have seen highly educated, well-meaning, human resource officers assume that just because employees have had the opportunity for training and education, the training job is done. We hope that by reading about the dire need of training by one organization with a strong human resources department and a staff of competent trainers, you will look closely at the training wants and needs of your own employees.

TRAINING DELIVERY SYSTEMS

If you are a human resource manager in a large organization, you probably have access to the services of a training department or of a coordinator or director of training. We usually think that an organization with about four hundred employees will need a person who can devote full time to the training function. Smaller organizations may have only a part-time person or no one while larger organizations will have large departments devoted specifically to training and career development.

Whatever the size of the organization, the person responsible for the training development function plays a key role. You want employees to have the knowledge, skills, and abilities to perform their jobs successfully. Those responsible for arranging for and/or conducting training also must have the requisite knowledge, skills, and abilities to perform the training-and-development function.

Lest you think that goes without saying, we will tell you about a recent experience. One of the authors received a phone call from a young woman, whom we will call Terri, who identified herself as the sister of a graduate student, Pete, at the author's university. Terri, a college graduate, was seeking a job. She had applied and been invited to interview for a position as a training-and-development coordinator for a large bank. Terri's degree was in business, but she knew nothing about training and development; in fact, she had never heard the term until she started her job search. Pete knew that the author was an expert in training and development and suggested that Terri call her. Terri's call began with the request for the author to tell her all about training and development over the phone so she would know what to say to get the job.

Because Terri is a person of color, we wondered if the bank's human resource officer has been so determined to seek employee diversity that he had lost sight of the necessity to hire people qualified for the particular job. To have hired Terri would have been to set her up for failure. As a person responsible for training and development, she should have the knowledge, skills, and abilities to carry out the following responsibilities.

1. determining training needs by analyzing individual performance problems, and by identifying future organizational skill needs;
2. designing and developing training programs and materials; or
3. arranging, contracting for, or purchasing training programs or materials;

4. delivering or arranging and contracting for the delivery of training programs; and

5. advising and counseling employees about their training needs and opportunities.[16]

It is very important to have people in training and development who understand how to assist others to increase their knowledge and skills as well as their potential for advancement. This understanding requires a knowledge of education-and-training theory and techniques.

The training-and-development function permeates all parts of the organization. Training may be remedial and useful for assisting employees to whom an organization is committed to meet performance expectations. It may provide basic literacy skills or it may enhance job execution. Training may provide means for employees to move from one department to another and from one job to another, so that workers experience the satisfaction of performing enriched jobs. Training may upgrade employees' skills, preparing them for new technologies, new legislation, and new policies. Training may enrich employees' lives and enhance their interpersonal skills. Training can assist workers to produce at higher levels, to supervise and to manage better.

We believe that training and development are the most undervalued activities in organizations today. We think that training often is not appreciated and that when corporate budgets get tight, training opportunities are usually the first to be cut back or eliminated. To denigrate or devalue training is like saying you don't need both feet to ride a bicycle, for training and development are the stabilizers and the support of all programs and all functions throughout your organization. We think there are ways to maximize the results of money spent on training programs, and we call these ways to your attention in an effort to assist you in having the best of both worlds in spending your training and development dollars.

Human resource managers are usually on mailing lists of people who regularly are deluged with vast amounts of slick training brochures advertising "great" and "wonderful" opportunities for you and your employees. For amounts of money ranging from the costly to the ridiculous, you can arrange for attendance at this or that. At even greater expense, you can bring the advertisers' representatives to your very own doorstep where they will provide in-house presentations to any and all of your employees.

Rather than engaging in corporate hand-wringing about the expense of training and its costs and benefits, we suggest that you look to the resources available through most colleges and universities. We have found again and again that college professors tend to be like the products in Sears catalog rated "Good," "Better," and "Best" at the most reasonable prices imaginable. Depending on the in-house resources you can access, you can hire experts from your local colleges or universities, to do anything from providing a specific workshop on a given topic to assisting you with the development and establishment of a complete educational program for your employees. In considering this option, remember that a college professor who is an expert on a subject may not always be a good teacher or a competent trainer.

Some college faculty tend to "profess" rather than teach. If they are accustomed to dealing with large classrooms full of bored freshman, they may patronize and alienate your employees. If they are accustomed to small groups of scholarly graduate students, they may speak in such esoteric terms that people feel overwhelmed. Between these two extremes, however, are a great number of extremely qualified, energetic, and competent adult educators. When you find them, capitalize on their abilities.

Often, we think, trainers settle for second-or third-rate outside experts because they do not have the time or the resources available to find truly skilled educators. There is a way. In fact, there are four sources: (1) specialized departments within a college or university; (2) specialized institutes within a college or university; (3) a College of Continuing Studies that is a part of most universities; and (4) a consortium of colleges, such as the Council for Adult and Experiential Learning.

Whichever of these options you might choose should have available the following services:

1. Project planning and design, during which educational experts meet with organizational representatives to identify special needs and to custom-design programs to meet those needs
2. An array of resource persons who have already demonstrated professional expertise and teaching competence
3. Assistance in promoting training opportunities to employees
4. Delivery of training programs on or off the job site
5. Evaluation of the value-added dimension of training
6. Access to college credits or continuing education credits for training participants
7. Special tuition rates for employees and management of the tuition accounting system
8. Tracking, evaluation, and quality control
9. Ongoing communication with your organization that includes progress reports on individuals and on each training session.[17]

To provide the best services possible for you, any contractor or consultant needs to know what you want from them. You need to think those requirements through carefully before initiating contact. Otherwise you may not get the kind of services that will be of most use for you or the type of educator who will best address your employee's needs. You should check the credentials and the references of a consultant or contractor as carefully as you do those of a full-time, regular employee.

Large organizations tend to have training facilities available within the company. Midsize and small companies usually do not. When you arrange with a college or university to provide training for you they will have meeting facilities available. If you contract with an individual faculty member, you may be responsible for coordinating the meeting logistics.

Good training of course costs money. So does bad training, but that's not the issue here. A major decision regarding who will pay and what percent will be paid must be made early in the planning as soon as you have an idea about total costs. If the training is in the organization's best interest, and you are requiring attendance, the organization needs to bear the total cost. If attendance at the training is voluntary, however, then you may want to consider some type of employee cost-sharing.

Organizations handle the cost of nonmandatory training in several ways:

1. The organization pays all and the employee attends on company time
2. The organization pays all, but the training is scheduled at a time that requires the employee to contribute some personal time to the event, such as, the training occurs on a Friday and Saturday
3. The employee pays for the training, and after successful completion, the organization reimburses the employee.

Support for employees to attain advanced education is usually structured in the same way.

The authors of *The 100 Best Companies to Work for in America* identify one of the characteristics of such a company that it expands "the skills of its people through training programs and reimbursement of tuition through outside courses."[18] Opportunities to access additional skills or to achieve educational goals inspire loyalty, commitment, and improved performance. An organization that pays for, or shares the cost of, such opportunities fosters employee satisfaction and loyalty.

PLANNING A TRAINING EVENT

If you do not have access to the services of professional logistics planners, you yourself can plan a training event. Plans should begin nine to twelve months prior to the actual date the event will occur. Later planning makes finding top-notch speakers and comfortable facilities much more difficult. For example, we received a phone call inviting us to conduct a workshop on administrative ethics for a large group of employees. When was the workshop scheduled? In two weeks. The most that we could do for this caller was to give her the same advice that we are giving you: If you really want a particular educator or a particular topic, allow plenty of time, and have alternate dates identified. Many of the really good trainers are already fully booked for the next year or more.

First, identify the purpose and theme of the training and the department or departments for whom the training is being planned. Next identify potential participants, decide on tentative dates and location, develop an agenda and forms to evaluate a session, identify potential educators, and prepare a budget. You will market the training as you finalize your plans.

Purpose and Theme

To be successful, a training event for which attendance is voluntary must be focused on a "hot topic," or be a part of a regular departmental or organizational meeting. It is best to choose your purpose and theme after employee evaluations or in consultation with either members of the target group or their supervisors. The purpose of the training must include the reasons that participants will benefit from it. Does it lead to some kind of certification? Will it enable employees to resolve current problems? Will it provide new marketable skills? Does it lead to promotion?

Employees are busy, as are you. Before expecting them to attend training events, you need to assess the value of that event for the employee and for the organization. You must, then, communicate that value so that potential attendees will in fact become participants.

Potential Participants

Unless participation in the training is mandatory, and during work time, the more potential participants you can identify, the more likely that the training will be well attended. Usually, from 20 percent to 50 percent of potential participants will actually attend training that is not obligatory.

The more clearly the purpose of the training event is related to their own positions and plans for themselves, the more likely are employees to participate. You will always hope that people choose to attend training to improve their current or potential performance. In order to facilitate participation that does actually lead to new skills or behavioral change, participants must both attend and get involved in the training event. You can encourage their personal investment by carefully choosing the times and days you schedule training.

Time

Choose a time for the training well in advance of your beginning planning stage. Before you announce the availability of the training, make certain that you have already arranged for a provider and a location. The person who recently called us had made the mistake of setting a day and finding a place before she found a speaker. We recommend that you schedule time and place around your chosen speaker's schedule, not the other way around. Decide how long the event will be, and if you will schedule it over a weekend. Critical issues to consider are dates, days, and locations.

Choose dates that do not conflict with major holidays. The months November through February can be problematic in northern states because of potential weather problems. Summer months, of course, compete with vacations. Remember that people do not like to leave their work site at special times and that it is very difficult for every member of a work team to be away from the job at the same time.

Often you cannot spare many people on weekdays or for a full week. For this reason, a good format for a five-day training session is Wednesday through Sunday or Saturday through Wednesday. This format has the advantage of having only committed and interested participants because they are devoting some personal time to the training activity.

If you do not have appropriate facilities within your organization, hold the training activity on a college or university campus, or in the college's off-campus professional education center if possible. You will save money, and participants will appreciate the educational aura that is not present in hotel meeting facilities.

If you operate in a large city, contact the administrative offices of several colleges or universities to see what services they offer. Request that they submit bids on planning for, designing, and conducting the training, as well as on such things as room rates, charges for meeting rooms, charges for meals and refreshments, and for audio visual equipment. Visit each one if possible to see what they have to offer. Insist on actually visiting the room(s) where your training will be conducted. Check the acoustics. Particularly check to see if the walls are solid enough to be sound barriers between your group and those in other rooms or in the hall. Check for adequate ventilation and climate control. Sit in the chairs. Make certain they are comfortable enough for several hours of sitting, and big enough to accommodate large people.

It is important for you to provide detailed directions to the personnel in charge of the meeting facility about the size and number of meeting rooms you will need and the way you want seating in those rooms arranged. You must tell them if you want a platform in front of the room, if you want a podium, and if you want one or more microphones. Many speakers will have preferences about such arrangements. You need to make certain that the facility personnel will accommodate teacher/trainer preferences.

Tasks

In conducting any kind of training event, three phases can be identified: before, during, and after the event. Each phase includes essential tasks.

Complete and thorough preparation before the event is essential. Your tasks are to:

1. develop the program and agenda;
2. prepare the budget;
3. coordinate with the meeting facility;
4. identify and contact trainer(s), to explain your needs and to solicit their proposal for meeting your needs;
5. market the training;
6. process registrations; and
7. prepare participant packets.

In consultation with department heads, union representatives, supervisors, and/or employee advisory groups, decide which topics people need and want training about. Prepare a tentative plan for addressing these needs, which includes target audience, ideal times, and preferred length of sessions. Then identify acknowledged experts in the field. This is where the resources of your local educational institutions will be useful.

Plan so that no one training room will accommodate more than thirty people at a time. It is not cost-efficient to fill a room with dozens of people who are literally lost in the crowd. This means that if a lot of people need or want a particular training opportunity, you will need to schedule several sessions.

Frequently training event schedulers become "penny wise and pound foolish." They try to cram many people into the same room to "hear a good speaker." Hearing a good speaker is not an event in which much cognitive learning takes place. Even less affective or skills learning occurs. When the costs and benefits of a training event are calculated, the benefits of small classes far outweigh the additional costs involved.

To market training opportunities successfully, plan on at least two announcements. Also use employee newsletters and bulletin boards to advertise to make as many announcements as possible. About four months before the event, circulate a brochure, with registration information and a tentative agenda to all potential participants. Send reminders after two months.

Set up a system for keeping records of all registrations. Prepare a folder, portfolio, or notebook for each participant. Include all relevant training event information and any reading materials or assignments. Also prepare a name tag for each participant. Do not assume that everyone will know everyone else. Use large type for the name tag.

During the Training Event

The following tasks must be done by either a member of your staff or a member of the contractor's staff during the event: coordinate with the meeting facility, register attendees, and coordinate resource persons. If the event lasts longer than one day, expect to meet daily with the facility contact person. In this way you can see that room arrangements, refreshments, and supplies are provided on time and correctly. Review these arrangements early in each morning before participants arrive.

Make certain that a table has been placed near the meeting area where participants can pick up packets and name tags and receive any necessary information. It takes about one minute for each participant to pick up materials. Plan accordingly, and set up your registration table well enough ahead of time that all can register before the event begins.

See that someone at the registration area is available to meet the trainers and direct them to the appropriate room and to offer any further help they may require. If you have concurrent sessions, it is a good idea to assign someone to be present in each session to assist the trainer with handouts, handle crowd control, climate control, malfunctioning equipment, and so forth. This assistant should also distribute and provide a collection area for evaluation forms.

After the Event

Four major tasks remain to be completed after each training event: (1) reviewing and summarizing evaluations; (2) preparing a financial statement; (3) paying the bills; and (4) thanking the resource persons. Make certain all of these tasks are completed within two months.

The participant evaluations are particularly valuable for you, for the trainer/educator, and for the representative of the organization that contracted to provide this particular training. Review evaluations carefully. Let participants know you read and respond to them. Provide feedback on trainer performance to the trainers themselves and to the department or consortium that they represent.

We once scheduled a training event called "Office Management Skills." The educator was a professor at a nearby university who had conducted secretarial training for other groups. We assumed that the list of workshops he had conducted and his academic credentials meant we were purchasing quality education. The evaluations soon indicated otherwise: the professor actually spent part of the training time "teaching" a group of competent adults the alphabet and how to use the phone book.

Perhaps an occasional dud is acceptable, but a few training events like the one reported here would soon sour an entire organization on any notions of training or development. In this case, however, the event was so bad that it has become a cult story, recorded in the annals of the organization, and a part of the shared memories of its members that has bound them together.

SUMMARY

Training and development is critical to the satisfaction and performance of employees at all levels of an organization. Training is a motivator and is essential to acquiring and maintaining skills necessary for optimal job performance. When you do not have an organizational trainer or training department, you can arrange for and manage a training event by following the steps presented in this chapter.

NOTES

1. Sarah Pennefather, "Key to Productivity," *Computer Data* 14, no. 7 (Canada, July 1989): 16–17.

2. Carolyn Ban, Sue Faerman, and Norma Riccucci, "Productivity and the Personnel Process," in Marc Holzer, ed., *Public Productivity Handbook* (New York: Marcel Dekker, 1992): 410–18.

3. Jennifer Powell, "What's My Role?" *Journal for Quality and Participation* (September 1989): 44–45.

4. "Skills Gap? What Skills Gap?" *Training and Development Journal* 44, no. 9 (September 1990): 9–12.

5. David Kearns, "Back to the Future of American Business," *Executive Excellence* 7, no. 11 (November 1990): 17–18.

6. Barry Sheckley, "The Adult as Learner: A Case for Making Higher Education Responsive to the Adult Learner," *CAEL News* no. 7, no. 8 (1984): 1.

7. Gail Sheehy, *Passages* (New York: Dutton, 1976).

8. See, for example, Jane Loevinger, *Ego Development* (San Francisco: Jossey-

Bass, 1976); Harry Lasker and Cynthia DeWindt, "Implications of Ego Stage for Adult Development," mimeograph (Cambridge, Mass.: Harvard School of Education, 1976); Robert McKenzie, "Center Focus," *The Antaeus Report* (Summer/ Fall, 1987); Catherine Marienau and Arthur Chickering, "Adult Development and Learning," in B. Menson, ed., *New Directions for Experiential Learning: Building Experience in Adult Development* #6 (San Francisco: Jossey-Bass, 1982); Arthur Chickering, "Adults as Learners," unpublished manuscript prepared for the Commission on Higher Education and the Adult Learner, 1983; Lee Knefelcamp and S. Stewart, "Toward a New Conceptualization of Commuter Students: The Developmental Perspective," in S. Stewart, ed., *Commuter Students: Enhancing Their Educational Experience, New Directions for Student Services* #24 (San Francisco: Jossey-Bass, 1983).

9. Richard Brostrom, "Training Styles Inventory," *1979 Handbook for Group Facilitators* (San Diego: University Associates, 1979): 91–98.

10. Data was collected using the inventory developed by Richard Brostrom (1979), which identifies preferred teaching roles.

11. To analyze responses, cross-tabs tables were constructed using the "Statistical Package for the Social Sciences."

12. David Kolb, *Experiential Learning: Experience as the Source of Learning and Development* (Englewood Cliffs, N.J.: Prentice-Hall, 1984).

13. Marienau and Chickering, "Adult Learning and Development."

14. See information in Chapter 1, Appendix A: Research Methodology.

15. Data from the employee responses were analyzed using the "Statistical Package for the Social Sciences." Occasions in which variation among responses was significant at the .01 to .10 levels are considered worth comment, as are situations in which a majority of the respondents reported a working condition that is less than desirable or that points to a problem.

16. This list is developed from a report of a survey of the American Society for Training and Development that is contained in Neal Chalofsky, *Up the HRD Ladder: A Guide for Professional Growth* (Reading, Mass.: Addison-Wesley, 1983): 66–70.

17. Adapted from the informational brochure of the Council of Adult and Experiential Learning (CAEL), which is an international nonprofit organization specializing in providing broad-based employee growth and development programs through the resources of college and university personnel across the United States. We highly recommend this resource, which can be re-accessed by writing or calling CAEL National Headquarters, 223 West Jackson, Suite 510, Chicago, IL 60606, telephone: (312) 922–5909.

18. Robert Levering, Milton Moskowitz, and Michael Katz, *The 100 Best Companies to Work for in America* (Reading, Mass.: Addison-Wesley, 1984): ix.

Chapter 6

The Benefits and Methods of Participation

Without involvement, there is no commitment.
Stephen R. Covey[1]

Participative methods of management in organizations have great potential to enhance job satisfaction and performance. As folk wisdom puts it, "People accept what they help to create." Participative methods, however, must be used with skill and careful thought about the intended results. Poorly designed and managed participative activities can do more damage than simply not using this approach at all.

We present here a brief discussion of what participation is, a discussion of the importance and benefits of participation in the U.S. context, and a typology of types of participation. The major portion of this chapter is devoted to the presentation of a set of propositions for how the human resource manager can design and guide an extensive participation effort, based on a participative strategic planning effort at Creighton University. The propositions provide knowledge about the design and management of participative activities that can be applied to more modest efforts.

THE MEANING OF "WORKER PARTICIPATION"

The term "participation" is a widely used but imprecise term. In relation to work in the European context, the term often refers to workers' participation in management, usually through formal mechanisms that permit workers' representatives to influence and even control decisions affecting the organization as a whole. In the United States, participation is usually thought of as a management style that permits subordinates to make or at least influence decisions about matters of importance to them—especially decisions about how they do their work.[2] We shall only be considering participation according to usage of the term in the United States.

Within the United States, there are two main schools of thought about participation. In one perspective, participation is the extent to which subordinates are able to influence decisions (or more frequently the extent to which they perceive themselves as influencing decisions). In the second context, participation concerns how decisions are made— that is, whether decisions are made by the boss, by subordinates, or jointly.[3]

From the perspective of influence, participation is a "process in which two or more persons influence each other in making certain plans, policies, and decisions which have future effects on all those making the decisions and on those represented by them." Processes such as joint decision making merely provide opportunity for influence, and that influence is the essence of participation.[4] From the perspective of process, decisions can be divided "among (1) those made by the superior (direction); (2) those made in some sense jointly by the superior and subordinates (consultation); and (3) those made that the superior lets subordinates make on their own (delegation). Similarly, decisions can be made on (a) an individual or (b) a group basis."[5]

Both influence and process are important, and they reinforce each other. The subordinates's influence and the boss's concern for subordinates transform mock participation into the real thing. Bosses who do not hold formal meetings with their subordinates may actually permit them more influence than bosses who hold frequent meetings in which they mastermind subordinates until the group comes up with the decisions the boss wants. The increased communication generated by the participation process leads to the expression of better ideas, which contributes to the quality of organizational decisions. But it is the feeling of influence that facilitates commitment to the decisions that are finally reached.[6]

On a day-to-day basis, participation may occur in many forms. It may occur in the locker room, at coffee breaks, or when a few workers and the supervisor gather socially after work. It may occur when two workers discuss how to do a job or when one person gives another tips on how to deal with quality control. It also occurs through de facto delegation when a supervisor neglects to pay attention to an able worker, who then corrects a serious problem on his or her own. It may also occur when the union steward and foreman discuss grievances or the workers unilaterally set production goals. Through its acts and omissions, management can do much to determine the form and shape of participation. The supervisors' open door or practices such as sharing coffee with subordinates along with *genuine* receptivity to new ideas may do more to encourage real participation than any regular series of formally scheduled meetings, although formal meetings are important too.[7]

BENEFITS OF PARTICIPATIVE MANAGEMENT

Participative management is a concept that has been discussed for decades in the management literature. Even in the 1920s, 1930s, and 1940s theorists were arguing that production improved when workers were involved.[8]

Employee involvement is one approach to improving productivity, and in recent years has become the most concerted effort ever to mobilize employees to enhance organizational performance. There are many names for the process ... but most are slight variations on the basic concept: problem-solving groups that contribute to productivity growth.[9]

Participation has been praised as a way to make work more interesting for workers and to encourage supervisors to be more democratic and treat employees with respect. Until recently, however, calls for instituting participative management have had little impact upon management. Now many managers and companies are practicing what has been advocated for decades: participation in one form or another.[10]

A major reason why organizations are more receptive to new approaches to management is the changing nature of the business environment in the United States, as we have discussed in Chapter 3. For the first time, U.S. companies are losing in the international competition for productivity and quality.[11] Survey data show a decided decline in the percent of employees who rate their companies and managements favorably. Among hourly employees, the favorable rating has dropped from about 40 percent in 1975–1979 to just over 20 percent in 1980–1984. Edward Lawler argues that America's top corporations have lost markets and experienced waning productivity, poor quality, and a lower rate of innovation because top management has been autocratic, not participative.[12]

Participative management appears to offer tremendous potential gains. In organizations where people at all levels think for themselves and manage their own work, jobs are more rewarding and satisfying. When people care more about how they do their work, they produce higher quality products.[13]

Three experts on management have described the benefits of participative management, as follows:

Experiments in the American workplace conducted throughout the 1970s and 1980s led us to one conclusion—quality, innovation, service to customers, and competitive performance in general were significantly enhanced when the work-place was redesigned and employees took charge. Additionally, employee in-volvement led to improved trust between management and labor, better organizational procedures and processes, improved decision making, and less resistance from workers to the introduction of new technology.[14]

There is no one solution for achieving increased people productivity. Success comes from a multitude of strategies: talking to your employees and letting them know your goals; listening to what your people say and letting them know their opinions are valued; acting on employee suggestions and grievances; seeking the cooperation of labor in creating innovative systems; and, finally, recognizing and rewarding those who contribute to your success.[15]

One way or another, the innovating organization accomplishes a high pro-portion of its productive changes through participation—masters of change are also masters of the use of participation.[16]

A TYPOLOGY OF PARTICIPATIVE APPROACHES

Discussions of participative decision making in organizations often suggest that decisions are either made in a participative or a nonparti-cipative manner. Decision-making styles, however, range from purely autocratic, or "top-down," to those that are highly participative, and "bottom-up." Knowing when to use which method is a part of the art of management.

Theorist Paul Nutt suggests the following decision models and their appropriate uses:

- MODEL 1—Bureaucratic: Decisions are made by those in power, which managers believe gives them decision-making power and responsibility.

- MODEL 2—Normative: Decisions are made by those in power, based on formal decision criteria, that assume that facts are dis-coverable and have been discovered.

- MODEL 3—Behavioral: Decisions are made by those in power by "satisficing," that is, recognizing that neither time nor resources are available to gather all relevant data.

- MODEL 4—Group Decision Making: Decisions are made with the input of a number of people, each of whom has some part of the information to facilitate decision making.

- MODEL 5—Equilibrium-Conflict Resolution: Decisions are made after group problem-solving, bargaining, persuasion, and polit-ical haggling.[17]

Models 1 and 2 should be used for decision making concerning the core technology; Models 3 and 4 are appropriate to the managerial level and its coordinating role; Model 5 is best utilized at the top levels of the organization.[18]

Participative methods of management, however, can cross organizational levels, diffuse the responsibility for results, and compound the information available. When people come together to participate in planning and decision making, that wonderful phenomenon called synergism takes place. The end product is truly greater that any decision that only one person might make.

Lawler's typology is similar. His "top-down" and "consultative" approaches are equivalent to Nutt's Bureaucratic and Normative approaches. What he adds to this list of decision-making possibilities is important to understanding participative management. These concepts are

- CONSULTATIVE-UPWARD COMMUNICATION: Individuals at the lower levels of the organization are expected to propose ideas and potential decisions to higher levels, but the ultimate decision-making power is always held by people at the top.

- CONSENSUS: Decisions are widely discussed in the organization and considered final only when everyone agrees that they are the right decisions.

- DELEGATION WITH VETO: Decisions are given to lower-level employees who make the decisions as a matter of course; However, high-level managers retain the power to reject a decision and ask the lower-level people to look at it again.

- DELEGATION WITH POLICY PHILOSOPHY GUIDELINES: Choices are given to lower-level employees and they make the decisions within certain constraints. Guidelines for decisions are often given that involve strategy, philosophy, or values.

- PURE DELEGATION: Decisions are given to the lower-level employees, and they are free to make them in whatever way they wish.[19]

The effects of each of these approaches are somewhat different and, depending on the decision to be made, any one of them may be the best style to use. An enormous range of decisions occur in every organization. Each approach has its strengths and weaknesses.

The strength of participative decision making is that it produces possibilities for multiple focus, creativity, empathy, cooperation, information, openness, and breadth of vision.

Participative decision making also has weaknesses: it can be indecisive, create difficulties in meeting deadlines, avoid detail, place overemphasis on process rather than results, and be overly intellectual.[20] Research indicates, however, that the strengths of participation outweigh its weaknesses.

Participating in decisions that affect you and those around you is a part of the concept of workplace as surrogate family. Participation affirms that your organization is not just "a mere aggregate of unconnected and impersonal assets, but rather is a set of relationships among persons of infinite worth."[21]

Participative management is complicated, but one helpful guide is Lawler's *High Involvement Management*, in which he suggests that you consider the following as a means of evaluating participation's value to your organization:

1. the type of decision-making changes that are instituted;
2. the type of knowledge that is developed in the work force;
3. the way in which rewards are affected;
4. the way in which the upward and downward flow of information is affected; and
5. how much of the organization is involved.

Lawler states that these issues must be considered in order to describe a participative program accurately and make reasonable predictions about its possibilities for success.[22]

USING WORKER PARTICIPATION

Both of the authors of this book have had extensive experience in designing and managing participative activities in organizations. In this, as in many other activities, experience is the best teacher. You will need to actually design and manage participative efforts to learn what really works and does not in your organization. This is what Karl Weick calls "retrospective rationality." As he says, you never really know what you're doing until after you do it. Because we believe that you can benefit from our experience, we present here what we have learned from an organization-wide, participative, strategic planning effort that involved over 350 people.

Many writers on organizational participation extol its virtues and suggest the benefits of many kinds of participative activities. The literature contains a great variety of suggestions about "what" participative activities are beneficial and why. Few, however, explain in informative detail how to manage participative processes.

Tremendous potential exists for negative experience and for the development of great cynicism about participative activities if they are mismanaged. To have no participation at all is usually better than badly managed participation. We provide you with a description of an effective means of managing participative activities. We have identified propositions to guide your efforts, and you can apply these in a variety of circumstances to achieve diverse purposes.

One of the most intensive and sophisticated kinds of participation is the development of an organization-wide strategic plan with extensive involvement from all areas of an organization. We describe such an effort within the structure of a set of propositions that will help you design and manage such a participative process.

Overview of Organization-Wide Participation

In May 1989, Creighton University (Omaha, Nebraska) initiated a massive bottom-up, top-down strategic planning effort with thirty-two committees representing every major area of the university. Over 350 people were involved in planning. A steering committee of top administrators, chaired by the president, guided the effort. The steering committee drafted a mission statement to guide the process and the thirty-two subcommittees did the same for their areas of responsibility.

The subcommittees examined the strengths and weaknesses, and opportunities and threats (SWOTs) in their areas of responsibility and made recommendations to the steering committee on how to improve the university in the next decade. The steering committee went away from campus for four and one-half days to shape the subcommittee recommendations into a plan. Several major initiatives resulted.

After the plan was reviewed by interested employees and the university board of directors, the planning subcommittees then shifted into the implementation phase. The subcommittees developed implementation plans that were approved by the steering committee. In addition to the major initiatives, over 300 smaller improvements were inaugurated.

Preconditions

Developing and managing an organization-wide participative strategic planning process is a very complex undertaking. Certain preconditions will greatly facilitate an effective process. They include the following:

1. The strong commitment of the chief executive officer to the participative process is the most critical precondition. A participative process puts substantial time and energy demands upon the participants at certain stages. In order to justify this com-

mitment and to maintain the momentum of the effort, the participants must be aware of the commitment of the chief executive officer.

2. The involvement of a staff member with group process facilitation skills in the design and management of the process is also a critical precondition. Too often the ability to facilitate groups is taken for granted. Facilitation is a learned skill, and a necessary one for successful participative management. Meetings must be designed very carefully so that the purpose of each meeting is clear and participants are able to make significant progress in achieving that purpose at each meeting. In addition to the use of facilitation skills in managing committee meetings, this staff member should develop and circulate guidelines for committee activities and materials explaining the purposes of meetings. Worksheets must be developed to enable committee members to have their ideas formulated independently prior to the meetings. While each planning effort must be unique, sample worksheets are provided in Appendix A: Planning Worksheets.

3. The approach to participative strategic planning must be flexible. Participative strategic planning is as much an art as a science. The process must fit the values and organizational culture of the institution as well as the administrative style of the chief executive officer. Because there are no comprehensive guidelines available for designing and managing such a process, each stage will have to be adapted and revised to suit the character of the institution and the particular purposes of the planning effort. Even though the process must be flexible, clearly defined goals and timetables must be identified. That "product is as important as process" must be a watchword.

Propositions for Designing and Managing a Participative Process

An organization-wide, participative, strategic planning effort requires a massive commitment of effort and time on the part of the chief executive officer and top administrators. Few useful guidelines are available on how to manage such a widely participative process. A great variety of management issues must be addressed to design and manage successfully. For you who want to learn how to develop an organization-wide participation effort or more modest participation activities, we present some guidance here.

In Table 6.1, we present a summary of seventeen propositions to assist you. Then, after each of the propositions is restated individually, we will discuss how the prescriptions in the propositions can be addressed in a strategic planning effort. Although the propositions apply to the management of a strategic planning process, the principles employed in managing this participative effort have wide application in other participative activities.

1. Help the chief executive officer design a structure for the planning process that will involve representatives of all major areas of the organization.
Participative planning must have either the direct involvement or strong support of the chief executive officer (CEO) of the unit for which the plan is being developed. Because extensive long-range planning, and participative planning in particular, are often new to administrators and organizations, such activities require strong support from top management or they may be carried out poorly. Poorly designed and administered participative activities may result in more harm than an absence of such efforts because they breed cynicism. While the quality of decisions and plans developed through participative efforts are usually superior to those developed on a narrow base of involvement, they do require substantially more time and effort. Without the strong support of top management, they may not receive the attention and effort they must have to succeed.

In the case of planning, the process must be designed and structured to meet the needs of the chief executive officer because top management must make the resources available to ensure the success of any plan. The choice of what subjects will be addressed in the planning effort and who will participate are key decisions that must be made by the CEO.

In one organization-wide planning process, the CEO selected thirty-two subject areas for planning subcommittees to address. Some of the subject-area subcommittees represented subunits of the organization, such as Public Relations, Marketing, and Buildings and Grounds. Others were broad issues that cut across the organization, such as Computing, Image and Reputation, and Work Force Diversity. Others addressed particular strengths or qualities of the organization, such as "Mid-West Values and Pride in Product." Other committees considered special constituencies of the organization: stockholders, customers, regulatory agencies, and competitors. Thus, planning subcommittees addressed the concerns of key operating units, key organization-wide issues, key strengths, and key constituencies.

The importance of selecting the correct focus for the planning effort through the selection of committee titles was brought home by revisions made by two committees in their titles. In both cases, they thought that the original title communicated too narrow a focus for the committee, and they received approval from the CEO to adopt titles indicating a broader scope of responsibilities for the committee. In addition, part

Table 6.1
Participative Planning Propositions

1. *Help the chief executive design a planning structure to involve representatives of all major areas of the organization.*

2. *Develop a planning structure that will keep top administrators involved and committed.*

3. *Select participants who see the broad interests of the organization.*

4. *Update the mission statement (or develop a new one, if one does not already exist) to guide the planning effort.*

5. *Initiate subcommittee activities and give them a sense of direction and a schedule.*

6. *Assist the planning subcommittees to develop mission statements for their areas of responsibility.*

7. *Help the subcommittees identify and rank their strengths and weaknesses, and opportunities and threats (SWOTs).*

8. *Help the subcommittees identify strategic issues.*

9. *Help the subcommittees develop recommendations to address the strategic issues.*

10. *Help to assure that subcommittee recommendations are reasonable and responsible.*

11. *Assist the subcommittees to meet their deadlines.*

12. *Assist the subcommittees to communicate their recommendations in a format that is reasonably readable and logical, and provide a means for higher-level administrators to review and respond to the subcommittee recommendations.*

13. *Enable the higher-level administrators to set priorities among the subcommittee recommendations and to produce a strategic plan document.*

14. *Solicit comments from the organization community and the organization's governing body.*

15. *Articulate the major themes of the strategic plan to the organization community and external constituencies.*

16. *Design a process to implement the strategic plan, and arrange for a review of the proposed process by higher-level administrators.*

17. *Assign accountability for the implementation.*

way through the planning process, two vice presidents created two additional committees to address issues that otherwise might have been neglected.

The design of a participative effort requires very thoughtful consideration. The inclusion or exclusion of particular subjects or groups in the participative effort communicates a message about the importance, or lack of importance, of these areas.

2. *Help the chief executive officer design a planning structure that will keep top administrators involved in, and committed to, the strategic planning process.*

3. *Help the chief executive officer select participants who are able to see the broad interests of the university, not just the interests of their own particular area.*

These two propositions are addressed together because although the design of a structure and the selection of participants are slightly different activities, they both serve to reinforce the commitment of higher-level administrators to the process. No plan can succeed without the commitment of higher-level administrators because they must make available the resources and means including the time commitments of staff members, that are critical to developing and implementing a plan.

If an organization undertaking a participative planning effort has a variety of administrative units representing diverse functions and constituencies, an organization-wide participative planning effort will have to have a number of subcommittees to address all key interests. In such circumstances, top administrators cannot be expected to participate directly in all of the meetings of each subcommittee. If top administrators do participate in the activities of some of the subcommittees, they should not serve as subcommittee chairs. One of the major benefits of widely participative activities is that members will bring a variety of new ideas and perspectives to their subcommittee. If top administrators chair these subcommittees, members may not feel free to share creative, unconventional, or controversial ideas. The administrators may participate as members, but the position of committee chairs should be in the hands of individuals who do not directly represent the interests of top administrators.

If top administrators do not participate in, or chair, the planning subcommittees, a mechanism is needed to assure them that the subcommittees will produce results that are responsive to their concerns. Planners have found that without some constraints on the process, subcommittees may develop recommendations that are either very unrealistic or not compatible with the broader concerns of the organization. One writer on university planning advised that "persons of constructive, action-oriented demeanor are preferable to professional curmudgeons, pedants, congenital contemplators, or other sorts of 'unplanners' who are lurking about, seeking the opportunity to become part of your planning process. A handful of 'unplanners' can scuttle an otherwise well-conceived planning process."[23] What is needed are people with fresh ideas and an "action orientation" who are not simply looking out for their own interests or the interests of one organizational unit or constituency only.

In the planning effort we are describing, the CEO designed a process for selecting participants for the planning subcommittees that recruited members with diverse viewpoints and who also had the broad interests of the organization in mind. He asked each of the top-level administrators to nominate members for each of the subcommittees that were to address planning issues of organization-wide concern. He then personally selected the members of each committee to bring a variety of perspectives to their work. Individual letters were written by the president to each committee member inviting him or her to join the effort. The president was extremely pleased with the high rate of acceptance of appointment to serve on these subcommittees.

The planning subcommittees included the administrators and experts with responsibilities for the subject areas of the subcommittees, but the president selected committee chairs who were neither experts nor administrators. The composition of these subcommittees assured that they would produce new and creative ideas, but that they would be generally realistic and would consider the best interests of the organization as a whole in their deliberations. The top administrators had confidence in these subcommittees because they themselves had nominated the members. The subcommittee members brought diverse ideas and perspectives to their work because they were selected from work units all across the organization. This ingenious design assured that the subcommittees would develop diverse, controversial, and creative ideas that at the same time would be generally practical and beneficial to the organization as a whole.

Another element in the design of the strategic planning process helped to assure the involvement and commitment of administrators to the effort. This was the creation of the Planning Steering Committee to guide the process. This committee consisted of all "higher-level" administrators. It was chaired by the president, and also included the assistant to the president and the assistant to the president for planning and institutional research, who served as the staff member who administered the business of the Planning Steering Committee. (For the sake of simplicity in usage, the "assistant to the president for planning and institutional research" shall instead be referred to as the "director of planning.")

This design of the structure for strategic planning, and the commitment of the president to the effort, were key factors in making the process effective. The effort had widespread credibility throughout the organization because of the diverse membership on the subcommittees and the involvement of the higher-level administrators in the selection of committee members. The planning subcommittees with organization-wide focus included almost 250 employees.

4. *Develop a participative process to update the mission statement (or develop a new one, if one does not already exist) to give the planning subcommittees a sense of direction.*

A mission statement should state the essential characteristics of the institution, articulate the philosophy and values that guide and inspire the organization, and state its purposes. It should also indicate how key types of organizational members contribute to the mission. The mission statement should be revised, or at least re-considered, every five years.

The mission statement is a "credo" that states the underlying philosophy of the organization, a philosophy to which the people in the organization are committed and that underlies every decision and every reaction to crisis.

An example of how mission affects actions is the Johnson and Johnson reaction to the 1982 Tylenol crisis. Their mission statement is in the form of a "credo," and it places responsibility to "doctors, nurses, patients," and "mothers" above all other responsibilities. With this as a guide, the company was able to react quickly to the Tylenol horrors, by simply pulling Tylenol from the shelves, then working to discover causes and ways to remedy.[24]

At our organization, early in the planning process, the president, an assistant to the president, and the planning director, jointly developed a mission statement worksheet to challenge the members of the Planning Steering Committee to reflect on the mission of the institution. This worksheet asked committee members to write responses to these questions or imperatives:

- Define the organization.
- Why should the organization exist?
- What should be the three to five most important principles guiding the life of the organization?
- What makes the organization distinctive or unique?

The responses were shaped into a mission statement draft. The Planning Steering Committee then met to suggest revisions. The revised statement was then distributed to each of the planning subcommittees as a "draft" to guide their planning efforts. Committees were told that this draft would be refined toward the completion of the planning process to recognize recommended changes in the mission or the character of the organization that might emerge from the planning process itself. In fact, the mission did not change, although the mission statement was condensed.

The mission statement draft served admirably to remind the planning subcommittees of the mission. Some of the subcommittee recommendations reflect the language in this statement. One planning subcommittee submitted recommendations for revising some of the language. The president circulated these suggestions to all planning participants, and when the final version of the mission statement was developed, it contained some of this language.

5. Assist the chief executive officer to initiate subcommittee activities and give them a sense of direction and a schedule.

A formal inauguration of subcommittee activities in planning by the chief executive officer is important because it emphasizes the importance of the planning process to the chief. It also helps to assure that participants in the process have a common conception of how the chief executive officer conceives the nature of the planning process and what the process is expected to accomplish for the institution.

In our example, the president met with the chairs of the subcommittees to initiate the process. The president simply explained the purposes and importance of the process, his expectations for it, and answered questions.

6. Assist the planning subcommittees to develop mission statements for their areas of responsibility.

Having each planning subcommittee develop a mission statement will assure that all subcommittee members have the same sense of the purpose of the subcommittee activities. This step is optional, however. If the subcommittee is in danger of bogging down in developing a mission statement, rather than letting the process lose momentum, the statement could be skipped. At our organization, we used worksheets with the same kinds of questions as for the organization's mission statement, slightly adapted for the subcommittees. Each committee did develop a mission statement.

7. Help the subcommittees identify and rank the strengths and weaknesses, and opportunities and threats (SWOTs) for their areas of responsibility.

A standard element in strategic planning is to examine strengths and weaknesses, and opportunities and threats—called SWOTs—relevant to the focus of the subcommittee. This action forces subcommittees to examine broadly both the environment of their function and how well the function is doing in this environment. Worksheets, based on models from a book by John Bryson, were used to have subcommittee members give thoughtful preparation to their task before the meeting of the sub-committee.[25] (See Appendix A: Planning Worksheets.)

Having subcommittee members do "homework" on worksheets in preparation for meetings is beneficial in two ways. First, meetings move along more quickly because participants have already spent time think-ing about the substance of the meeting. The number and variety of SWOTs being developed quickly gives members a sense of accomplish-ment. Second, having members reflect independently prior to the meet-ing helps to assure that a more varied and diverse set of ideas are presented than if participants follow along the first two or three trains of thought that are put forth in the meeting.

A technique that injected some very productive fun into the planning process was adapted by the Planning Director from the Bryson book. This was the "Snowcard Process," in which each subcommittee member writes out the strengths and weaknesses, opportunities and threats of the committee's subject area on 5-inch by 7-inch cards before the meet-ing. At the meeting, one person posts along the wall his or her list of "strengths," starting a column for each one, and explains each one a bit, unless it is self-evident. The next person then posts similar "strengths" in the same columns, or starts new columns for new ones that are not similar. The bolder members will get up first and serve as models and encouragement for those who might be a little shy.

This activity is fun because people enjoy getting up to talk about their items and moving around is stimulating. When everyone is finished, the "strengths" have been organized into a logical pattern, which saves the facilitator, or chair, substantial time. In our experience, this process usually takes two or more meetings because chairs usually wanted to limit meetings to no more than an hour or an hour-and-a-half.

Once the subcommittee completed identifying SWOTs, and they had been listed, a worksheet was prepared that instructed each subcom-mittee member to assign fifteen points to the most important of any of the SWOTs, fourteen points to the next most important, and so on. These worksheets were then collected by the chair or the planning di-rector, and a complete composite ranking was developed for the total group of SWOTs.

8. Help the subcommittees identify strategic issues.

Once the ranked list of SWOTs has been prepared, strategic issues are developed. Strategic issues are simply a distillation of the most im-portant SWOTs. Issues can be identified simply by looking for "themes" among the SWOTs. Committee members can examine the list of the top SWOTs to identify similar concerns. Top SWOTs can be grouped to-gether and then summarized as an issue.

This summary of strategic issues is often facilitated by the fact that in many instances a strength can be viewed from another perspective as a weakness, or an opportunity, or a threat. For example, a strength such as "employees are strongly committed to the organization and are motivated to work hard" could also be viewed as a weakness if they become overworked, or burnt out. "Commitment" could also be an opportunity when employees talk with prospective workers and help recruit new high-quality staff members. Another example is that an important strength of an institution is its excellent reputation, but this could also be viewed as a weakness if current excellence causes employees to become complacent.

9. Help the subcommittees to develop recommendations to address the strategic issues.

Once the strategic issues have been identified, the subcommittee is ready to develop recommendations to address them. Preparing recommendations is usually straightforward and is especially satisfying because the earlier work of the subcommittee is now coming to fruition in a practical and tangible form.

The person coordinating the planning process should develop guidelines for formulating recommendations. In our process, the planning director prepared a recommended format for the reports, in consultation with the president. He used an actual set of recommendations prepared by a committee that had moved ahead of the others in their planning effort to demonstrate the contents of a report and how it should be organized. This example then served as an easily comprehensible model for the reports that the other subcommittees would prepare.

10. Help to assure that subcommittee recommendations are reasonable and responsible.

One complaint often made about strategic planning efforts is that recommendations are too idealistic or unrealistic. While it is important to ask planning participants to dream creatively, recommendations that are too idealistic may be of little use.

In our planning process, five factors helped to assure that recommendations were reasonably practical. First, because the subcommittee members were nominated by higher-level administrators, they tended to be individuals who had proven their practicality and strong interest in the broader good of the organization through service on other committees. Through experience they knew the problems, the needs and realistic means for improving the organization.

Second, although many subcommittee members were selected to bring fresh, nonexpert ideas to the subcommittee, some members of the subcommittees did have substantial expertise. Members with expertise were usually a key to shaping recommendations that were reasonably practical as well as idealistic.

Third, the subcommittee members knew that their recommendations would be reviewed by the president. They knew that if their recommendations were too unrealistic, the president would remind them of that. This, we believe, fosters a conscientious and thorough consideration of options. Even so, there were some "off-the-wall" suggestions.

Fourth, the Planning Director assisted many of the subcommittees as facilitator. He used a variety of group-process techniques that allowed all subcommittee members to participate in reaching agreement on recommendations. Usually the group will have enough collective sense to discard totally impractical suggestions. Most did. The really weird ideas that did make the final report were so strange that they injected levity rather than frustration. The president himself enjoyed citing the recommendation for a domed arboretum to be built near the administration building as a sanctum for meditation. Most recommendations, however, were laudable and very practical.

Fifth, the subcommittee members knew that the members of the Planning Steering Committee would be reading their reports and the subcommittees would be asked to make formal presentations. This put another subtle pressure on members to be reasonable and professional.

11. Assist the subcommittees to meet their deadlines.

Because planning involves looking ahead rather than dealing with the urgent issues of the moment, it is sometimes set aside in the press of daily activities. Typically, one or two subcommittees will be slow in completing their activities. A variety of means to help subcommittees to meet their deadlines may be necessary.

In our organization, developing and communicating the schedule of the entire planning process to the subcommittee chairs was the most basic means of keeping the process moving. Also, memos were sent to all subcommittee chairs to remind them of upcoming deadlines. Sharing progress reports of subcommittees that were on schedule was a subtle reminder to other subcommittees that they had a deadline to meet. If reports still were not appearing, the Planning Director would then call the chair to inquire about progress and to offer assistance.

Sometimes there is no substitute for personal contact. In one case, the planning director simply undertook to do the actual listing of SWOTs for the chair, just to keep the process moving. For the ultimate laggards, repeated calls to the chair would do the trick. If a meeting was upcoming in which the subcommittee was expected to report, that was the ultimate motivator to keep on schedule. Peer pressure is powerful. Not to have had completed subcommittee assignments would have been very embarrassing.

12. Assist the subcommittees to communicate their recommendations in a format that is reasonably readable and logical, and provide a means for higher-

level administrators to review and respond to the subcommittee recommendations.

In a bottom-up, top-down structure with several subcommittees preparing reports for higher-level administrators, it is important that the reports be readable, comprehensible, and complete. Participative strategic planning is an activity that is new and unfamiliar to most people at all levels of the organization. They need assistance in preparing reports that are neither too simplistic nor too complex to be useful and that also document briefly some of the steps reached in arriving at recommendations (such as listing the SWOTs considered).

In our process, the planning director prepared a recommended format for the reports, in consultation with the president. He used an actual set of recommendations prepared by a committee that had moved ahead of the others in their planning effort to demonstrate the contents of a report and how it should be organized. This example then served as an easily comprehensible model for the reports that the subcommittees would prepare.

Subcommittees presented recommendations to the Planning Steering Committee in a series of four meetings. Each planning subcommittee had twenty minutes to present its recommendations. The members of the Planning Steering Committee had previously read the reports, a letter from the president that raised questions and commented on the report, and responses of the subcommittee (if any) to the president's comments. At the meetings the members of the Planning Steering Committee asked questions for clarification and made comments on the recommendations. At the end of each meeting, the president asked the members of the Planning Steering Committee to comment on the themes and common issues they detected in the report presentations. The comments made were extremely valuable as a way in which members of the Planning Steering Committee identified the strengths of the recommendations, but also as a way in which they shared with each other their reservations about some proposals. It was a means for members to express disagreement without being directly confrontive.

13. *Assist the chief executive officer to design a process that will enable the higher-level administrators to set priorities among the subcommittee recommendations and to produce a strategic plan document.*

Once the strategic planning subcommittees have presented their recommendations, the higher-level administrators need to select those that should have the highest priority for implementation, and shape them into a document that will communicate these priorities to the organization's governing body, the organizational community, and external constituencies. Top administrators should leave the work site for a few days and nights to interact as a group in a "planning conference" to produce a planning document. They should meet in a location that is far enough away to discourage running back to office or home. As a group they need to develop a sense of community as a basis for developing a common conception of the major challenges and opportunities confronting the institution. An expert, neutral facilitator is a crucial ingredient here. This person should be from outside the organization and have no direct stake in the institution. The role of this facilitator is to help design and manage the planning conference. This will assure that no subcommittee recommendation or subunit of the organization will receive more favorable consideration than any other due to the manner in which issues are addressed or considered.

At our organization, the Planning Steering Committee went away from the campus for four-and-a-half days to a hotel in a city almost a four-hour drive away for a planning conference. An expert facilitator from outside of the organization worked with the planning director and the assistant to the president to design a planning conference at which the Planning Steering Committee would shape the major features of the strategic plan. The facilitator worked closely with the planning director in reviewing the subcommittee reports to understand the major issues of organization life and the values of the institution.

Two documents were prepared to provide background for the planning conference. One was a review of the major accomplishments of the organization and changes that had occurred in the previous ten years. The other document was a compilation of statements about the organization in documents that are distributed to the general public. These documents reminded the planning participants of the major achievements of the organization over the previous ten years and the major features as represented to outsiders.

At the planning conference, the top administrators briefly summarized the major features of the plan recommendations for their own area. Participants then raised questions and suggested minor revisions in each proposal. Committees were formed to review the recommendations of each of the planning subcommittees to select and summarize those that should receive the highest priority for implementation. Participants then, as a body, reviewed, revised, and approved statements that would become the text of the strategic plan draft. In a few instances, the participants in the planning conference made the recommendations even more ambitious than in the original subcommittee recommendation.

Next, members were asked to identify major themes that seemed to pervade the various reports. Five major organization-wide themes were identified. Members also formed a subcommittee that drafted a revision of the organization's mission statement. The conference participants as a group revised and adopted a mission statement.

Conference participants listed the major capital projects needed. Each individually assigned a ranking to these projects. The ranking was tabulated to produce an overall ranking of the capital projects.

To assign accountability for followup in implementing the strategic plan, each member of the Planning Steering Committee was assigned to be an "Oversight Person" to be responsible for implementation for two or more planning subcommittees.

As a final event in the planning conference, a text of the draft strategic plan was prepared with the assistance of two secretaries from the president's office. Two members of the organization's board of directors then went over the entire text and asked questions and made suggestions and comments.

14. Help the chief executive officer design a process to allow the organization community and the organization's governing body to review and comment on the strategic plan.

Once the planning conference is completed, final corrections to the document should be made. Members of the organization community and members of the organization's governing body should be given an opportunity to review and comment on the document.

In our organization, a draft of the plan document was circulated to all members of the Planning Steering Committee for any final revisions, and each strategic planning subcommittee chair received a copy for review. Other members of the campus community were invited to review copies available for inspection in selected sites throughout the organization and to send comments to the Planning Director. Revisions were made in light of these comments, and the draft was distributed to the organization's governing body for review. The fact that very few—and only minor—revisions were suggested attests to the great value of broad involvement in preparing, reviewing, and revising the strategic plan. The president communicated comments by the governing body to the members of the Planning Steering Committee to guide plan implementation activities.

15. Assist the chief executive officer to articulate the major themes of the strategic plan to the organization community and external constituencies.

Strategic planning documents intended to guide plan implementation are often fairly detailed and specific. They may be arrayed according to organizational units and subcommittee structures. Therefore, the strategic plan should be articulated in terms of broader themes for easier comprehension by both those in the organization community who were not a part of the planning process and by those outside of the organization.

At our organization, the president prepared a summary statement of the strategic plan in terms of an overarching goal and supporting goals. The overarching goal was to be the outstanding organization of its type in the United States. The other goals covered all aspects of the plan. These included such concerns as recruitment and retention of diverse professional, technical, and support personnel; the key features of the product niche; the key resources needed to make the organization more effective and efficient; the commitment of the organization to preserve its traditions; and goals for improving image.

16. Assist the chief executive officer to design a process for the implementation of the strategic plan, and arrange for a review of the proposed process by higher-level administrators.

Once the major themes of the strategic plan have been articulated and approved, the institution is ready to move into the implementation phase. Actual implementation of plans can be difficult because the planning process has moved from the dreaming phase into the follow-through stage. The excitement of dreaming and thinking ahead may be lost in the more pedestrian activities of simply carrying out plan recommendations. One of the great strengths of a broadly participative planning process, however, is that many, many recommendations require few resources for implementation, and if they are not controversial, they require no formal review before implementation. We found that even before a formal implementation phase had been initiated, over 260 recommendations were already in the process of being implemented. The momentum generated by the extensive time and effort devoted to a widely participative planning effort was extremely gratifying as well as a strong validation of this approach to planning.

In our process, a design for implementation was developed by the planning director and the assistant to the president, in consultation with the president. The proposed design, an implementation schedule, and a description of job responsibilities of all participants was circulated to the Planning Steering Committee. (See Appendix B: Planning Process Tasks for the job descriptions.) This committee met to review and approve the implementation process.

The first stage of implementation was to restructure the planning subcommittees into implementation subcommittees. Members of the strategic planning subcommittees were thanked for their service and invited to continue as members of the implementation subcommittees (a substantial majority of subcommittee members agreed to continue serving in the implementation phase). The responsibility for managing the subcommittees was then shifted from the nonexpert, lay chairs to the administrators or staff persons who are responsible for the subject areas of the subcommittees. These individuals were then named as "implementors." The oversight persons, who were all higher-level administrators, were reminded that they would need to review the implementation plans before they received final approval.

The planning director distributed copies of the implementation schedule and the job description of participants to all the implementors, committee chairs and members of the implementation committees. He met with each of the implementation committees to inaugurate the process and be sure they understood their responsibilities.

To initiate the implementation process, each implementation subcommittee was asked to sort its recommendations into those already being implemented, those that would be initiated or addressed during the coming calendar year, and those that would have to wait until later for implementation. The subcommittee members were asked to give particular attention to the recommendations emphasized in the plan document developed at the planning conference held by the Planning Steering Committee. The sorted recommendations were identified as "implementation outlines."

Each subcommittee then prepared a summary report. The planning director compiled the summary reports into a master Implementation Outline that was then circulated to all of the members of the Planning Steering Committee. This summary document was particularly valuable as a record of the planning commitments of all of the strategic planning subcommittees. In addition, it was a record of the large number of recommendations that had already been implemented even before the formal initiation of implementation.

An all-afternoon meeting was arranged for the Planning Steering Committee at which each of the implementors made a very brief review of their implementation outline. At the end of that meeting, members of the Planning Steering Committee were asked to name issues that were unresolved and that would need additional work. Four such issues were identified. Later, members of the Planning Steering Committee were asked to nominate members to task forces that would address each of the four issues.

The implementation schedule included dates when each of the implementation committees would report on their progress. They prepared reports to the president, who responded to each report individually. The planning director then summarized all of the reports in a standard format to make them easier to read, and distributed a notebook with the reports to each member of the Planning Steering Committee. A meeting of the Planning Steering Committee was held to review progress in implementation and briefly review how plan priorities might have changed in the past few months. Committee members were reminded that the four task forces would be preparing reports for a future meeting of the Planning Steering Committee.

17. Design means to assign accountability for the implementation of the strategic plan and to maintain momentum in implementation.

Strategic plans are of little use unless they lead to actual plan implementation. A frequent complaint about planning is that once plans are developed, they are frequently put on a shelf to gather dust. This is especially likely to happen if the plans are too idealistic, unrealistic, or are too vague to connect with the specific needs of the organization. This neglect may also occur if the planning process has not been strongly endorsed by the chief executive officer or if there has been little involvement in developing the plan on the part of those who will implement the plan or who will be affected by the plan.

Means are needed to assure that responsibility for implementation is clearly assigned and that plans are carried forward as intended. This does not require rigid adherence to plan intentions. The organization and its environment are constantly changing, and flexibility is needed to assure that plan implementation is responsive to unexpected obstacles or unforeseen opportunities. New and pressing problems may make original intentions unrealistic. Some plan components may turn out to be less feasible or desirable than expected. What is needed is assurance that substantial efforts are made to move forward with implementation of most plan commitments.

At our organization, a key element in establishing accountability for implementation was the description of the job responsibilities of those who would be involved in plan implementation—which included oversight persons, implementors, committee chairs, and committee members. (See Appendix B.)

An implementation schedule included points at which the implementation committees would prepare reports to the president and the Planning Steering Committee on their progress. These reporting responsibilities and target dates helped to remind the implementors of their accountability to the president and the Planning Steering Committee. An especially effective means of assuring accountability was an awareness that the president would be responding individually to each report at certain stages in the process.

In preparation for the first progress report meeting of the Planning Steering Committee, the planning director prepared summary reports in a standard format to make it easier for members of the Planning Steering Committee to review them. His memos and calls to implementors were reminders of accountability through the review of the reports by the Planning Steering Committee.

What we have just described is the successful effort of one organization to involve its members in an organization-wide participative planning effort. The question, of course, that you want answered is "Did all this investment in involvement increase productivity?" For our organization, it is too soon to tell, although we expect that it will.

Evidence exists, however, to indicate that involvement and participation of organizational members in planning and decision making is in fact a means for increasing productivity in both the public and the private sectors. Some examples will serve to illustrate.

PARTICIPATION EQUALS PRODUCTIVITY

The concept of productivity "appears to be simple—improving the ratio of outputs (work done, products distributed, services rendered, impact achieved) to inputs (labor, capital, materials, space, energy, time, and so on)—a productivity program actually covers a range of subjects and strategies."[26]

Marc Holzer, Executive Director of the National Center for Public Productivity, has developed ten steps to productivity improvement: (1) obtain top management support, (2) locate models, (3) identify promising areas, (4) build a team, (5) plan the project with the team, (6) collect data, (7) modify plans based on team discussions, (8) expect problems, (9) implement, (10) evaluate and publicize results.[27] Participation of people in productivity teams is crucial to improving productivity.

At Wilton Development Center in New York State, trust between labor and management is viewed as critical. This trust is built in cooperative efforts that are centered in an umbrella Quality of Work Life Committee whose function is to "address facility-wide issues and to provide support to the many joint committees and teams at all organizational levels."[28]

The City of New York has been working to improve productivity. In an article titled, "Productivity Gains through Employee Participation at the New York City Department of Sanitation," the deputy commissioner explains, "The workers, more than anyone else, know what is wrong. They may not be able to tell you how to fix the problems, but they certainly know when things are not right. We wanted to capture that intelligence."[29] In sum, the time that participation takes, is time invested not used up. Its return is manyfold.

This chapter has discussed participative management in terms of organization-wide strategic planning. We believe this to be an effective method of fostering community, improving satisfaction by giving meaning, and in improving performance of individual members. Others, however, would prefer to use other types of group participation. In the next section we discuss and evaluate "the new mantra of management reform: 'TQM.' "[30] We acknowledge that Quality Circles have also been a popular form of participative management, but as "enthusiasm (for them) has dropped off in recent years,"[31] we do not include a discussion of them here.

TOTAL QUALITY MANAGEMENT

Total Quality Management (TQM) reflects the trend toward employee participation in organizational management:

TQM is based on the theory that the greater the involvement an employee has in determining organizational goals, the more committed he or she is to continually improving the process to achieve them. Total Quality Management encourages participation, teamwork, and better quality of results by providing incentives to increase the success of the whole enterprise.[32]

TQM is also an organizational philosophy that is driven by the needs of customers, whether those customers are the final purchasers of products, or dependent departments within the organization. The philosophy assumes that things can always be improved and that people who do the jobs are the best qualified to identify problems and solutions. TQM gurus tell us that the cost of quality in typically managed U. S. business has been 25 percent to 40 percent but that successful installation of TQM will reduce that cost to less than 10 percent.[33]

Understanding TQM requires looking at the three words that comprise it: *Total* refers to the entire organization and begins at the top with the chief executive and all top administrators who must take the tremendous time required to learn TQM before passing it on to their subordinates; *Quality* demands that the organization meet the customer's demands, without error; and *Management* refers to facilitating the production process.

TQM is the brainchild of W. Edwards Deming who, rejected by United States business in the 1950s, took his ideas to Japan. His fourteen quality improvement principles have been widely publicized recently.[34] *U.S. News & World Report* describes "America's belated embrace of a prophet."[35]

TQM requires a long-term commitment throughout the organization. Emphasis is placed on changing structure, process, and attitudes. Rather than assessing organizational culture to determine where changes need to be directed, *a priori* assumptions prompt focus on what is done, rather than who is doing it. What is left unmanaged, we believe, are the feelings of the people without whom no process is carried out. TQM proponents approach an organization with preconceived notions about what the problems are: process and structure. They seem often to ignore that people will resist change due to fear and that they need to resonate with change efforts and problem diagnosis:

TQM defines your COPQ so that your ROI can increase. In order for the QIP to work the PDCA must be followed. The QFD provides a matrix which in essence is the SPC for TQM. . . . Flow charts, cause and effect diagrams, check sheets, Pareto charts, scatter charts, histograms, run charts, control charts, are all methods of viewing the numbers. . . . TQM is not just quality circles discussing a problem.[36]

Advocates of TQM say that everyone in the organization will have to buy into it or leave. They believe that all problems will be solved as the process is changed. They talk about training a lot, and they do a lot of training. They attempt to empower workers with knowledge and with participation.[37] They also use a lot of numbers and slogans, enough that "the overuse and abuse of jargon can strangle an organization."[38]

Implementing TQM involves three phases: planning, improvement, and control.

- Quality Planning contains the following steps: (1) determine who the users/customers are; (2) determine their needs; (3) develop a response to those needs; (4) develop processes to implement the response; and (5) operationalize the processes.

- Quality Improvement requires these steps: (1) evaluate actual quality performance; (2) compare actual performance to goals; and (3) act on the differences.

- Quality Control includes these steps: (1) establish necessary infrastructure; (2) select improvement projects; (3) establish a team for each project; (4) provide motivation, resources, and training necessary to diagnose the causes, generate a solution, and establish controls to maintain the gain.[39]

Much of TQM has merit. It involves people throughout the organization, beginning with top executives. A Quality Council begins to organize teams. The philosophy begins to trickle down. Managers are transformed from givers of orders to participators with employees in problem solving. Here, as with other forms of participative management, obstacles can arise. "Middle managers may feel most threatened by changes like these, since they may fear that TQM will take away some of their power. They are used to telling people what to do and how to do it."[40] TQM, on the other hand, empowers workers and seeks to please both internal and external customers.

We approach TQM with caution, however. Like management consultant Mark A. Abramson, we are "skeptical of three-letter acronyms."[41] Abramson states, further, "What I object to is when the process gets in the way of the outcome . . . people begin to think that the objective is 'to fulfill your TQM plan,' or something like that, instead of changing the way they approach their mission."[42]

A series of interviews conducted by two graduate students at the

University of Nebraska at Omaha revealed that TQM is often misunderstood among the rank and file. For instance, one TQM team was assigned to choose a new copy machine, and another was ridiculed when a decision they made became costly. Team members did not appear to be as excited as the consultants who are pushing TQM, nor as informed about the process as they needed to be.

TQM has worked well in Japan; however, the Japanese culture and the American one are vastly different. Here we are competitive and ambitious, moving from company to company and place to place to advance ourselves. There, employees make a lifetime commitment to one company. Americans expect more from their employers in benefits, wages, and opportunities.

American managers must realize that TQM is not a quick fix. It is an effort in organizational change that requires complete and total commitment, expects no mistakes, and is intolerant of error, even errors that lead to ultimate learning. TQM operates from an underlying philosophy that the fourteen Deming principles will be appropriate for every organization at every point in time. Enthusiasm for it is fueled by horror stories, such as: (1) two million documents will be lost by the IRS this year; (2) twelve babies will be given to the wrong parents each day; (3) 22,000 checks will be deducted from the wrong bank accounts in the next sixty minutes; and (4) 268,500 defective tires will be shipped this year.[43]

Certainly, such quality failures should and must be corrected. TQM, however, is not the only way to correct errors, nor has it yet been demonstrated to live up to claims of the TQM zealots. The prestigious Malcolm Baldridge National Quality Award, established in 1987, is a means to identify and reward companies who have successfully implemented TQM. An area where all applicants for this award have fallen down is human resources training.[44]

We recommend that TQM be viewed as one and only one approach to participative management. We believe that it will be most effective if an identified need for it emerges from the organization-wide strategic planning process. When TQM is suddenly grasped by top managers then dumped upon the rank and file, resistance is predictable and natural. People accept what they help to create. An organization's people are the best source of ideas and solutions for that organization.

We are all unique. No magic formulas apply. Vast corporations such as Xerox, Ford Motor Company, and the federal government are far different in structure and in culture than small businesses, hospitals, and local government. Each type of organization was established to produce a good or service. Each type of organization employs people for that purpose.

These people are the greatest resource. Their input and their enthusiasm is essential. Their resistance can be lethal. Organizational-change theorists have long known that rational explanations of why and how things need to change are not nearly as effective as solutions that emerge from the people themselves.[45] Participative management is a bottom-up approach to problem solving. TQM is a top-down approach, unless it is the solution of choice of those throughout the organization. We advise caution.

SUMMARY

Participative management is a means by which both satisfaction and performance can be enhanced throughout an organization. We have offered the example of an organization-wide strategic planning process because we believe in its efficacy. We have discussed TQM, and we reiterate that TQM is a solution that might emerge from participative planning, but it is only one solution. We urge creativity.

No matter what participative processes you use or what product or service you produce, your major resource is people. In order to remain competitive in today's market, in order to produce the level of quality you want, training for your employees is essential.

NOTES

1. Stephen R. Covey, *The 7 Habits of Highly Effective People: Powerful Lessons in Personal Change* (New York: Simon and Shuster, 1989) 143.

2. George Strauss, "Managerial Practices," in J. Richard Hackman and J. Lloyd Suttle, *Improving Life at Work: Behavioral Science Approaches to Organizational Change* (Santa Monica, Cal.: Goodyear Publishing Co., Inc., 1977): 323–24.

3. Ibid., 326.

4. Ibid.

5. Ibid., 327.

6. Ibid., 328.

7. Ibid., 325.

8. See, Mary Parker Follett, "The Giving of Orders," F. J. Roethlisberger, "The Hawthorne Experiments," Douglas McGregor, "The Human Side of Enterprise," and Chris Argyris, "Organizational Behavior," all in Jay Shafritz and Albert Hyde, eds., *Classics of Public Administration* (Oak Park, Ill.: Moore Publishing, 1978).

9. James Bowman, "Quality Circles in the 1990s," in Marc Holzer, ed., *Public Productivity Handbook* (New York: Marcel-Dekker, 1991).

10. Edward E. Lawler III, *High-Involvement Management* (San Francisco: Jossey-Bass, 1986) 1.

11. Ibid., 13.

12. Ibid., 10.

13. Ibid., 3–4.

14. Joseph H. Boyett and Henry P. Conn, *Workplace 2000: The Revolution Reshaping American Business* (New York: Dutton, 1991): 234.

15. L. William Seidman and Steven L. Skancke, *Productivity: The Proven Path to Excellence in U.S. Companies* (New York: Simon and Schuster, 1990): 50.

16. Rosabeth Moss Kanter, *The Change Masters: Innovation and Entrepreneurship in the American Corporation* (New York: Simon and Schuster, 1983): 241.

17. Paul Nutt, "Models of Decision Making in Organizations and Some Contextual Variables Which Stipulate Optimal Using," *Academy of Management Review* 1, no. 2 (April 1976): 84–98.

18. Ibid.

19. Lawler, *High-Involvement Management*, 22–23.

20. Phillip Hunsaker and Johanna Hunsaker, "Decision Styles in Theory and Practice," *Organization Dynamics* (Autumn 1981), 23–36.

21. From the draft preamble to the Creighton University Policy Statement on Employee Family and Medical Leave (October 24, 1991).

22. Lawler, *High-Involvement Management*, 27–28.

23. Donald M. Norris and Nick L. Poulton, *A Guide for New Planners* (Ann Arbor, Mich.: The Society for College and University Planning, 1987), 21.

24. Robert Levering, Milton Moskowitz, and Michael Katz, *The 100 Best Companies to Work for in America* (Reading, Mass.: Addison-Wesley, 1984), 162.

25. John M. Bryson, *Strategic Planning for Public and Nonprofit Organizations: A Guide for Strengthening and Sustaining Organizational Achievement* (San Francisco: Jossey-Bass, 1988).

26. Marc Holzer, "Building Capacity for Productivity Improvement," *Public Productivity and Management Review* 15, no. 2 (Winter 1991), 113–22.

27. Ibid, 115–16.

28. Susan Grace and Marc Holzer, "Labor Management Cooperation: An Opportunity for Change," in Holzer, ed., *Public Productivity Handbook*, 487–98.

29. Ronald A. Contino and John Giuliano, "Productivity Gains through Employee Participation at the New York City Department of Sanitation," *Public Productivity and Management Review* 15, no. 2 (Winter 1991): 185–90.

30. Graeme Browning, "Quest for Quality," *National Journal* (December 12, 1991): 3071–74.

31. Bowman, "Quality Circles for the 1990s, 502.

32. Michael Milakovich, "Total Quality Management for Public Service Productivity Improvement," in Holzer, ed., *Public Productivity Handbook*, 581–82.

33. Paula Wells of Wells Engineering, TQM Consultant, personal conversation, 1991.

34. See, W. Edwards Deming, *Out of the Crisis* (Cambridge, Mass.: Center for Advanced Engineering Study, Massachusetts Institute of Technology, 1986); A. C. Rosander, *The Quest for Quality in Service* (Milwaukee, Wis.: American Society for Quality Control, 1989); and Mary Walton, *The Deming Managment Method* (New York: Putman Publishing Group, 1986).

35. "The Man Who Gave Japan the Business," *U.S. News & World Report* (April 22, 1991): 65.

36. Gwen Thorpe and Janet Anderson, "Total Quality Management," Unpublished paper, University of Nebraska at Omaha, 1991, 23–24.

37. See J. M. Juran, *Juran on Leadership for Quality* (New York: The Free Press,

1989) and J.M. Juran, *Juran on Planning for Quality* (New York: The Free Press, 1988).

38. Thorpe and Anderson, 24.

39. Paula Wells, personal conversation.

40. David Carr and Ian Littman, *Excellence in Government* (New York: Coopers and Lybrand, 1990): 132.

41. Browning, "Quest for Quality," 3073.

42. Ibid.

43. Natalie Gabel, "Is 99% Good Enough?" *Quality* (March 1991): 40–41.

44. Thorpe and Anderson.

45. See, Edgar Schein, *Process Consultation*, vols. 1 and 2 (Reading, Mass.: Addison Wesley, 1987 and 1988).

APPENDIX A: PLANNING WORKSHEETS

The purpose of examining Strengths and Weaknesses, Opportunities and Threats (SWOTs) relevant to the function, program, or area of concern of our committee is to develop an understanding of the external and internal environmental factors that constrain or that open opportunities for different strategies. Many contingencies may be both opportunities and threats. It depends on how you look at a situation: "When you get lemons, make lemonade."

Directions: In preparation for the next meeting, respond to the following questions. These worksheets are intended simply to prepare your thinking for the meeting.

1. Identify two to five opportunities relevant to the area of concern of our committee. These may be opportunities for new activities, ways of doing things differently or of reaching new markets, or new uses for existing facilities, and so forth. Think of "opportunities" broadly and imaginatively—we will get more realistic later. Use a phrase or sentence to describe each briefly.

a.

b.

c.

d.

e.

2. Identify, and describe in a brief phrase or sentence, two to five threats relevant to the area of concern of our committee.

a.

b.

c.

d.

e.

3. Identify, and describe in a brief phrase or sentence, two to five internal strengths of our organization relevant to the area of concern of our committee now.

a.

b.

c.

d.

e.

4. Identify, and describe in a brief phrase or sentence, two to five internal weaknesses of our organization relevant to the area of concern of our committee.

a.

b.

c.

d.

e.

APPENDIX B: PLANNING PROCESS IMPLEMENTATION

Overview of Implementation Planning Process

Here are the key steps in the planning process.

1. Summarize responses to the draft strategic plan of the employees.

2. Summarize responses to the draft strategic plan from the Board of Directors.

3. Circulate all summarized responses to the Planning Steering Committee.

4. Poll chairs and committee members of Strategic Planning Committees to see if they wish to continue participating in the planning process. Strategic Planning Committees become Implementation Committees.

5. Members of the Planning Steering Committee appoint Implementor(s) to be responsible for implementation.

6. The Planning Steering Committee reviews the proposed implementation planning process, considers responses to the draft strategic plan, and approves a document that becomes the guide for implementation.

7. Orientation meetings for Implementor(s) and Implementation Committee Chairs are held to acquaint them with the implementation process.

8. The Planning Coordinator meets with each Implementor and Implementation Committee in a joint meeting to get them started and to answer questions on the implementation process.

9. The Implementor(s) meet with Implementation Committees to consider adding members to the committee. These should be individuals who can bring expertise to implementation planning and implementation.

10. Implementors, in consultation with Implementation Committees, develop an "Implementation Outline" that includes recommendations that are proposed to be implemented.

11. Set a date due for "Implementation Outlines" to be submitted to the Planning Coordinator, who immediately circulates them to the members of the Planning Steering Committee. Ask members to consider whether any recommendations are inconsistent with the priorities previously established, and to watch for possible duplication of recommendations.

12. Schedule a Planning Steering Committee meeting in about one month for Oversight Persons or Implementor(s) to present "Implementation Outlines."

13. Once "Implementation Outlines" are reviewed by the Planning Steering Committee, the Implementor(s), in consultation with the Implementation Committees, develop "Implementation Procedures."

14. Implementors send "Implementation Procedures" to Planning Coordinator within another four to six weeks.

15. Planning Coordinator distributes composite report of "Implementation Procedures" from all Implementors to the Planning Steering Committee within the next four to six weeks.

16. Oversight Persons and Implementors send "Implementation Progress Report" to the Chief Executive Officer within three months.

17. Office of the Chief Executive Officer prepares a "Progress Report on Organization-Wide Implementation" within five to six weeks and circulates it to the Planning Steering Committee.

18. The Planning Steering Committees meets for an annual review of the "Progress Report on Organization-Wide Implementation" and the implementation process. (We suggest that this meeting be held away from the organization, preferably in another city or at a retreat center).

Implementation Responsibilities

Oversight Persons, Implementors, and Implementation Committee members and Chairs have different responsibilities in implementation planning.

Oversight Persons:

1. are responsible to see that plans are implemented;

2. appoint an Implementor or Implementors to be directly responsible to supervise implementation;

3. monitor the activities of the committees over which they have oversight responsibilities;

4. appoint members of the organization, if nominated by Implementor(s), to join the Implementation Committees. These are individuals who can bring expertise to implementation planning and implementation;

5. interpret which recommendations not specifically contained in the strategic plan document are consistent with the priorities set at the retreat;

6. examine "Implementation Outlines" of various committees to determine means for combining efforts or for assigning only one committee with

responsibility when there is potential for duplication or overlap of recommendations from different committees;

7. participate in the Planning Steering Committee review of "Implementation Outlines";

8. review "Implementation Procedures" established by the Implementor(s);

9. locate financial resources in operating budgets to carry out implementation; and

10. advise the Implementor(s) on where to find nonfinancial resources to carry out implementation.

Implementors:

1. are appointed by Oversight Persons to Implementation Committees (in some cases the Oversight Person will also be the Implementor);

2. direct implementation planning and keep Oversight Persons apprised of progress (in many instances, the Implementor(s) will actually carry out implementation);

3. become Chairs of Implementation Committees if the Chair of the Strategic Planning Committee has resigned;

4. invite Oversight Persons to meetings of Implementation Committees when needed;

5. convene the Implementation Committee in consultation with the Chair of the Implementation Committee;

6. assign responsibility to keep minutes of meetings and to send copies to the chief executive's office;

7. nominate members of the organization, if any, who should be appointed by the Oversight Person to join the Implementation Committee. These are individuals who can bring expertise to implementation planning and implementation;

8. in consultation with the Chair of the Implementation Committee and committee members, obtain background information and data that will enhance implementation planning and plan implementation, if necessary;

9. in consultation with the Chair of the Implementation Committee and committee members, develop and write "Implementation Outlines," establish and write "Procedures for Implementation," and write an "Implementation Progress Report."

10. in consultation with the Chair of the Implementation Committee and committee members, revise "Implementation Outlines" in light of review by Planning Steering Committee.

Chairs of Implementation Committees:

1. poll committee members to determine who wishes to continue on the committee when the Strategic Planning Committee becomes the Implementation Committee;

2. are the primary advisors to the Implementor(s);

3. interpret the Strategic Planning Committee report to the Implementor(s), if needed;

4. advise the Implementor(s) on members of the organization, if any, who should be nominated for appointment by the Oversight Person to join the Implementation Committee. These are individuals who can bring expertise to implementation planning and implementation;

5. assist the Implementor(s) in obtaining background information and data that will enhance implementation planning and plan implementation, if necessary;

6. assist the Implementor(s) to develop the "Implementation Outlines";

7. assist the Implementor(s) in revising the "Implementation Outlines" in light of the review by the Planning Steering Committee, if necessary;

8. assist the Implementor(s) in establishing "Implementation Procedures"; and

9. assist the Implementor(s) in preparing the "Implementation Progress Report."

Members of Implementation Committees:

1. advise the Implementor(s) on members of the organization, if any, who should be appointed by the Oversight Person to join the Implementation Committee, these are individuals who can bring expertise to implementation planning and implementation;

2. assist the Implementor(s) in the development of the "Implementation Outline";

3. in consultation with the Implementor(s), obtain background information and data that will enhance implementation planning and plan implementation, if necessary;

4. assist the Implementor(s) in the establishment of "Implementation Procedures"; and

5. assist the Implementor(s) in preparing the "Implementation Progress Report."

Planning Coordinator

The Planning Coordinator meets with the committees to explain the implementation process and to assist them in developing "Implementation Outlines," "Implementation Procedures," and "Implementation Progress Reports."

Portraits of Satisfied and Dissatisfied Employees

> Effective managers . . . behave in such a way that subordinates, peers, and supervisors get the help they need in order to get things done.
>
> Edgar Schein[1]

An excellent way to understand job satisfaction and performance better is to talk with employees about their work. If you want to know what helps them to perform well and what hinders their performance, you need to ask. If you want to understand what is going on in your organization, you should enter into a collaborative process where you and your employees jointly examine the characteristics of jobs and their relation to the greater organization.[2] In other words, in order to learn about your own organization, ask those who work in it.

Often we become convinced that our view of the organization is the same as everyone else's, but each of us stands in only one part of the whole. We are like the proverbial blind men surrounding an elephant. In that parable, a group of blind men are asked to describe an elephant. One feels the trunk, and says, "Oh, my! An elephant is like a snake—narrow and flexible." The second, standing near the elephant's leg, says, "Oh no, my friend, the elephant is like a tall marble pillar, round and very sturdy." The third blind man, as he felt the elephant's tusk, laughed aloud at his friends' ignorance. "This elephant," he said, "is curved and firm, like a sword." Each blind man felt only a part of the whole and judged that all of the elephant was as that part with which he came in contact. Too often, that is how we learn about, and then describe, the organization's functions, strengths, and weaknesses.

If you truly want to learn about the satisfaction of employees, go to each or to several and ask them. If you truly want to understand their problems in producing quality, and really want to congratulate them on their successes, go to them and visit. We have talked about the value of participation in decision making, planning, and in instituting Total Quality Management. We encourage you to talk to your employees on a regular basis.

We did just that. We were surprised at how readily and how fully they shared with us when we started our conversation by simply saying, "Tell me about your work." We interviewed six workers in Omaha, Nebraska, in spring 1991. We learned about the characteristics of their jobs and of their organizations that foster and impair job satisfaction and performance. We wanted to know what contributed to their ability to balance the two. We wanted to know if they would view their jobs as "good work."

Two of our interviewees are blue-collar workers. Three are white-collar, and one is a professional. Four are male; two are female. Five are white; one is black. They work in jobs which range from a machinist on a shop floor to an office manager. Their stories illustrate the complexity of meaningful work, the sources of job satisfaction and dissatisfaction, and the individuality of those who perform it.

The interviews were unstructured, and each one took an average of one-and-a-half hours to complete. Once the workers presented their perspective on their work, probing questions were asked to explore the dimensions of their jobs from two perspectives. One framework was to identify the presence of the job characteristics of task identity, task significance, skill variety, autonomy, and feedback. These are the components of a job that were identified by Hackman and Oldham as those that foster job satisfaction.[3]

The second framework for questions was based on Soelle's conception of "good work," which can be described as a situation in which workers are able to be themselves and utilize their own unique talents, in which workers have developed meaningful relationships in their work setting, and in which workers believe that their work contributes to a greater good, a better world. A final question, simply put, in the interviews was, "If you had a child, would you want your child to have a job like yours?"

In the following pages we present their stories, with names and job locations changed to maintain anonymity. The stories are followed by a section that reflects on the similarities and differences in the stories. The report ends with a commentary on what we learned from the interviews about balancing job satisfaction and performance and about the merits of doing "good work."

Mark Madison, Machinist (age 27): I'm a machinist. I always thought I'd have a job where I sit behind a desk and wear a white shirt and tie, but I sort of lucked into this, I guess.

I was eighteen when my Mom remarried. The guy was all right, but I didn't want to live in his house, so I figured this would be a good time to go it on my own. I couldn't find a job in Kentucky, where I lived, but my uncle said there was lots of work in California, so I figured, why not?

Well, I'd been in California about six or eight weeks and hadn't found anything, when my uncle told me he'd seen an ad on a bulletin board where he works. I decided to apply, what the heck? Well, I applied for and passed a lot of tests to be a machinist apprentice. I was an apprentice for four years. That meant 7,400 hours of training and 30 units of college.

I'm proud of that. I'm good at what I do. I work from blueprints to set up a machine and the tooling, then I run the job. The run is boring, and repetitive, but I like making prototypes. I'm good at what I do, and the engineers in R and D [Research and Development] will come to me with an idea, and I put it together from start to finish. There's a certain pride in that; I mean, that's you, you can say "I did this" and feel proud.

There's a lot of pressure in my work. We work with expensive microwave tubes and parts. I've known people who got fired for just one mistake. Management sets the standards. If they say you have two hours to set up and six hours to do the run, then you have to do it in that time. There's a lot of pressure to meet standards within 90 to 100 percent. If you really have to push to meet the standards, there's a lot of stress. I've never seen anyone badly hurt. I had to have a few stitches once. But I've heard stories.

They have safety teams that check about every two weeks, but I think it's a very unhealthy work environment. Those machines get really hot, and we clean them with chemicals. Sometimes, the smoke's so bad I'll yell, "Hey, you tryin' to barbecue some meat over there?" They have fans, but the blades are covered with a black soot.

If you'd let it, the stress could really get you down. Mostly I've learned to just do my job and not complain. When I get upset, I just grit my teeth and say to myself, "Keep your mouth shut and keep working." I'm trying to be at peace with myself.

My boss is a good man. He really cares. We can go to him if we're having problems. He's been doing kind of what you're doing—asking questions about what we like and don't like about our jobs. He really tries. That makes it a good environment to work in.

We make radiation machines to treat cancer, microwave tubes for TV, radar systems for the military—stuff like that. We're high tech. I earn $18.05 hourly. That includes a two-dollar night differential, but I like the night shift. I've got more autonomy. I think we work harder on night, but we don't have someone breathing down our neck all the time.

I really like the people I work with. I don't know anyone but my family except the people I meet at work. If I could have stayed in Kentucky, where I grew up, it'd probably be different. I mean I'd know people. But out here? No way. I like the guys I work with, though. We play golf together. Sometimes we go to Reno.

I'll probably be doing this same job, or one like it five years from now. But I don't want to spend the rest of my life as a machinist. If I ever have a son, I wouldn't want him to be a machinist. We don't get respect. I mean if I meet someone away from work, and I say I'm a machinist, they laugh or say something like, "Oh, does that mean you can fix my car?"

People tend to stay in their jobs where I work. I've been there for eight years, and I'm the second youngest man. My company's in transition and there's been some layoffs. But my friends and I have a motto, "A good machinist is never out of work." And I'm good.

Lou Williams, Authorization Agent (age 29): I've been at this job for twenty-three months. I worked part time when I was going to college, then I quit school and went full time. I sit in a large room at a computer terminal and verify that credit card holders have enough money in their accounts to cover their purchases. I also enter data into the computer.

This job is dull, boring, and repetitive. The money is pretty good. I make $7.50 an hour and the fringe benefits are great, especially the health insurance. What I really like is my supervisor. She's employee-oriented and friendly and flexible. She treats me like a responsible person. Sometimes she lets me get by with stuff, like when I'm a little late and she doesn't report me.

The customers are idiots. They're rude and I can't half understand what they say. I don't think they can understand me. I hate it. I just want to hang up on them. Some of them are really insulting. When I'm just following the rules and decline a charge because the customer doesn't have the money, they blame me, like it's my fault or something.

The room I sit in has rows of computer terminals and a tall dais in the center. People are put in teams and the teams are supposed to sit together. They think that'll make us like the jobs better. It doesn't. The supervisors walk around the room and somebody monitors the calls electronically on a random basis. Knowing that they might be listening does make me more conscious of treating the customers well.

I don't get any personal satisfaction, and I don't have many friends here. My friends are the people I knew before I started working here. You can't make friends because you don't have time. You can't talk while you're working. Oh, you might see someone in the break room, but not often. A lot of people work part time, and there's a lot of turnover. There's hardly anyone here who was here when I started.

This is a good company, and I'd like to stay with the company, but not in this department. First, I have to work off my "occasions." They give you an "occasion" when you miss work. Then you have to work off the "occasion" by not even being late any day for a month. They won't let you transfer to another job when you have "occasions." My supervisor tells me that no other department would want me if I have a lot of "occasions," because they want someone they can depend on.

I've always been a dependable person, but this job is so boring that I really have to make myself go to work. I get insulted by customers. I get headaches. I have a callus on my wrist. I would say that I have absolutely no job satisfaction but I have good pay and benefits. If I decide to finish college, they'll pay my tuition. I'm thinking about that.

I wouldn't advise a friend to work here. They don't require any particular level of education. They teach you how to use their computers. Then they try to play games to get you to come to work. For instance, if you come to work for two weeks without missing, and don't even take a break when you're entitled to, they give you a little gold key. The keys are like green stamps. You can save them, but most people don't want to. I throw mine away when I get them. They're an insult. With eight keys, I can get a soap-on-a-rope. Big deal. I'm not going to play their reindeer games.

I think there are things they could do to make this a better place to work. For one thing, I'd like them to give you information about the whole system and how your own job fits into it. And I'd like them to change the kind of job I do so it's not so rep.titive.

I'm not proud of what I do, and I sure wouldn't want a kid of mine to do it, but it's a job.

Steve Simmons, Security Guard (age 42): I've worked in this company as a Security Guard for more than fifteen years. The job's a good one—especially for someone like me with only a high school education. Most places I'd only make minimum wage. I was really glad when I passed the test for this job. Most people don't want to work in security, but I thought, "Why not? It'd sure pay better than the other jobs I can get."

Well, I passed the test with, you might say, flying colors. When I went for my interview, the personnel officer asked me if I was free to work nights and swing shifts. I said, "Sure." Everybody had said that they always start the new recruits on the worst hours, but I didn't think nights would be too bad. I could be home in the day with my wife and kids.

About, my job. I wouldn't really say it's a career, but I wouldn't want to quit it or do something else either. It's a tough job and people don't appreciate what we do, but I feel like I make a difference. There's some people who get into security because they're on this power trip, you know? But, then a lot of us really care. A good security officer learns to balance the power with wisdom. Not everybody can, of course. I guess, that's why part of the selection process is a psychological test.

For the past several years, I was assigned to the unit that checks people's credentials when they come in the building. We're also the ones that make certain that the bank deposits are carried safely out of the building. We sort of stand in a line, and the people carrying the money pass between us to the truck. We have to be able to take a lot of stuff off the people who see us. They think they can intimidate us, or they'll act like they're going to steal the money as a kind of joke.

We have to stay calm and in control no matter what happens. That can be tough. We just stick together though. We like to say, "We're the normal ones. Everybody out there is a shithead." Sometimes I wonder.

Since last September, though, I've been a "teacher." I got assigned to work with the new drug-abuse prevention program. I had to pass a test, then they gave me intensive training on drugs and alcohol, and on how to teach. I was really proud when I passed the teaching test. A lot of people don't.

I wear my uniform and go to the company's different sites around the city to teach our employees about drugs and alcohol. I'm horrified that they thought the people here needed this kind of education. They all seem okay to me. But I love doing this. I never knew teaching could be so hard or so rewarding.

Now, I'm more a part of the training department than I am security. The different places I go to always include me in their meetings and invite me to their parties. They make me feel like I'm a part of their work group too. I love working with all these different people. It's like I finally have the perfect job.

My job sure doesn't absorb all my life though. I like to go hunting and fishing. I'm also taking horseback riding lessons. I don't know why. I just like to stay busy.

I'm not really friends with the other security officers. We're in the union together, but we don't socialize. For relaxation, I do things with my wife and people we know outside the company. My wife and I go out a lot—we really get the good from our "Pleasure Pack," and we like to play games at home—"Trivial Pursuit," "Pictionary." We've got a pinball machine and a pool table in the basement. Come on, let's go downstairs and play pinball.

Ron Gillespie, Purchasing Agent (age 27): I work in the Purchasing Department at my company. This has been a great job for me. I started four-and-a-half years ago, working half-time for minimum wage. Then, after about two years, a real job came open. I applied, took the test, and got the job.

This is the perfect job for me right now. The pay's not much, $6.80 an hour, but the company pays my college tuition, gives me free insurance, and vacation and sick leave days. My boss supports me in going to school, so no matter when a class I need is scheduled, he lets me arrange my work hours around class times.

I have a lot of responsibility in my job. Anyplace else, I'd get paid a lot more. I pay invoices, maintain computer accounting records for all orders, send rejected supplies back, and keep the CD ROM data base updated. This has given me knowledge about purchasing, accounting, and computers that I could never have learned in school. I figure it'll help me when I go to graduate school.

I'd say I'm sort of satisfied with my job. I really like how it complements school. It pays tuition. It's near the campus. I can schedule my work around school. It's not physically hard. I wear a white shirt and tie to work, and, it pays better than any job I've ever had. The only thing I wish was different is the money. I wish it paid more money.

I really think this job is a good one. It's varied enough and changes often enough to be challenging. At the same time, I can use many of the skills I already have. I especially like being the first one to know what's being bought for the different departments.

On a scale of 1 to 9, I'd rate my supervisor a 7 1/2. Sometimes she gets on me for talking too much. I can talk and work too, but she says I disturb my coworkers by talking. She gives too much negative feedback. She sees the exception and plays up every mistake you make, instead of bragging on the 99 things you did right. This keeps you on a tightrope. Sometimes I wonder if she's jealous because she's pretty much stuck where she is, and I'm on my way up.

I think a supervisor should be like a football coach. She needs to let people know when they mess up, but also cheer and brag when you do well. When you do a good job and no one says anything, you want to say, "Why the hell do anything?" I hope when I'm a supervisor I can remember to say, "Thanks, good job," or "What happened here?" You've got to work it both ways.

My working conditions are good. I wish I had a window, is the only thing. We work underground, and that could get claustrophobic, but with school and everything, I'm in and out, so I don't let that get to me.

I like the people I work with, but we're not really what you'd call friends. We wouldn't have anything in common outside of work. None of them are in school, except Janet, and she's just taking classes on "marriage and the family" and stuff like that. Everybody's married and most of them have a kid. But they're nice. We enjoy working together. The women are all the time bringing cookies or candy or something. Linda's on the organizational task force on women's issues—she think's she's a radical feminist, or something. I like to tease her about that. She never knows if I'm serious or trying to get her upset. I guess you'd say, we're operating with different priorities and this shows outside of work.

If I had a kid in college, I'd want him to get a job just like this. In fact, I would highly recommend it to anyone who is trying to get through school. I wouldn't change a thing about this job. Of course, I know I'm not going to spend the rest of life in it. This job meets my immediate needs, but I've known it was temporary from the beginning. It's a means to an end.

Mary Miller, Research Associate (age 35): This is the best job I've ever had. It's not the money—I've earned more in other jobs. What I like is being treated with respect and encouraged to use my own ideas and initiative. I don't even have a job description. Basically I'm doing research on workload and job satisfaction for the employees in this company. I helped design the survey instrument we're using. I set up the data analysis program, and I meet regularly with the director and his staff. I also supervise the data entry person. My own supervisor is good to let me take the ball and run with it. I know my own limits and I ask for help when I need it. He trusts me.

I've had a couple of really awful jobs so I can appreciate this one. When I was working on my Bachelor's Degree, I wanted to teach history. Student teaching changed that. I'm a really quiet, very shy person. Being in front of a class was intimidating. I'd be prepared, and think I was doing OK, then the supervising teacher who always sat in front of the room would just interrupt with, "I'm bored. These children are bored. You're going to have to do something to entertain us. We're all going to sleep." I'd be just devastated.

In my last job I was a legal secretary. My boss wanted me to keep my ideas to myself and follow orders. He wanted no initiative, so I just rocked along, feeling worse and worse about myself. I experienced a lot of pain. I endured it. We had been through a recession, and I was grateful for the job. I spent eight years in that job, being scared because my husband couldn't find work, and I had a regular paycheck. I was the security.

Finally, I got the courage to file for divorce, quit that job, and found this one. It's the best thing I've ever done. I'm able to build technical skills and use the knowledge I have. It's a good growth- and confidence-builder. I've been way down on self-confidence, and it's good to see that I know something. I do things I'm proud of. I can reach out and say, "That was my idea."

For the first time in my life I have a job that lets me be who I am. I like to work independently, and in this job I can. But I'm also learning to work as a part of a team. I am starting to become comfortable with who I am, and to know what I'm good at. I like the people I work with. At the office, we're not just colleagues. We're friends. But we never see each other outside of work.

I really think what I do makes a difference. I'm working on a survey and report that examines job satisfaction and workloads. If the organization follows our recommendations, this will be a better place to work for hundreds of people.

If I ever had a kid like me, I'd recommend this job. It'd be perfect. At first I saw it as an escape from the last job. I didn't really know what I was getting into. I was just so miserable. Remember the ice storm last week? In the old job I would have been thrilled to be snowed in. In this one I wanted to be at work. I love this job and I love the way people treat me.

Laura Larence, Office Manager (age 37): I manage the minority development office. I'm only on a three-fourth-time appointment. They expect me to use the other one-fourth time to go to school to finish my doctorate. This company gives me free tuition. I'd say for three-fourth-time and the tuition, I'm paid a just wage, but I sure hope they plan to increase it when I go on full time. (Laughs.)

Going to school means I don't really have a life. I'm making a lot of personal sacrifices so my kids won't have to. Their life's been hard enough. I don't get enough sleep, and I don't do anything for me, ever. Going into my office and working to help other people have better lives makes me feel like I'm me, you know, the human being I really am.

I love my job. I like seeing end results and feeling fulfilled. When I'm here at work, I can be me. I can joke and be at ease. I always tell the people who work for me that I'm going to do my very best for them, and that I hope they'll do their best for me too. That way we'll all grow. It generally takes the new people about two weeks to learn to see me as a human being, and not as a black woman sitting there talking at them. I really care about them. Most of them figure that out and then we're OK.

I am very loyal to this organization. My supervisor and my coworkers have faith that I'm a credible human being. They believe in me. That's important right now. I'm just breaking free from being married for fifteen years to an abusive husband. Being beaten a lot doesn't do much for your self-esteem.

I always look for the good side. Having an abusive husband pushed me toward the Lord and gave me the courage to get this job. I really love the Lord and I've come to trust Him completely. If I'd had a happy marriage, maybe I wouldn't have. I'm a part of a church family that really supports me, and that helps too.

I don't have much of a life beyond this office. Between my own school and my kids and dealing with that crazy I used to be married to, there's no time for me. I'd say I have four burdens. I'm a black woman trying to raise three kids alone. I work and go to school. No wonder I'm tired all the time!

Which burden is heaviest? I'd say it depends on the day. Most times, though, it's the kids. I want to make them credible God-fearing human beings. All else is secondary. There are so many negativities. This is the burden I bear alone. I have no one to share it. And I worry. Am I doing enough? Am I doing it right?

School gets heavy too. I'm taking six-hours credit toward my doctorate. I have to drive 120 miles round trip two nights a week to classes. Last week I spent thirty hours on a budget exercise alone! That doesn't count the hours I had to spend doing the reading and driving back and forth.

The job is OK most of the time. It gets a little crazy sometimes. Other than that, I really like what I do. I can be me, and I feel like I make a difference. Working in minority development means I'm contributing to making this world better.

I spent the whole part of my developmental life trying to get past seeing being a black female as a burden. You do bump into the system because you're black. Some of the employees outside this office think I don't know as much. They don't realize I have to know twice as much because I'm black, and I work much harder. I want to know so much and be so good that people will not even see a black person in front of them, but will just hear the words I say.

I bring a different perspective to my job than white people do. I've had different experiences. That's what managing diversity is about. I want people to see that being different is not a handicap. It's an asset because it helps see a broader part of the problem and different kinds of solutions.

Despite what they say, though, people see black and stereotype me. The other day I had a meeting at one of our installations across town. I got caught in traffic and I was running late. I didn't have time to fix my hair before I ran into the receptionist area. When I arrived and said I was there for a meeting with her boss, the receptionist looked at me, and said, "You can't be meeting with anyone here. I've never seen you before. Let me see some identification." She acted like she was afraid because I am black. When you encounter that stuff enough times, you just let it be other people's problem, not yours.

This job is a blessing for me. It's helped me professionally, and it's helped me put my life back on track. I wish I had time to socialize outside the office, but I don't have a life. I will someday, though.

JOB SATISFACTION AND PERFORMANCE

Five of the people we interviewed described themselves as satisfied with their jobs. All six stated that they are productive. In this section we examine the characteristics of their jobs in relationship to the theoretical constructs that lead to job satisfaction, and we discuss the effects that the various job components have on these peoples' performance. We believe these issues are relevant for you to consider, as they point to job elements that you can manipulate.

Table 7.1 is a matrix that summarizes the characteristics of each job of our interviewees. At a glance, you can see each job's components and whether or not that component has a positive or negative effect on the job's incumbent. We want to point out that whether the effect is recorded as negative or positive depended on the perception of the jobholder. That is, of course, true of the jobs and their incumbents in your organization as well.

All of the people we interviewed except the authorization agent thought that what they did was significant. They could identify a completed job, and say that "this is my product." They used a number of skills to complete their jobs.

In authorizations, however, each task is generated by a random phone call, over which the agent has no control. He knows that already some of the company's clients are using technology that directly accesses a computer that handles credit decisions similar to the ones he makes. Soon his job will be obsolete, and he finds no sense of accomplishment and no sense of pride. Could he?

We like to think that even a job rapidly being replaced by technology can be enriched so that job incumbents can identify with what they do and feel that it is significant. For example, could an authorization agent be responsible for a certain group of credit card holders? of a specific geographic area? Could he be involved in the totality of an account, perhaps approving the original application, processing charges, issuing billing and recording payments? When asked, this agent said he'd like to see more of the total picture. We believe that providing that view will be more conducive to productivity and to regular attendance than will the little keys and pins in the "reindeer games."

We define the characteristic of "autonomy" as being able to work independently, and as having control over one's own time. In the interviews we conducted, the office manager and the research associate seemed to have the most long-term autonomy. Now that the security guard is assigned to training and development, he experiences this kind of freedom as well, and the difference in his satisfaction level was evident. The purchasing agent is given the freedom of flexible scheduling, and the freedom to balance the tasks of purchasing within his own time constraints. These four people reported greater satisfaction than did the two confined to one place and one machine-generated task.

Both the machinist and the authorization agent described the pressure and stress from being confined to one spot until given permission to move from it. They feared making mistakes, and they had no say in setting time or performance standards. One had been injured. The other

Table 7.1
Job Characteristics Matrix

JOB CHARACTERISTICS	Machinist	Authorization Agent	Purchasing Assistant	Office Manager	Security Guard	Research Associate
TASK SIGNIFICANCE	x	0	x	+	+	+
TASK IDENTITY	+	0	+	+	+	+
SKILL VARIETY	+	0	x	+	+	x
AUTONOMY	0	-	x	+	+	+
FEEDBACK	+	-	-	+	+	+

KEY: x = job incumbent feels neutral about the existence of this characteristic
+ = job incumbent feels positive about the existence of this characteristic
- = job incumbent feels negative about this characteristic
0 = this characteristic does not exist in this job

complained of headaches. Their routinized work over which they had no control caused physical distress.

Our interviewees received feedback about their performance in different ways, and for different reasons. Mark, the machinist, said that the fact that his boss listens to him makes his job less frustrating than it might be. The authorization agent saw his supervisor as very important to his job satisfaction. Her treatment of him as a "real person" was what made his job bearable. The purchasing agent, on the other hand, was frustrated by his supervisor's "negative feedback." He explained that his supervisor "plays up every mistake you make, instead of bragging on the 99 things you did right. This keeps you on a tightrope." Conversely, one of the things that made the research associate like the job she now has better than any other was that her "supervisor is good to let me take the ball and run with it. He trusts me." What a difference a supervisor can make!

Were the satisfied people we interviewed more productive than the dissatisfied one? We have no basis for determining, except their self-reports, and their description of their attendance records. The dissatisfied employee says he misses often, and he has to make himself go to work. The ones who believe that their jobs are significant rarely miss work.

The employees whose supervisors trust them and work with them report a commitment to do well. The employees whose supervisors give only negative feedback resent it. As the purchasing agent remarked, "When you do a good job and no one says anything, you want to say, "Why the hell do anything? "

What he—as well as all the employees we interviewed and we ourselves—wants is a supervisor who can remember to say, "Thanks, good job," or "What happened here? " These few interviews did indeed indicate that satisfaction and performance are greatly influenced by the characteristics of the job itself, and by the behavior of a supervisor.

GOOD WORK

We also wanted to know if the people we interviewed had managed to find "good work," and if that had any effect on their satisfaction or performance. The characteristics of good work, and their presence or absence in these peoples' jobs is shown in Table 7.2.

Three of the employees described in this report view their work as completely "good" in Soelle's terms: They are able to be themselves and utilize their own unique talents; they have developed meaningful relationships in their work setting; and they believe their work contributes to a greater good, a better world. Four state they are satisfied with both the conditions of their job and the situation in which they work. All

Table 7.2
Good Work Matrix

GOOD WORK ELEMENTS	Machinist	Authorization Agent	Purchasing Assistant	Office Manager	Security Guard	Research Associate
JUST WAGE	+	+	+	+	+	+
FREEDOM TO BE ONESELF	0	0	+	+	+	+
INTERACTIONS AT WORK	0	0	+	+	+	+
CONTRIBUTES TO A BETTER WORLD	+	0	+	+	+	+
FREEDOM FROM PHYSICAL OR MENTAL VIOLENCE	-	-	#	#	#	#

KEY: + = job incumbent feels positive about the existence of this characteristic
      - = job incumbent believes this conditions exists and does harm
      0 = this characteristic does not exist in this job
      # = the potential for this characteristic to exist is ever present

believe they earn a just wage, and all wish they earned more. None see the place they now are as the pinnacle of their career. Each hopes for more.

Of those interviewed, only one is experiencing alienation. Lou, the authorization agent, is trapped on a treadmill of repetitive, routine, and dehumanizing tasks. His work is not "good." He is not satisfied. There is no joy in producing, for Lou neither plans nor envisions his product. Neither vision nor responsibility has been entrusted to him, and he has no control of his own time. In the language of job satisfaction, he has no task significance, no task identity, no skill variety, no autonomy, and little feedback. His work is "bad" because it does not allow him to be himself and use his own talents; it does not promote meaningful relationships; and he does not see how it might contribute to making this a better world. After talking to Lou, we began to characterize the large rooms full of people confined to computer terminals and telephones as the sweat shops of the twentieth century.

The other people we interviewed all have control of their time, to some extent. They experience task identity, task significance, skill variety, a great deal of autonomy and some feedback. They also are a part of planning, with a vision they can bring into reality in both their jobs and their personal lives.

The term "good work" implies that those who work are free from both physical and psychic violence. This violence might be overt. It might be subtle. When violence is present, people act to resist or overpower it. Violence occurred regularly in the workplaces of four of our interviewees: the authorization agent, the security guard, the machinist, and the office manager.

Lou (authorization agent) escapes with sarcasm and frequent absences. Steve (security guard) dealt with the psychic violence by bonding with coworkers and spending nonworking hours in various recreational escapes. Office Manager Laura has chosen to ignore the subtle racism that can do violence to her spirit. Steve lived with the threat of physical violence too, but he was prepared, armed, and trained. He is glad to be away from it. While the machines used by Mark, the machinist, can do violence, it is an overt, predictable kind of assault that he is very much aware of and that safety teams work hard to prevent. In the computer room, the violence is so subtle it can go undetected. In law enforcement and the machine shop, it is a known enemy.

The other workers in our study did not report having to cope regularly with violence, but their stories reveal that the potential for violence is always present. Ron (purchasing assistant) talked with us about verbally abusive customers. Both Mary (research associate) and Laura (office manager) described hostile and rude employees, and offensive workers in other departments.

We wonder what the organizations of our interviewees are doing to prevent or overcome the potential violence to their employees. We suspect that those in positions to make a difference have never thought about the workplace in these terms. We hope that you will look around your organization, talking to your workers, looking for ways that potential for workplace violence can be minimized or eliminated.

Regarding control of personal time and freedom to be oneself, it seemed that those who had some discretion were more satisfied than those who had little or none. Lou has no control over his own time. He answers phones when they ring, inputs appropriate computer data, gets a reply, responds, and the cycle repeats over and over and over. The image of a treadmill comes to mind, and Lou calls his work drudgery. That is not good work.

Mark has only a partial control over his time. He is confined to meeting the time-limit standards set by management, and he is reluctant to say what he thinks. His freedom from the treadmill comes in the part of his job where he works from blueprints, and when he works with the research and development department. He often holds back comments he would like to make, so holds his personality in check. He sometimes has "good work."

Most of the time, the others say, they can be themselves. Laura feels free when she is in her office. Mary feels free when she is sheltered away from people, able to work alone. Ron enjoys the flexibility of arranging his own schedule, and appreciates the encouragement he gets toward reaching his personal goals.

It was interesting to note that those who had some discretion over time at work reported greater levels of satisfaction. Neither Lou nor Mark had the freedom even to get up and stretch except at scheduled breaks. Such "nose to the grindstone" approaches to work design are often thought to get higher levels of productivity. Lou called these approaches "reindeer games." Blind obedience, while it might be expected by some supervisors, does not lead to greater productivity.

Often employees who have little say and little discretion will adapt their behavior in ways that act to the detriment of accomplishing good things for the organization. Workers are people first, employees second. When they are frustrated, they act in ways to minimize their own pain. Often these actions slow down production, or minimize the particular worker's contribution.[4]

Soelle asserts that "Work should be a joy in our lives."[5] Neither the machinist nor the authorization agent would want a child of theirs to do the jobs they do. Even though the machinist takes pride in his product, he is not proud of his blue-collar status and finds joy in his work only when he can say, "This is me. I did that." The two people who are using their jobs as a means of finishing college believe the jobs are ideal for that purpose, not for the rest of their lives. Their joy comes from both their work and the dreams that the work can help fulfill. The office manager is so overburdened by life's responsibilities that she has no time to rejoice in the work that she sees as a blessing. The security guard, until his recent assignment in training and development, had carefully separated work and personal life, finding a superficial joy in the toys and activities his work buys.

Soelle states, "Those who come to understand the goal of work as fulfilling the needs of their neighbors tend to experience a transformation in their entire approach to work."[6] That transformation was most evident in Steve Simmons's story. As a security guard, he felt alienated. "We're the normal ones. Everybody out there is a shithead," he said. Then he got a chance to work in substance-abuse prevention. When he talks about helping save people from drugs, he glows with pride. This same transformation was obvious in Laura Larance's description of her role in minority development, Mary Miller's account of the application of her research to real world problems, and Mark Madison's description of the special assignments he completes for research and development.

Both of the women interviewed told tragic stories. Both had been in unhappy marriages that contributed in some way to their entry into the work force. For them, work was sanctuary. Mary described herself as "the only security." Laura said, "My husband's abuse pushed me to this job." The men reported, however, proactively seeking employment. The women described their entry into the world of paid employment as a reaction to an unjust and unhappy home situation from which they sought freedom.

Neither of the women started their adult lives expecting to have careers. They each married someone who they thought would take care of them, and they each found their own stereotypes of marriage roles were unrealistic. Mary's husband could not find a job. Laura's husband was "crazy" and worked only sporadically. They are both in the work force because at the time they entered it, they believed they had no choice. Now, they really do not. Nor would they want to go back to the role of housewife.

The role that "good work" plays in making life in and away from the workplace meaningful is obvious. "Good work" is a condition that organizations do not often consider or address. We hope that now that you have been introduced to its possibilities, you will strive to make your organization one in which people find it.

SUMMARY

In this chapter, and throughout this book, we have described the complexities of the concepts of job satisfaction and performance. We believe that the people who work with, and for, you are complex and diverse. They are people who want to find satisfaction in their work. Most of them want to perform.

The keys to both job satisfaction and job performance are you, the supervisors in your organization, and the support you provide. When you value participation, affirm diversity, and establish a workplace environment of mutual commitment, you enable yourself and your employees to balance job satisfaction and performance.

NOTES

1. Edgar Schein, *Process Consultation: Lessons for Managers and Consultants* (Reading, Mass.: Addison-Wesley, 1987).

2. Thomas Cummings and Edgar Huse, *Organization Development and Change*, 4th ed. (St. Paul, Minn.: West Publishing, 1989).

3. J. Hackman and G. Oldham, "Development of the Job-Diagnostic Survey," *Journal of Applied Psychology* 60, no. 2 (April 1975): 161.

4. Willa Bruce, *Problem Employee Management* (Westport, Conn.: Quorum, 1990): 19.

5. Dorothy Soelle, *To Work and To Love* (Philadelphia: Fortress Press, 1989): 84.

6. Ibid., 107.

Further Reading

Abramis, David. "Fun at Work." *Personnel Administrator* 34 (November 1989): 60–63.

Adams, Roscoe. "Management, Analysis and Planning for Skill Development in the 90s." *Advanced Management Journal* 4, no. 4 (Autumn 1990): 34–40.

Agor, Weston. "Intrapreneurship and Productivity." *The Bureaucrat* (Summer 1989): 41–45.

Alexander, Elmore, Marilyn Helms, and Ronnie Wilkins. "The Relationship Between Supervisory Communication and Subordinate Performance and Satisfaction Among Professionals." *Public Personnel Management* 18 (Winter 1989): 415–29.

Arwine, Don. "Human Resource Managers Should Prepare for 'Big One.'" *Modern Healthcare* 20 (August 27, 1990).

Asch, Beth. "Do Incentives Matter? The Case of Navy Recruiters." *Industrial and Labor Relations Review* 43 (February 1990): 89s–106s.

Asplund, Gisele. *Women Managers: Changing Organizational Cultures.* Chichester, England: John Wiley and Sons, 1988.

Axline, Larry. "People, Productivity, and Profits." *Personnel Administrator* 29 (November 1984): 113–17.

Badham, Richard. *Theories of Industrial Society.* London: Croom Helm, 1986.

Balk, Walter, Geert Bouckaert, and Kevin Bronner. "Notes on the Theory and Practice of Government Productivity Improvement." *Public Productivity and Management Review* 13 (Winter 1989): 117–31.

Beaty, D. "Reexamining the Link Between Job Characteristics and Job Satisfaction." *The Journal of Social Psychology* 130, no. 1 (1989): 131–32.

Becker, Thomas, and Richard Klimoski. "A Field Study of the Relationship between the Organizational Feedback Environment and Performance." *Personnel Psychology* 42 (Summer 1989): 343–58.

Belcher, Hohn. "The Role of Unions in Productivity Management." *Personnel* 45 (January 1988): 54–58.

Bergmann, Thomas, Joyce Grahn, and Robert Wyate. "Relationship of Employment Status to Employee Job Satisfaction." *Akron Business and Economic Review* 17 (Summer 1986): 45–50.

Berl, Robert, Terry Powell, and Nicholas Williamson. "Industrial Salesforce Satisfaction and Performance with Herzberg's Theory." *Industrial Marketing Management* 13 (February 1984): 11–19.

Bernstein, Paula. *Family Ties, Corporate Bonds*. Garden City, N.Y.: Doubleday, 1985.

Best, Fred, and Kay Eberhard. "Education for the 'Era of the Adult' " *Futurist* 24, no. 3 (May/June 1990): 20–26.

Bezold, Clement, Rick Carlson, and Jonathan Peck. *The Future of Work and Health*. Dover, Mass.: Auburn House Publishing Co., 1986.

Bigelow, John, Thomas Cummings, William Notz, Paul Salipante, Suresh Srivastva, and James Waters. *Job Satisfaction and Productivity*, 2d ed. Washington D.C.: Comparative Administration Research Institute, 1977.

Blau, G. and K. Boal, "Conceptualizing How Job Involvement and Organizational Commitment Affect Turnover and Absenteeism." *Academy of Management Review* 12, no. 2 (1987): 288–300.

Bokemeier, Janet, and William Lacy. "Job Values, Rewards, and Work Conditions as Factors in Job Satisfaction Among Men and Women," *The Sociological Quarterly* 28, no. 2 (September 1987): 189–204.

Bottger, Preston, and Irene Chew. "The Job Characteristics Model and Growth Satisfaction: Main Effects of Assimilation of Work Experience and Context Satisfaction." *Human Relations* 39, no. 6 (1986): 575–94.

Bottger, Preston. "Effects of Assimilation of Work Experience on Growth Satisfaction." *Human Relations* 41 (1988): 603–17.

Brass, Daniel. "Technology and the Structuring of Jobs: Employee Satisfaction, Performance, and Influence," *Organizational Behavior and Human Decision Processes* 35 (April 1985): 216–40.

Brooke, Paul, Daniel Russel, and James Price. "Discriminant Validation of Measures of Job Satisfaction, Job Involvement, and Organizational Commitment." *Journal of Applied Psychology* 73, no. 2 (1987): 139–145.

Brown, D. S. "Reducing Dysfunctionalism: Another Way of Improving Productivity." *Public Productivity Review* (1988): 117–22.

Burack, Elmer. "Corporate Business and Human Resources Planning Practices: Strategic Issues and Concerns." *Organizational Dynamics* 15, no. 1 (Summer 1986): 73–87.

———. "A Strategic Planning and Operational Agenda for Human Resources." *Human Resources Planning* 11, no. 2 (1988): 63–68.

Burden, Dianne. "Single Parents and the Work Setting: The Impact of Multiple Job and Homelife Responsibilities." *Family Relations* 35, no. 1 (January 1986): 37–43.

Callahan, S. D., and A. Kidd. "Relationship Between Job Satisfaction and Self-Esteem in Women." *Psychological Reports* 59, no. 2, Part 1 (1986): 663–68.

Calpin, J. P., B. Edelstein, and W. Redmon. "Performance Feedback and Goal Setting to Improve Mental Health Center Staff Productivity." *Journal of Organizational Behavior and Management* 9, no. 2 (1988): 35–38.

Carsten, Jeanne, and Paul Spector. "Unemployment, Job Satisfaction, and Employee Turnover: A Meta-analytic Test of the Muchinsky Model." *Journal of Applied Psychology* 72, no. 3 (1987): 374–81.

Casey, D. "Job Satisfaction Is on the Rise." *Public Management* 72, no. 7 (August 1990): 22–24.

Champagne, Paul, and R. Bruce McAfee. *Motivating Strategies for Performance and Productivity: A Guide to Human Resource Development.* Westport, Conn.: Quorum Books, 1989.

Chermis, C., and J. Kane. "Public Sector Professionals: Job Characteristics, Satisfaction, and Aspirations for Intrinsic Fulfillment through Work." *Human Relations* 40 (1987): 125–36.

Chisholm, Rupert, and Robert Munzenrider. "Evaluating a Public Sector Productivity Improvement Effort: An OD Approach," *Public Administration Quarterly* 13 (Spring 1989).

Chusmir, Leonard. "Increasing Women's Job Commitment," *Personnel* 63 (January 1986): 41–44.

Coates, Joseph, Jennifer Jarrett, and John Mahaffie. "Workplace Management 2000," *Personnel Administrator* 34 (December 1989): 50–55.

Cohen, Steven. *Effective Public Manager: Achieving Success in Government.* San Francisco: Jossey-Bass, 1989.

Copeland, Lennie, "Staffing: New Rules for the Multicultural Workplace." *The Journal of Staffing and Recruitment* (Summer 1989): 21.

Cotton, John, David Vollrath, and Kirk Froggatt. "Employee Participation: Diverse Forms and Different Outcomes." *The Academy of Management Review* 13 (January 1988): 8–22.

Cotton, John, David Vollrath, Mark Longneck-Hall, and Kirk Froggatt. "Fact: The Form of Participation Does Matter." *Academy of Management Review* 15, no. 1 (January 1990): 147–53.

Courtney, Rosalyn. "A Human Resources Program That Helps Management and Employees Prepare for the Future." *Personnel* 63 (May 1986): 32–35 + .

Crispell, Diane. "Workers in 2000." *American Demographics* 12 (March 1990): 36–40.

Curry, James, Douglas Wakefield, and James Price. "On the Causal Ordering of Job Satisfaction and Organizational Commitment." *Academy of Management Journal* 29 (December 1986): 847–58.

Cutchin, Deborah. "Municipal Executive Productivity: Lessons from New Jersey." *Public Productivity and Management Review* 13, no. 3 (Spring 1990): 245–70.

Cutler, David, James Poterba, and Louise Sheiner. "An Aging Society: Opportunity or Challenge?" *Brookings Papers on Economic Activity* (1990): 1–73.

Das, B., and A. Mital. "The Moderating Effects of Production Feedback and Standards on the Relationship Between Worker Job Attitudes and Productivity." *Journal of Human Ergology* 18, no. 1 (1989): 33–39.

Deem, Rosemary, and Graeme Salaman, eds. *Work, Culture and Society.* Philadelphia: Open University Press, 1985.

Deeprose, D. "Three Key Elements of a Productivity Program," *Supervisory Management* 34, no. 11 (November 1989): 7–11.

Dixon, J. Robb, Alfred Nanni, Jr., and Thomas Vollmann. *The New Performance*

Challenge: Measuring Operations for World Class Companies. Homewood, Ill.: Dow Jones-Irwin, 1990.

Dole, Elizabeth. "New Incentives for a Changing Workforce: Resources Where Employers Can Get Help." *Business and Health* no. 1 (January 1990): 10–20.

Dressel, David. "Office Productivity: Contributions of the Workstation." *Behavior and Information Technology* 6, no. 3 (July-September 1987): 279–84.

Drucker, Peter. "How to Make People Decisions," *Harvard Business Review* 63 (July/August 1985): 22–24+.

Dunn, Samuel. "What the 90s Labor Shortage Will Mean to You." *Training* 22 (June 1985): 39–41+.

Eisenberger, R., P. Fasolo, and V. Davislamastro. "Perceived Organizational Support and Employee Diligence, Commitment, and Innovation. *Journal of Applied Psychology* 75, no. 1 (1990): 51–59.

Erikson, Kai, and Steven Vallas, eds. *The Nature of Work: Sociological Perspectives.* New Haven: Yale University Press, 1990.

Eubanks, Paula. "Workforce Diversity in Healthcare: Managing the Melting Pot." *Hospitals* 64 (June 20, 1990): 48+.

Ezorsky, Gertrude, and James Nickel, eds. *Moral Rights in the Work Place.* Albany: State University of New York, 1987.

Farrant, A. W. "You Need Good Subordinates." *Supervision* 51, no. 5 (May 1990): 17–20.

Feldman, Stevan. "How Organizational Culture Can Affect Innovation." *Organizational Dynamics* 17, no. 1 (1988).

Finchamn, Robin, and Peter Rhodes. *The Individual, Work and Organization.* London: Weidenfield and Nicolson, 1988.

Foo, C. T. "Perceptions of Corporate Productivity Practices." *Omega International Journal of Management Sciences* 18, no. 4 (1990): 355–64.

Frank, Howard. "Volcker versus Niskanen: Reflections on the Limited Use of Financial Incentives in the Public Sector." *Public Productivity and Management Review* 13 (Winter 1989): 187–93.

Freedman, Sara, and James Phillips. "The Effects of Situational Performance Constraints on Intrinsic Motivation and Satisfaction: The Role of Perceived Competence and Self Determination." *Organizational Behavior and Human Decision Processes* 35 (June 1985): 397–416.

Fryxell, Gerald, and Michael Gordon. "Workplace Justice and Job Satisfaction as Predictors of Satisfaction with Union and Management." *Academy of Management Journal* 32 (December 1989): 851–66.

Gattiker, Urs. *Technology Management in Organizations.* Newbury Park, Cal.: Sage, 1990.

Gavin, Frank. "Employee Turnover: The Silent Cancer." *The Bureaucrat* 19, no. 1 (1990): 53–55.

Geber, Beverly. "Managing Diversity." *Training* 27, no. 7 (July 1990): 23–30.

Goodmeasure, Inc. *The Changing American Workplace: Work Alternatives in the '80s.* New York: AMA Membership Publications Division, 1985.

Gorden, Michael, and Richard Arvey. "The Relationship Between Education and Satisfaction with Job Content." *Administrative Science Quarterly* 33 (March 1988): 61–81.

Grant, Phillip. "Exploring the Relationships Between Motivation, Satisfaction and Performance." *Personnel Administrator* 28 (July 1983): 55–59.

———. "The Do's and Don'ts for Getting Top Performance." *Management Solutions* 33 (May 1988): 22–26.

Greenberger, David, Stephen Strasser, Larry L. Cummings, and R. B. Dunham. "The Impact of Personal Control on Performance and Satisfaction." *Organization Behavior and Human Decision Processes* 43 (February 1989): 29–51.

Greidanus, John. "The Cost of Human Resources: Controlling the Size and Productivity of the Work Force." *Public Utilities Fortnightly* 121 (March 31, 1988): 17–20.

Grey, Ronald, and Peter Gelford. "The People Side of Productivity: Responding to Changing Employee Values." *National Productivity Review* 9 (Summer 1990).

Grey, Ronald, and Peter Gerona. "The Bias of Productivity: Responding to Changing Employee Values." *National Productivity Review* 9 (Summer 1990): 301–12.

Gutknecht, Douglas, and Janet Miller. *The Organizational and Human Resources Sourcebook.* Lanham: University Press of America, 1986.

Guy, Mary. "High Reliability Management," *Public Productivity and Management Review* 13 (Summer 1990): 301–13.

Hackman, J. Richard. *Groups that Work and Those that Don't.* San Francisco: Jossey-Bass, 1990.

Hanson, Sandra, Jack Martin, and Steven Tuch. "Economic Sector and Job Satisfaction." *Work and Occupations* 14 (May 1987): 286–305.

Harper, Kirke. "The Future Environment." *The Bureaucrat* 19, no. 2 (Summer 1990): 20–22.

Harrick, Edward, and Gene Vanek. "Alternate Work Schedules, Productivity, Leave Usage, and Employee Attitudes: A Field Study," *Public Personnel Management* 15, no. 2 (Summer 1986): 159–69.

Hartman, Curtis, and Steven Pearlstein, "The 1987 Inc./Hay Employee Survey: The Joy of Working." *Inc.* 9, no. 12 (November 1987): 61–63 + .

Hendricks, Dale. "Career Development: If We Know What It Is, Why Don't We Do It?" *Industrial Management* 32, no. 1 (January/February 1990): 10–15.

Heneman, Robert, David Greenberger, and Stephen Strasser. "The Relationship Between Pay-for-Performance Perceptions and Pay Satisfaction." *Personnel Psychology* 41 (Winter 1988): 745–59.

Hennecke, Mark. "The People Side of Strategic Planning," *Training* 21 (November 1984): 24–25 + .

Herron, Laura. "The New Game of HR: Playing to Win (In an Era of Labor Shortages)." *Personnel* 66 (June 1989): 18–20 + .

Herzberg, Frederick. "Workers' Needs: The Same Around the World." *Industry Week* 234 (September 21, 1987): 29–30 + .

Hirschorn, Larry. *The Workplace Within: The Psychodynamics of Organizational Life.* Cambridge, Mass.: MIT Press, 1988.

Hodgson, Alan. "The Civil Service Road to Job Satisfaction." *Personnel Management* 17 (October 1985): 54–57.

Hodson, Randy. "Gender Differences in Job Satisfaction: Why Aren't Women More Dissatisfied?" *The Sociological Quarterly* 30, no. 3 (Fall 1989): 385–99.

Hoffman, William, Larry Wyatt, and George Gordon. "Human Resource Planning: Shifting from Concept to Contemporary Practice." *Human Resource Planning* 9, no. 3 (1986): 81–96.

Hollenbeck, J., C. Williams, and H. Klein. "An Empirical Examination of the Antecedents of Commitment to Difficult Tasks." *Journal of Applied Psychology* 74, no. 1 (February 1989): 18–23.

Holzer, Marc, ed. *Public Productivity Handbook.* New York: Marcel-Dekker, 1991.

Holzer, Marc, and Arie Halachmie. *Public Sector Productivity: A Resource Guide.* New York: Garland Publishing, 1988.

Honeycutt, Alan. "Creating a Productive Work Environment." *Supervisory Management* 34 (November 1989): 12–16.

Hooper, John, Ralph Catalanello, and Patrick Murray. "Shoring Up the Weakest Link." *Personnel Administrator* 32 (April 1987): 49–55 + .

Hopkins, Anne. *Work and Job Satisfaction in the Public Sector.* Totowa, N.J.: Bowman and Allanheld, 1988.

Hughes, Charles. "The Three-Legged Stool: A Balanced Approach Is Best." *Personnel Administrator* 32 (November 1987): 32.

Hutchins, Robert. "Seniority, Wages, and Productivity: A Turbulent Decade." *Journal of Economic Perspectives* 3, no. 4 (Fall 1989): 49–64.

Jenkins, Stephen. "Turnover: Correcting the Causes." *Personnel* 65 (December 1988): 43–48.

Johnson, Tom. "Do More with Less by the Year 2000." *Risk Management* 37 (June 1990): 81–82.

Kanter, Donald, and Phillip Mervis. *The Cynical Americans: Living and Working in an Age of Discontent and Disillusionment.* San Francisco: Jossey-Bass, 1989.

Kanter, R. "The New Workforce Meets the Changing Workplace: Strains, Dilemmas, and Contradictions in Attempts to Implement Participative and Entrepreneurial Management." *Human Resource Management* 25, no. 4 (Winter 1986): 515–37.

Kanungo, Rabindra. "An Alternative to the Intrinsic-Extrinsic Dichotomy of Work Rewards." *Journal of Management* 13 (Winter 1987): 751–66.

Karasek, Robert, and Tores Theorell. *Healthy Work: Stress, Productivity, and the Reconstruction of Working Life.* New York: Basic Books, 1990.

Katzell, R. A., and D. E. Thompson. "Work Motivation: Theory and Practice." Special issue of *Organizational Psychology* 45, no. 2 (February 1990): 144–53.

Kchut, Andrew, and Linda DeStefano. "Mirror of America." *The Gallup Report* 288 (1989): 22–28.

Keawood, Anthony. "Human Resources in the 1990s." *Business Horizons* no. 1 (January/February 1990): 74–80.

Kelley, Robert. "Managing the New Workforce." *Machine Design* 2, no. 9 (May 10, 1990): 109–18.

Kelly, John, and Chriss Clegg, eds. *Autonomy and Control at the Workplace.* London: Croom Helm, 1982.

Kiechel, Walter. "How Important Is Morale, Really?" *Fortune* 119 (February 13, 1989): 121–22.

Kim, Jay. "Effect of Behavior Plus Outcome Goal Setting and Feedback on Employee Satisfaction and Performance," *Academy of Management Journal* 27 (March 1984): 139–49.

Klein, H. "Job Satisfaction in Professional Dual Career Couples." *Journal of Vocational Behavior* 32, no. 3 (1988): 255–68.

Kochan, Thomas, ed. *Challenges and Choices Facing American Labor*. Cambridge, Mass.: MIT Press, 1985.

Kovach, Kenneth, and John Pearce. "HR Strategic Mandates for the 1990s," *Personnel* 67 (April 1990): 50–55.

Krantz, Les. *The Jobs Rated Almanac*. New York: World Almanac, 1988.

Kravetz, Dennis. *The Human Resources Revolution: Implementing Progressive Management Practices for Bottom Line Success*. San Francisco: Jossey-Bass, 1988.

Kulik, Carol, Greg R. Oldham, and J. Richard Hackman. "Work Design as an Approach to Person Environment." *Journal of Vocational Behavior* 31, no. 3 (December 1987): 278–96.

Lee, Raymond, and Elizabeth Wilbur. "Age, Education, Job Tenure, Salary, Job Characteristics, and Job Satisfaction: A Multivariate Analysis." *Human Relations* 38, no. 8 (August 1985): 781–91.

Leonard, Jonathan. "The Changing Face of Employees and Employment Regulation." *California Management Review* 31 (Winter 1989): 29–38.

Levering, Robert. *A Great Place to Work: What Makes Some Employers So Good, and Most So Bad?* New York: Random House, 1988.

Levine, David. "Participation, Productivity, and the Firm's Environment." *California Management Review* 32, no. 4 (Summer 1990): 86–98.

Levinson, D. R. *Working for the Federal Government—Job Satisfaction and the Federal Employee*. Washington, D.C.: Merit System Protection Board, 1990.

Lincoln, James. "Employee Work Attitudes and Management Practice in the U.S. and Japan: Evidence from a Comparative Survey." *California Management Review* 32, no. 1 (Fall 1989): 89–106.

Liou, K., R. Sylvia, and G. Brunk. "Non-Work Factors and Job Satisfaction Revisited." *Human Relations* 43, no. 1 (1990): 77–88.

Locke, Edwin, David Schweiger, and Gary Latham. "Participation in Decision Making: When Should It Be Used?" *Organizational Dynamics* 14, no. 3 (Winter 1986): 65–79.

Loverd, Richard. "The Challenge of a More Responsible Productive Public Work Place." *Public Productivity and Management Review* 13, no. 1 (Fall 1989): 43–59.

Lunneborg, Patricia. *Women Changing Work*. Westport, Conn.: Greenwood Press, 1990.

Mahler, S. A. "How Working Single Parents Manage Their Two Major Roles." *Journal of Employment Counseling* 26, no. 4 (1989): 178–85.

Maidment, R. "Decision Making: When Not to Involve Employees." *Supervisory Management* 34, no. 10 (October 1989): 33–35.

Manzini, Andrew, and John Gridley, "The False Economies of Unplanned Layoffs." *Personnel* 63 (March 1986): 25–26 +.

Martin, Jack, and Constance Shehan. "Education and Job Satisfaction." *Work and Occupations* 16 (May 1989): 184–99.

Matzer, John, ed. *Productivity Improvement Techniques: Creative Approaches for Local*

Governments. Washington, D.C.: International City Management Association, 1986.

Mawhinney, T. "Job Satisfaction as a Management Tool and Responsibility." *Journal of Organizational Behavior and Management* 10 (1989): 187–93.

McAfee, R. Bruce, and Myron Glassman. "Job Satisfaction: It's the Little Things that Count." *Management Solutions* 33 (August 1988): 32–37.

McArthur, Kent. "Management Productivity." *Journal of the Society of Research Administrators* 19 (Summer 1987).

McDaniels, Carl. *The Changing Workplace: Career Counseling Strategies for the 1990's and Beyond.* San Francisco: Jossey-Bass, 1989.

McGee, Lynn. "Innovative Labor Shortage Solutions." *Personnel Administrator* 34, no. 12 (December 1989): 50–60.

McGee, Linda. "Keeping Up the Good Work." *Personnel Administrator* 33 (June 1988): 68–72.

McGuire, Jean, and Joseph Liro. "Flexible Work Schedules, Work Attitudes, and Perceptions of Productivity." *Public Personnel Management* 15 (Spring 1986): 65–73.

Miller, Katherine, and Peter Monge. "Participation, Satisfaction, and Productivity: A Meta-analytic Review." *Academy of Management Journal* 29 (December 1986): 727–53.

Mischkind, Louis. "Seven Steps to Productivity Improvement." *Personnel* 64 (July 1987): 22–30.

Misra, P., and N. Jain. "Self-esteem, Need-achievement, and Need-autonomy as Moderators of the Job Performance–Job Satisfaction Relationship." *Perspectives in Psychological Research* 9, no. 2 (1986): 42–46.

Modic, Stanley. "Whatever It Is, It's Not Working." *Industry Week* 238 (July 17, 1989): 27.

Morf, Martin. *The Work/Life Dichotomy: Prospects for Reintergrating People and Jobs.* Westport, Conn. Quorum Books, 1989.

Moore, Helen. "Job Satisfaction and Women's Spheres of Work." *Sex Roles* 13, nos. 11/12 (November-December, 1985): 97–105.

Morrill, Douglas, Jr. "Human Resource Planning in the 1990s." *Best's Review (Prop/Casualty Insurance Edition)* 91, (July 1990): 104–10.

Mottaz, Clifford. "Gender Differences in Work Satisfaction, Work-related Rewards and Values, and the Determinants of Work Satisfaction." *Human Relations* 39, no. 4 (April 1986): 359–78.

———. "Age and Work Satisfaction." *Work and Occupations* 14, no. 3 (August 1987): 387–409.

Naff, Katherine, and Raymond Pomerlean. "Productivity Gainsharing: A Federal Sector Case Study." *Public Personnel Management* 17 (Winter 1988): 403–19.

Naisbitt, John, and Patricia Aburdene. *Re-inventing the Corporation: Transforming Your Job and Your Company for the New Information Society.* New York: Warner Books, 1985.

Neil, Cicily, and William Snizek. "Gender as a Moderator of Job Satisfaction." *Work and Occupations* 15, no. 2 (May 1988): 201–19.

Neuman, George, Jack Edwards, and Nambury Raju. "Organizational Development Interventions: A Meta-Analysis of Their Affect on Satisfaction and other Attitudes." *Personnel Psychology* 42 (Autumn 1989): 461–89.

Newsome, W. B. "Motivate, Now!" *Personnel Journal* 69, no. 2 (February 1990): 51–55.

Nicholson, Nigel, and Gary Johns. "The Absence Culture and the Psychological Contract—Who's in Control of Absence?" *The Academy of Management Review* 10 (July 1985): 397–407.

Niehouse, Oliver. "Participation in Decision Making: When Should It Be Used?" *Supervisory Management* 31, (February 1986): 8–11.

Nkomo, Stella. "Strategic Planning for Human Resources: Let's Get Started." *Long Range Planning* 21, (February 1988): 66–72.

Nordstrom, R., T. Lewissohn, and R. Hall. "Productivity in the Public Sector: A Discussion of the Issues." *Public Personnel Management Journal* 16, no. 1 (1987): 1–6.

Norris, Dwight, and Robert Niebuhr. "Attributional Influences on the Job Performance–Job Satisfaction Relationship." *Academy of Management Journal* 27 (June 1984): 424–31.

Norris, William. "Productivity and Cooperation." *Public Productivity and Management Review* 13 (Summer 1990): 295–99.

Occupational Outlook Quarterly. "Outlook 2000: The Labor Force." *Occupational Outlook Quarterly* 33 (Fall 1989): 4–11.

Oldham, Greg, Carol Kulik, and Maureen Ambrose. "Relations Between Job Facets Comparisons and Employee Reactions." *Organizational Behavior and Human Decision Processes* 38 (August 1986): 28–47.

Organ, Dennis. "A Restatement of the Satisfaction-Performance Hypothesis." *Journal of Management* 14 (December 1988): 547–57.

Packer, Arnold, and Sar Levitan. "Skills Shortage Looms: We Can Handle It." *HR Magazine* 35, no. 4 (April 1990): 30–42.

Paul, Robert, and Yar Ebadi. "Leadership Decision Making in a Service Organization: A Field Test of the Vroom Yetton Model." *Journal of Occupational Psychology* 62, no. 3 (September 1989): 201–11.

Pennefather, Sarah. "Key to Productivity." *Computer Data* (Canada) 14, no. 7 (July 1989): 16–17.

Personnel Administrator, Editors, "Outlook for the 90s: Special Report." *Personnel Administrator*. 34 (December 1989): 50–76.

Petty, M. M., Gail McGee, and Jerry Cavender. "A Meta-analysis of the Relationships Between Individual Job Satisfaction and Individual Performance." *The Academy of Management Review* 9 (October 1984): 712–21.

Poister, Theodore, and Gregory Streib. "Municipal Manager's Concerns for Productivity Improvement." *Public Productivity and Management Review* 13, no. 1 (Fall 1990): 3–11.

Pollock, Marny. "Participative Decision Making in Review." *Leadership and Organizational Development Journal* 8, no. 2 (1987): 7–10.

Powell, Gary N. *Women and Men in Management*. Newbury Park: Cal.: Sage Publications, 1988.

Press, Mike, and Don Thomson, eds. *Solidarity for Survival*. Nottingham: Spokesman, 1989.

Pritchard, R. D., S. Jones, P. Roth, K. Steubing, and S. Ekeberg, "The Evaluation

of an Integrated Approach to Measuring Organizational Productivity."
Personnel Psychology 42 (Spring 1989): 245–70.

Reddy, Brendan. *Teambuilding: Blueprints for Productivity and Satisfaction.* NTL
Institute for Applied Behavioral Sciences and University Associates, Inc.,
Bethel, Maine, 1988.

Redwood, Anthony. "Human Resource Management in the 1990s." *Business
Horizons* 33 (January-February, 1990): 74–80.

Rice, Robert, Dean McFarlin, and Debbie Bennett. "Standards of Comparison
and Job Satisfaction." *Journal of Applied Psychology* 74, no. 4 (1989): 591–
98.

Roberson, L. "Prediction of Job Satisfaction from Characteristics of Personal
Work Goals." *Journal of Organization Behavior* 11, no. 1 (1990): 29–41.

Robertson, Ivan. *Motivation and Job Design: Theory, Research, and Practice.* London:
Institute of Personnel Management, 1985.

Rollins, Thomas, and Jerrold Bratkovitch. "Productivity's People Factor." *Personnel Administrator* 33 (February 1988): 50–57.

Romzek, Barbara. "Personal Consequences of Employee Commitment." *Academy of Management Journal* 32 (September 1989): 649–61.

Rudd, Nancy, and Patrick McKenry. "Family Influences on the Job Satisfaction
of Employed Mothers." *Psychology of Women Quarterly* 10, no. 4 (December
1986): 363–72.

Saltzman, Amy. "The New Meaning of Success." *U.S. News & World Report* 109
(September 17, 1990): 56–58.

Sandy, William. *Forging the Productivity Partnership.* New York: McGraw-Hill,
1990.

Sashkin, Marshall. *A Manager's Guide to Performance Management.* New York:
AMA Membership Publications Division, 1986.

Sayles, Leonard. "Managerial Productivity: Who Is Fat and What Is Lean?"
Interfaces 15, no. 3 (May/June, 1985).

Scott, Dow, and Steven Taylor. "An Examination of Conflicting Findings on the
Relationship Between Job Satisfaction and Absenteeism: A Meta-
analysis." *Academy of Management Journal* 28 (September 1985): 599–612.

Shapira, Zur. "Task Choice and Assigned Goals as Determinants of Task Motivation and Performance." *Organizational Behavior and Human Decision
Processes* 44 (October 1989): 141–65.

Shore, Lynn, and Harry Martin. "Job Satisfaction and Organizational Commitment in Relation to Work Performance and Turnover Intentions." *Human
Relations* 42, no. 7 (1989): 625–38.

Siegel, Gilbert, Ross Clayton, and Sarah Kovoor. "Modeling Interorganizational
Effectiveness." *Public Productivity and Management Review* 13, no. 3 (Spring
1990): 245–70.

Smith, M. P., and Nock, S. "Social Class and the Quality of Work Life in Public
and Private Organizations." *Journal of Social Issues* 36, no. 4 (1989): 59–75.

Spencer, Daniel. "Employee Voice and Employee Retention." *Academy of Management Journal* 29 (September 1986): 488–502.

Staw, Barry. "Organizational Psychology and the Pursuit of the Happy Productive Worker." *California Management Review* 28 (Summer 1986): 40–53.

Steele, Fritz. *Making and Managing a High Quality Workplace: An Organizational Ecology*. New York: Teachers College Press, 1986.

Tait, Marianne, Margaret Padgett, and Timothy Baldwin. "Job and Life Satisfaction: A Reevaluation of the Strength of Relationship and Gender Effects as a Function of the Date of the Study." *Journal of Applied Psychology* 4, no. 3 (June 1989): 502–7.

Townsend, Patrick. *Commit to Quality*. New York: John Wiley and Sons, 1990.

Turek-Brezina, J., C. Pettibone, and D. Tanner. "The Federal Executive Dilemma—I Like My Job but. . . ." *Government Executive* 21 (1989): 58–59.

Valorns, George. "Beating the 1990s Labor Shortage." *Training* 27, no. 7 (July 1990): 32–35.

Vanderslice, Virginia, Robert Rice, and James Julian. "The Effects of Participation in Decision Making on Worker Satisfaction and Productivity." *Journal of Applied Social Psychology* 17, no. 2 (February 1987): 158–70.

Warren, Alfred B., Jr. "Creating a Competitive Workforce." *Economic Development Review* 8, no. 1 (Winter 1990): 10–12.

Watson, Collin, Kent Watson, and John Stowe. "Univariate and Multivariate Distributions of the Job Descriptive Index's Measures of Job Satisfaction." *Organizational Behavior and Human Decision Processes* 35 (April 1985): 241–51.

Weaver, Charles, and Michael Mathews. "What White Males Want from Their Jobs: Ten Years Later." *Personnel* 64 (September 1987): 62–65.

Wegmann, Robert, Robert Chapman, and Miriam Johnson. *Work in the New Economy*. Alexandria, Va.: American Association for Counseling and Development, 1989.

Wells, Don. *Empty Promises: Quality of Working Life Programs and the Labor Movement*. New York: Monthly Review Press, 1987.

Wending, Wayne. "Responses to a Changing Workforce." *Personnel Administrator* 33 (November 1988): 50–54.

Withey, Michael, and William Cooper. "Predicting Exit, Voice, Loyalty, and Neglect." *Administrative Science Quarterly* 34 (December 1989): 521–39.

Witt, L. Alan. "Sex Differences Among Bank Employees in the Relationships of Commitment with Psychological Climate and Job Satisfaction." *Journal of Applied Psychology* 116, no. 4 (October 1989): 419–26.

Wood, Bob, and Andrew Scott. "Gentle Art of Feedback." *Personnel Management* 21, no. 4 (1989): 48–51.

Wright, Wayne. "Overcoming Barriers to Productivity." *Personnel Journal* 66 (February 1987): 28–34.

Wygant, Alice, and O. W. Markley. *Information and the Future: A Handbook of Sources and Strategies*. Westport, Conn.: Greenwood Press, 1988.

Yankelovich, Daniel, and John Immerwahr. "Putting the Work Ethic to Work." *Society* 21, no. 2 (January/February, 1984): 58–76.

Yaverbaum, Gayle, and Oya Culpan. "Exploring the Dynamics of the End-User Environment: The Impact of Education and Task Differences on Change." *Human Relations* 43, no. 5 (May 1990): 439–54.

Zakon, Alan. "Pushing the Limits Can Improve Performance." *Management Review* 77 (May 1988): 18–20.

Zeitz, G. "Age and Work Force Satisfaction in a Government Agency: A Situational Perspective." *Human Relations* 43, no. 5 (May 1990): 419–38.

Index

committee presentations, in
participative planning, 184
committees: and deadlines, 183; in
implementation process, 187–88;
need for skill in managing, 174;
quick sense of accomplishment,
181; use of in participative
planning, 175
communication: by computer, 98–99;
electronic, 89; improved, through
participation, 168
communications revolution, 94
community, 135
Companies that Care, 133
comparable-worth debates, 68
compensation, 23–24
competition, increased, 90
competitive edge, 8, 14
competitive environment, 17
competitive position, 100–101
competitive standards, new, 90
competitiveness, elements of, 90
computer technology: need for work
design in use of, 108; office
restructuring (CAD), 97–98; in
tractor assembly plant, 96
computer-aided engineering (CAE),
advantages of, 98
computer-based technologies,
management of, 110
computer-driven manufacturing, 97
computers, 94–111; applications in
flexible manufacturing, 97; and
competitive position, 100–101;
contributions to economic
production of, 93; contributions to
productivity, 96; dependence of
economy upon, 93; desktop, 100–
101; enhanced by
telecommunications, 95; facilitate
communication to integrate firms,
98–99; help to keep inventory
down, 98; impact of, 94–95; impact
on banking and insurance, 95;
impact upon agriculture, 95–96;
impact upon offices, 99; to reduce
overloading of reporting systems,

101; speech recognition by, 96;
uses of in everyday life, 95
conference, 185
Conn, Henry P., 118 n.40, 195 n.14
consensus, and participation, 171
consultants, 142, 147, 158–59
consumers, demands of, 90
Contino, Ronald A., 195 n.29
contract, 132–34
control, decentralization of, 110–11
control systems, impact of upon
manufacturing, 96
controversial ideas, and participative
planning, 177
Cooper, Terry, 137 n.7
cooperation, and participation, 171
Copeland, Lennie, 74 n.36
corporate America, 133
corporate culture, 46
costs of poor performance of Routine
Producers, 105–6
Council for Adult and Experiential
Learning, 158, 165 n.17
covenant, 132–34
Covey, Stephen R., 194 n.1
creativity, and participation, 171
Creecy, Robert, 74 n.43
Creighton University, 134
Cuba, 49
cultural diversity, 45, 51
cultural heritage, 59; United States,
37–38
cultural messages, 60
cultural minorities, 47
culture, 33, 47, 51, 56; American, 23,
123, 169; corporate, 46; defined,
39–42; minority, 38, 50;
organizational, 38–39, 61, 66, 134;
shock, 39; workplace, 48
Cummings, T., 29 nn.35, 38, 30 n.44,
218 n.2
currency, value of, 88

data, cost of storing, 95
data interchange, electronic, 98
data processing workers, work
problems of, 106–7, 117 n.17
Davis, Donald, 118 n.52

About the Authors

WILLA M. BRUCE is Associate Professor of Public Administration at the University of Nebraska at Omaha where she teaches administrative ethics, organizational behavior, and organizational development. She is Mid-West Representative to the National Council of the American Society for Public Administration and 1993 Chair of the Ethics Committee. She has published in numerous professional journals and has published two previous books with Quorum, *Problem Employee Management* (1990) and, with Christine Reed, *Dual Career Couples in the Public Sector* (1991).

J. WALTON BLACKBURN is Assistant to the President for Planning and Institutional Research at Creighton University. He has over fifteen years of experience in community, regional, and university planning, including work for the High Council for Urban Planning of Iran. He has published in such journals as *Policy Studies Journal*, *Review of Public Personnel Administration*, and *Public Personnel Management*.